A Real Boy

W d

Praise for *A Real Boy*:

'This wonderfully honest book tells us a great deal, not only about autism, but also about the extraordinary tolerance and unselfishness that is borne out of unequivocal love. At the same time, it reveals some uncomfortable truths about the struggle it takes to access the rights of those with disabilities in our so-called civilized society.'

Jane Asher, President of the National Autistic Society

'Absolutely brilliant. We laughed and cried. We recognized so many familiar situations ... *A Real Boy* helps to promote a greater understanding of autism to those who don't understand the condition.'

Marina Blore, Trustee, Wishing Well House
www.wishingwellhouse.co.uk

For more photos of David and his family, please visit
http://www.flickr.com/photos/arealboy/

A Real Boy

HOW AUTISM SHATTERED OUR LIVES – AND MADE A FAMILY FROM THE PIECES

Christopher Stevens with Nicola Stevens

Authors' note: we wrote this book together, just as we've brought up David together. Chris had his hands on the keyboard most of the time, so our story is told in his voice.

Michael O'Mara Books Limited

First published in 2008 by
Michael O'Mara Books Limited
9 Lion Yard
Tremadoc Road
London SW4 7NQ

A CIP catalogue record for this book is available from
the British Library.

Papers used by Michael O'Mara Books Limited are natural,
recyclable products made from wood grown in sustainable forests.
The manufacturing processes conform to the environmental
regulations of the country of origin.

ISBN: 978-1-84317-266-6

1 3 5 7 9 10 8 6 4 2

Designed and typeset by E-Type

Printed and bound in Great Britain by Cox & Wyman,
Reading, Berks

www.mombooks.com

With special thanks to David's inspirational teachers
and to all the staff at Briarwood school, for their
dedication, patience and support.

Prologue

The little boy on his mother's hip was gazing around the nursery. He had blond curls, and green eyes, and his mouth was open in an enquiring 'o'. When she put him down, he clung to mum's arm for a few seconds before bravely standing on his own, his red anorak zipped up, as the nursery teacher beamed at him.

'He'll be fine,' the teacher declared. 'Look at him – he can't wait for you to be gone so he can start playing with all these toys. Isn't that right, David?'

So we went. We'd debated all morning whether we should leave with a fanfare of goodbyes, or slip out unseen – in the end we decided on a loud, 'See you later, David,' and a smart exit. We'd never left him with anyone before, not even his grandparents, but it wasn't as if this step was unexpected. We'd been trying for eleven months to find a preschool place for David. This one seemed ideal: a small class, a sunny playground, experienced staff who listened to our welter of instructions. During the half-hour tour, our three-year-old son had investigated the paint pots and the piano, inspected the selection of scooters, and helped himself to a jam tart from the kitchen.

Home from home, we said. He'll be bringing his suitcase and moving in, we said.

The staff smiled patiently while we convinced ourselves. They're used to fussy families in north Bristol. It's usual for both parents to cross-examine the nursery leader, and ask for archives of the Ofsted reports – we probably seemed less neurotic than some, since we hadn't brought an Oxbridge admissions tutor and a feng shui consultant.

And after all, the first session was only an hour. We'd cope, somehow. Strong coffee was probably the answer, so we drove to Starbucks.

'This is the first time,' commented my wife, Nicky, as we settled into a sofa in the basement, 'that we've been in a cafe without a toddler, for five years.'

She checked her mobile, to make sure there hadn't been any distress calls from the nursery. There was no signal. We were completely separated from our children. We felt like we'd eloped.

The relaxed mood evaporated as we drove back to the nursery and parked, even before we switched off the engine. David was screaming. It was unmistakably him. No other child could achieve that high, sustained sound, like a buzz saw going through plate glass.

We had to ring the doorbell three times before anyone heard us. The noise in the nursery was deafening. We were used to it, and it still had the capacity to stun, to drive all thoughts and words out of our brains. The assistant who came to the door, a girl in her late teens, gaped at us, and we gaped back.

David was in the front room, with the two senior teachers. All the other children had been herded into the art room, behind a heavy door across the hall. Our son

8

was spreadeagled on his back with his head thudding into a teacher's lap. He was trying to squirm out of her grip, so that he could smash his head on the floor instead.

His face was flushed, but it was an old flush, an exhausted red, as if he was running out of energy for this struggle.

His shrieks broke off for a couple of seconds, as he heaved a breath.

'I think he's calming down,' the teacher gasped.

'Was it worse than this?' I asked. She nodded, her eyes wide, and the back of David's skull thumped into her leg again. Nicky knelt, talking to him, trying to hold his hands, but he had no idea that we'd come back.

'It started about two minutes after you left,' the teacher said. 'There was no warning – suddenly he was screaming, overturning all the tables and chairs, and nothing would make him stop.'

'We'll take him home,' I said.

'That would be best,' the teacher agreed, fervently. She handed David's red coat to Nicky.

There was something odd about the coat. It wasn't damaged, it wasn't dirty ... it just looked different from usual.

Its zip was undone.

'When you took David's coat off,' said my wife, struggling to slide David's arm into a sleeve as he thrashed, 'did you unzip it?'

'We didn't explain about that,' I said.

Nicky's jaw was set as she wrestled David's other arm into the coat. With his head hammering against her shoulder, she seized the ends of the zip, slotted them together and slid the fastener up to his chin.

The screaming stopped.

David collapsed backwards into his mother's arms. He sighed once. And then he fell asleep.

'I should have warned you,' I told the teacher. 'I thought I'd said, I must have forgotten, there was so much to explain ...'

'David can't stand to have his zip undone,' said Nicky. 'He wears the coat outside, indoors, to bed, everywhere except the bath.'

'But he must take it off sometimes,' the teacher protested. 'We didn't want him getting too hot.'

'Sometimes he'll let you lift it over his head. But it has to stay zipped.'

She picked him up. He was very small, for someone who could make that much noise.

'I wish,' I said, as we strapped him into his car seat, 'that he came with an instruction book. *David: An Owner's Manual* ... like those car books, with 3D diagrams to show which bits are missing in his brain and a trouble-shooting guide – look up "unprovoked screaming" in the index and there'd be a whole chapter of diagnostics.'

'It's our fault,' said Nicky. 'We should have warned them about his zip. Poor David, he couldn't believe it was happening.'

I shook my head. 'There's too much to explain. If we'd mentioned the zip, we'd have forgotten something else. And most of it is so hard to accept: I'm sure they didn't take me seriously about having to sing "Here We Go Round The Mulberry Bush" before he'll let you change his nappy. What we really need,' I repeated, 'is a "David manual".'

Eight years later, this is the manual. The book that

should have come with the boy. It's a step-by-step primer on a language that can't be spoken with words or gestures. And it's an assembly guide, for building an extraordinary family out of everyday components.

It isn't a 'misery memoir'. The supermarket shelves are full of them this year: stories of childhood neglect and brutal upbringings. If you're looking for that kind of book, put this one down – no one ever neglected David. He's the centre of attention. He's also the most blissfully happy little boy in the world, usually ... and when, for any reason, he isn't, we all get to hear about it.

So forget about 'misery'. And 'memoir' is the wrong word too – this isn't a book of memories, because the tales in these pages are still our daily experiences. It's more like a travelogue, the diary of an expedition which started as a trip to Mothercare and became an exploration of the uncharted jungles of parenthood ... or a voyage to a land where there was no communication, and every idea was inside out.

Most of all, it's a book about life with our son. He's different from all the other children, but that doesn't make him any less human. He's still a real boy.

One

The call from the hospital came late in the afternoon, just after I'd left for work. Nicky bottled up the news until halfway through the evening, when she couldn't hold it back any longer. She dialled the newspaper's front desk and asked to be put through to me, which she had never done before. When I answered the phone, she couldn't speak. She just sobbed.

I told the editor that my wife was unwell, and slipped away. When I reached the flat, Nicky had stopped crying. She was on the sofa, wrapped in a white linen-and-lace dressing gown, clutching a scrap of paper, with her knees up and our dog's muzzle resting mournfully on her toes.

On the scrap of paper, she had jotted the results of a blood test done earlier that week at the maternity hospital. Our unborn baby was thirteen weeks old, big enough on the sonar scan to look not merely human but, we prided ourselves, a lot like his parents. We were sure he was a boy – it was the way he was lying on his back, with his legs crossed casually, one arm thrown sideways as though reaching for a snack.

The scan had taken twenty minutes, the blood test barely twenty seconds. We hadn't expected it or wanted it, but it was offered and to refuse might have seemed rude. 'It's just routine,' the nurse had said dismissively, as if the notion that anything could be wrong with our baby was too far-fetched to be worth dignifying with a discussion.

And now the results were back, and they showed the probability that our baby had Down's syndrome was more than double the average. Nicky and I were first-time parents-to-be at twenty-nine, and the chances that our child would suffer from a chromosome abnormality should have been one-in-600. Instead, the blood test indicated it was one-in-250.

We talked about everything this might mean. It meant, statistically, that Nicky could have 250 babies, demonstrating a production-line efficiency which even rabbits would have to admire, and only one solitary child would have Down's. It also meant, in practical terms, that our unborn baby either did or didn't have the extra 'chromosome 21' which causes the syndrome; the test results couldn't affect that.

Ultrasounds, further into the pregnancy, might indicate more clearly whether our baby would be born disabled. In the meantime, the foetus would be growing, developing, becoming more like us. If we discovered, at any time in the next six weeks or so, that this baby had Down's syndrome, we could opt for a termination. The pregnancy would stop ... if we decided to do that.

There was a test for Down's which could be done straight away. It was called amniocentesis, and the hospital had already made an appointment with Nicky for us to discuss it with a doctor. It was a crudely simple procedure where a tissue sample was taken from the womb with a long needle.

'We like to have a chat with the mums first,' the doctor told us, 'because of the slight risk of complications.'

'What kind of complications?' we asked.

'In a tiny minority of cases, the test can trigger a miscarriage – we're not sure why.'

'How tiny?'

'About 1 per cent.'

'So you're recommending that we take a one-in-100 chance of killing our baby, to discover if we've lost the one-in-250 lottery for Down's syndrome?'

As soon as I started to speak, the doctor raised his hand, but I was too worked up to hold my tongue. Nicky looked as agitated as I felt. Before that moment, I couldn't have imagined any circumstance that would make me lose my temper with a doctor.

'I'm not "recommending" anything,' he said. 'This is just a chat.'

'Even if it is … you know,' Nicky said, 'I don't think I could … you know.'

And I did know. I knew completely. I couldn't put it into words either, but I knew we'd made a commitment to the life we had created inside her. We wanted all the best in the world for it. If that meant facing up to the worst, we'd try our hardest.

Six months later, James was born. He was perfectly healthy. He's fourteen now, and he still lies on his back with his legs crossed, occasionally reaching for a piece of fruit or a biscuit.

When James was nearly two, Nicky had the first ultrasound on our second child. This one hid its personality better. It looked strong, and healthy, and fast asleep. 'Right number of heads, anyway,' I joked.

Nicky chose not to have the blood test. She'd reached that decision a long time ago. We wanted everything to be right for our new baby. And if, God forbid, there was anything wrong, we didn't want to hear about it.

The first time I saw my wife, she was on a bus and I wasn't. It was a two-second glimpse, of an exceptionally pretty girl with a bow in her hair – gone in a moment, and it summed up everything that was suddenly good about life. If I'd never seen her face again, I think I would still remember the girl on the bus, twenty-five years on.

I'd started a college course in Cardiff that week, after seven bleak years at a boys-only grammar school: lessons in economics and classics, from masters who wore gowns and praised Enoch Powell, had given way to anecdotes and banter, disguised as tutorials in journalism, by lecturers who smelled of pubs and Woodbines. I was filled with optimism. Life was brimming with hope. Even the buses were looking good.

The girl with the bow was standing on the college steps next morning, prettier than ever, chatting to a friend. Naturally, I strolled over with a confident smile to introduce myself … or I would have done, if I could have been sure of saying, 'Hi, I'm Chris,' without swallowing my tongue. Instead, I spent six weeks gazing at her across the refectory at lunchtimes, blushing and burying my head in my jumper whenever I caught the girl's eye, until her friend sent a message via my friend that, if I didn't stop staring, they might have to get the college security staff involved.

I managed to blurt out enough words to avoid arrest,

but I don't think I completed a sentence until our first date, on a rainy Bonfire Night: outside Cardiff Castle, she pronged my face with the side of her umbrella. 'Don't worry,' I said, 'I've got another eye.' And she laughed – not because I had an umbrella sticking out of the side of my head, but because she thought I'd said something funny.

I remember our first kiss, and our first meal, and so many other firsts that it has taken me half a morning to write this sentence ... but the best of them all was the first time I made her laugh.

She's still endearingly dangerous with an umbrella.

By the time we were both twenty-one, I had a job on the Cardiff evening paper and Nicky was studying at the city's university, and we were living together. Some couples evolve a quiet companionship, based on mutual under-standing, where the truth of the relationship is revealed in what's unsaid. That wasn't us. We talked all the time. I'd known for certain that I was in love when she spent three hours describing the characters in a movie she'd seen the night before (it was *Ryan's Daughter*, with John Mills, and I still haven't seen it because it could never live up to Nicky's retelling). We didn't go to nightclubs or parties much, because we couldn't talk easily there, and we rarely fell asleep before three, because our conversations wouldn't cease, even though I had to be up at six to catch the bus. That was my fault, mostly – I never could shut up. I can hold my tongue until I start talking, and then I can't stop. 'This boy has verbal diarrhoea,' the gym teacher wrote on my first report. 'His mouth should be taped shut.'

The five words I've heard most often from Nicky are, 'Can I say something now?'

She completed her degree and got a job on a local radio

station, Red Dragon, as a researcher, and then as a presenter of the weekly slot on disability issues. Neither of us is disabled – she simply found the work engrossing, and soon took a post at Bristol University, organizing courses for adults with disabilities. We moved across the Severn, buying the smallest flat in the grandest house in Clifton. It was a Regency mansion built on the spoils of empire, with a ninety-foot entrance passage that extended from the house to the road so that ladies would never be exposed to the elements (or the rabble) when they alighted from their carriages.

Our apartment was ten times less spacious than the hall. It was so cramped that, to squeeze into the kitchen, you had to sidle in, left foot first – if you went right foot first, you'd have your back to the cooker, and there wasn't room to turn round. We couldn't get our sofa through the front door, so we bought another, which was more like a wicker dog-basket: the dog hogged it, and we just sat on the bed.

We loved the place. Friends would say, 'It's so tiny, don't you feel like you're always on top of each other?' And we'd just grin.

Nicky wanted a white wedding. She got one: we were married in Lapland, in February 1993, so far above the Arctic Circle that the days were only a few hours long and the nights were lit by spectral green rivers across the sky, the aurora borealis.

On the morning of our wedding, we dressed in the outfits we had prepared and packed so carefully, and walked from our cabin across a trail of packed ice, in temperatures of 40 below zero, to the hotel reception, where a trio of Lapp reindeer herdsmen were waiting to take us to the ceremony in a nearby village. They took one look at Nicky's beautiful dress of silk and velvet, which had cost her many weeks' salary, and months of designing, fitting and fretting. And they burst out laughing.

'You can ride with the reindeer in these clothes,' offered the youngest of the Lapps, in careful English, 'but when we arrive at the village, you will need a funeral, not a wedding.'

They produced snowsuits padded with rings of insulation like tractor tyres. Then they stood back, smiling, and waited to watch the bride change out of her dress.

I chased them outside, into the snow. They had their revenge on the ride to the village, when I stepped out of the reindeer sleigh to take a photograph and sank up to my neck in a snowdrift.

The words of the Finnish ceremony were beautiful. We pledged to love and support each other, with one goal above all the others: to bring up a family. It matched our private reasons for getting married. We had lived together for seven years, and now we wanted to have children.

After the ceremony, the hotelier, Jussi, gave us a reindeer's antler and explained it was a traditional Lapp fertility symbol. We didn't need Nicky's degree in psychology to work out why, but Jussi added: 'Place this under your bed and you will have boys.'

'What if we want a girl?' Nicky asked.

Jussi looked baffled. He consulted with the herdsmen, and came back: 'For a girl, hide a hammer under the bed. But not a sledgehammer … a hammer like this.' He crooked two fingers.

'A claw hammer?'

I thought I'd understood, but maybe something was lost in the translation – because, after the honeymoon, we put the antler under our bed in Bristol, and James was born within a year. Later, we slipped a hammer beneath the springs ... and produced a demolition specialist.

Our one-bed flat was too tiny for a family, or even a cot. By the time Nicky was six months pregnant, we knew we had to move urgently: she couldn't get into the kitchen. But the apartment had already been on the market for a year, and despite dozens of viewings, we'd had no offers. House sales were in a slump, interest rates had been as high as 15 per cent, and we were resigned to selling for less than we'd paid. Most of the people who shuffled through our nest waving the estate agent's details seemed to want nothing more than an afternoon's free sightseeing.

With only weeks before the baby was due, my father came to the rescue with a loan which, in effect, made him the temporary owner of a bijou flatlette that had been, we now saw from the title deeds, converted from a stairwell. We moved across the city, to a terraced house with three bedrooms and a kitchen long enough to go bowling in.

James arrived on 24 February 1994. We were happier than I had ever hoped to be. He was an exemplary baby. The women who ran the toddler group in the church hall at the end of our road called him 'Smiler', and that was a feeble understatement, like nicknaming Liberace 'Flashy' or Genghis Khan 'Grumpy': we had the sunniest, cuddliest, cheerfulest baby in Bristol. And though we did our best to conceal it, keen observers might have detected a smidgeon of smugness about us. We had wanted this baby so much – we'd followed all the medical advice with superstitious fervour, and lived an ascetic life devoid of alcohol but steeped in folic acid, and broken the bank to give him the finest cot from John Lewis in a freshly painted nursery in a warm house on a safe street. Despite the scare we'd had after the blood test, our little boy had been born perfect. And a secret part of us felt that he was perfect because we'd done everything right.

Nicky went back to work two days a week, as a careers adviser for teenagers; I was working the evening shift on the city's daily paper, and having the most fun of my life during the day – trundling a pushchair, heating bowls of puréed fruit, waltzing round the community hall at Baby Ballet. One baby wasn't going to be nearly enough, we decided. We needed at least eight, in matching sailor outfits, arranged in order of height, and singing harmonies. If we kept doing everything right, eight shouldn't be too demanding. To hurry things along, we might try for twins next time.

By James's second birthday, Nicky was six months pregnant and her friends were all saying she was too big for mere twins – there had to be triplets in there at least. She probably had a whole tray of buns in the oven. And there were bunfights: kicking, wrestling, stamping. Even under a T-shirt, her tummy looked like Giant Haystacks and Kendo Nagasaki, trapped inside a SpaceHopper.

The scans showed only one baby, and we couldn't be sure of its gender. James had left us in no doubt – he'd projected such a definite personality from the womb. We'd sing to him, or play him Mozart and Chopin, or chat away to help him learn to know our voices, as the baby books recommended, and he would reward us with a stretch and a wriggle. Not a Fight-Club Tag-Match Frenzy … just a wriggle. This second baby was immune to chamber music and indifferent to our coos. James would stretch his arms around Mummy's tum and press his ear to her skin, and we'd say: 'Can you hear anyone? Does it sound like a brother or a sister?' And James would look puzzled and shake his head, and his mystery sibling would stay as still as a stone. But later, when Nicky was lowering herself into the car or trying to sleep, the baby would start to churn.

By seven months, it had stopped being funny. The baby was so heavy, and lay so awkwardly, that Nicky had searing back pains. By eight months, she could barely get out of bed. Physiotherapy didn't help, and the GP could only advise her to lie still and wait. When her labour finally started, she didn't seem nervous – however tough the birth would be, at least it meant an end to the pregnancy.

And it was tough. Seventeen hours passed before her contractions were coming frequently enough for the maternity hospital to admit her, in the early hours of 18 May 1996. It took another ten hours of agony before the baby emerged. At the end, Nicky was close to collapse and I was hallucinating from tiredness: the ward was a medieval torture den, and the consultant with his rack of tubes and needles was the inquisitor. My wife was screaming and her feet were in grey iron stirrups; of the reality of those memories I am certain. This was not the teary, hug-filled scene that greeted James's birth.

The baby bellowed when the midwife sponged away the blood. The consultant gave a weak cheer. He didn't look like Torquemada now: he looked like a doctor who'd been afraid that the infant which had been so uncooperative would be stillborn. While he attended to Nicky, I held my new child.

'Boy or girl?' I asked. Even now, staring at the baby's bruised face, I couldn't tell.

'I never thought to check,' said the midwife. 'Shall we look? Good heavens ... definitely a boy.'

'You're here now,' I whispered. 'I'm your dad.'

His blue eyes were open and pointed in my direction, but I didn't have the feeling he was really looking at me. I thought that he, like me, must be stunned.

We called him David. It was one of a dozen possibilities we'd toyed with – Isobel, Greta and Ingrid were non-starters now, and he was too blond to be a Ewan (if you're wondering, Ewans can be gingery or dark, but not blond: that wouldn't be right). David seemed a serious, purposeful name, suited to a gravely unsmiling baby who spent his first five days eating, sleeping and looking as if he didn't fully approve of the arrangements.

And then he started to cry.

For the next eight months, David didn't sleep for longer than forty minutes at a stretch, and there was never less than three hours between naps. When he woke, he wanted to feed: Nicky was breast-feeding him and he didn't so much suckle as attack his meal, like a lion laying into a zebra. After that, he cried. If we held him, he grizzled and whimpered and bleated and moaned, and these pitiful noises gradually built into a head-splitting wail which went on, and on, until it burned itself out and David fell asleep. For forty minutes.

If we didn't hold him, he'd start with the head-splitting wail and stoke it up from there.

We had expected difficult nights. Broken sleep is part of the deal with a new baby. It's a stock image of life for young marrieds, like a fifties cartoon drawing – dishevelled mum pacing the floor at 3 a.m. with a bundle of howling terylene, while dad is sprawled in an armchair, open-mouthed and snoring. We'd been there with James, and it had felt like a game.

Nothing about the shattered days and nights which

followed David's birth was fun. We kept telling each other that he'd soon settle into a rhythm and that, till then, we'd have to put up with feeling tired. But it was hard to imagine a baby who could shriek like that would ever learn to stop. Without saying so out loud, we both expected it to get worse, and it did: David's screams were full of frustration, as if he was going to need a much bigger mouth and stronger lungs before he could really express himself.

We had, after six weeks of howling, evolved a makeshift set of coping mechanisms. The first focused on James. The new baby had disrupted his life as much as ours (that, too, was part of the deal, we kept saying: it's what little brothers are meant to do). We made sure we continued to take James to the nursery clubs, dance sessions, soft plays and coffee mornings where his admirers gathered. Since friends couldn't be expected to admire 15lb of ululating, steaming-mad infant, we didn't take David. It set the pattern for the next decade: divide and conquer.

The second survival technique exploited a chink in David's armour-clad resolve to scream himself blue: he eased off when he was travelling. We'd put him in his pram for a trek to the park, to give the neighbours a break from his noise, and before we reached the corner he'd be starting to settle. If we timed the circuit well, he'd gaze at the sky for a mile or so, with a face full of suspicion and mistrust, as though he couldn't see what was stopping the clouds from falling on him. And as we arrived home, he'd be asleep, which would give us forty minutes to microwave a meal and wolf it, or pass out on the sofa.

To fool him into thinking he was on an expedition, we'd roll his pram up and down the kitchen, or rock him in his car seat on the kitchen table. He needed constant movement, but these tricks lulled him. Sometimes he would go whole minutes without screaming.

We needed a holiday. Ideally, we needed one of those holidays where the parents fly off to Turkey for two weeks, locking their children in the house with a fridgeful of chocolate yoghurts and Diet Cokes. We settled for a family break in north Wales, where my mum and dad had a chalet on a caravan park overlooking Cardigan Bay. It was spectacular and it was free, which was only slightly more expensive than we could afford. The chalet was a four-hour drive away, but we thought we'd be all right, since David liked travelling. We were half right. He gazed out of the window all the way to Builth Wells, our midway point, where he reached a decision.

Perhaps, after a couple of hours, he had realized this wasn't the way to the park; perhaps he thought that, if he stayed silent any longer, his larynx would start to lose its protective coating.

The rest of that journey has burned straight through my memory and left a hole. I remember it the way I remember falling down steps as a child and putting my teeth through my face: I can picture moments, but I can't feel the pain. The brain has a safety mechanism that prevents us from dredging up agonies and going insane.

I know that we drove for two more hours, up the Wye valley and over the mountains to the coast road, trapped in a tin box with a scream that was too painful to be heard: it drilled into the skull. I remember it took all my concentration to keep the car on the road, and that I could relax enough to breathe only when David, on the passenger seat beside me, stopped to draw breath. I remember that Nicky and James were huddled on the back seat, hugging and crying, both with their fingers in their ears.

Around Machynlleth, the sporadic rain turned torrential. We wound up the windows and sealed the noise in tighter, with the wipers thrashing on the windscreen and the water distorting the hillsides around us. The storm, the scream and the claustrophobia merged in a rippling hallucination, which deepened when the rain tore away a windscreen wiper.

We reached our seaside town with me half-standing to see through the patch cleared by the remaining wiper. I parked on the promenade to let James and his mum run into a cafe. He'd been promised the first ice cream of the holiday, and neither of them looked like they cared about a drenching when they escaped from the car and hurried across the road.

David's screams were no longer constant. They flared up, but he had been awake since Bristol, and he was gradually giving in to sleep. I looked into his mouth. It was raw. Then I caught a flicker of his eyes, before he screwed up his face and bawled again. In that brief glance, his irises hadn't looked blue. I knew that when I'd held him on the morning he was born, I'd gazed at his swollen, creased face and thought, 'Blue eyes, like his brother.' And since then … I couldn't remember looking directly in David's eyes.

That was a guilty thought. I'd spent many hours with James, before he could talk, staring into his face and trying to guess his thoughts. Was this a sign that I loved David less?

When Nicky and I were trying for a second child, I had nursed an unspoken fear: how could I feel the same adoring affection for any baby but James? It was like a real version of the silly, sulky game Nicky and I used to play – 'If I died and you got married again, would you love her as much as you love me?' (The correct answer to that one, I'd learned, wasn't, 'I'd love her differently,' but, 'I could never remarry!')

It was easy to stroke the blond fuzz on David's scalp and forgive him for the brain-skewering headache. I'd forgive his brother anything, after all, and I had to treat them equally. But how could I claim I loved the baby as much as the toddler, if I couldn't even be sure of the colour of his eyes?

I held David's hot little hand between my thumb and forefinger, and promised him I'd never love him any less than James. When he looked at me, he'd know I meant it.

But I couldn't catch his glance again. When his eyes were open, his irises rolled away from me. At one moment, I thought they were brown; the next, they seemed blue, but bloodshot and red-rimmed. Craning my neck and chasing his gaze as it flickered, I couldn't get that connection, the bond I'd experienced so often with James. And I blamed myself.

It wasn't till David was asleep that I could lift one eyelid, and discovered his eyes were blue but turning green, like his mother's. I watched him for twenty minutes, his face calm and fearless now, as the rain washed down the windows in folds.

And after a while I realized that I did love him. I knew he mattered more to me than I could ever matter to myself, and that was just how I defined my love for James and for Nicky. Loving David felt different – but then, I supposed, he was a different child.

Two

The question everyone asks is, 'When did you first know?' At its core, there is our instinctive dread of the invisible: 'When did you realize there was something else, something terrible, something unseen?' Parents of young children ask it with the most urgency, not troubling to disguise their interest as polite small talk: 'How old was he when you found out?'

We usually say that we knew something was badly wrong before David was two years old.

'Oh, Josh/Lilly/Mike is nearly three,' they assure us. 'And Jessie's almost six – we were a bit worried when she was late starting to talk, but she's fine now.'

Perhaps the parents of children with physical disabilities have to nod and grin their way through similar conversations. Perhaps, if David or James· had been born with a deformity, couples with babies on the way would be asking, 'Could you see it on the scans? It wasn't, like, a complete shock when they were born? Because Sarah's had the first scan, and it looks pretty normal …'

Parents with healthy children are permitted to ask crass and insensitive questions. It's their fear talking, their desperate need to believe that nothing bad can happen to their babies. I believe parents of disabled children are permitted to give crass and insensitive answers: otherwise, I'm contributing to the unhelpful myth that babies with special needs are always born into families of saints.

So I say, 'One child in six has some sort of learning difficulty or disability in this country. That means, for a family with three kids, there's a 50/50 chance that something will be up with one of them. Disability is normal. It's everywhere. We just don't talk about it.'

And the truth was that, despite the years Nicky had spent working with disabled students, neither of us gave a conscious thought to the possibility that our baby was screaming because something was badly wrong with his brain. When David wasn't howling, he was adorable. I once showed him off as he slept, at the church hall toddler group, and a veteran mum, whose oldest was a superannuated eight, said: 'Enjoy it while it lasts – he'll be grown up before you know it.'

And I said, 'I wish I could freeze-dry him, and keep him a baby for ever.'

That was a decade ago. I have no memory for jokes, but I remember that quip. I heard myself say it, and it sounded dangerous, too cocky to be clever. It sounded like a lie, too – what I really wanted was to help David grow up.

I must have made dozens of silly remarks that week: I do, every week. Half my conversation, with people I don't know well, is smart-aleckery. But that joke sticks in my mind, and it can only be because, at some level which my conscious mind would not acknowledge for many months, I already suspected David would always be a baby.

The first time we dared face the idea that there might be

something wrong with him – something trivial, something easily righted – he was sixteen months old. The community nurse gave him the once-over, weighing him, prodding him and listening to his lungs. She asked how many words he'd mastered, and we said, 'One. "A-duh." It means "dog". His brother had about a hundred words at this age, but then David was much earlier to walk – they all have different talents, don't they?'

The nurse made a note, showed David some flashing lights and spinning toys, and then stood behind him and called his name.

He didn't react.

She called again, more sharply. Then she rang a handbell.

David ignored her.

'He knows it's you,' we said. 'He's too smart to be fooled by that one.'

The nurse shook her head. 'He ought to turn round. It should be instinct. And his speech is slow to develop … Have you noticed any hearing problems?'

Had we noticed? The whole street was painfully aware that David had suffered a series of ear infections. The screams that signalled physical pain were even more piercing, even more relentless, than his usual howls of protest at the injustice of existence. On our last visit to the surgery, our GP had hurried out to discover what could make a child scream so awfully – and we were still in the foyer. We hadn't even reached the waiting room. The same day, one of our neighbours had commented, pointedly, that she'd heard our child crying all night: she lived seven doors away.

Every ear infection had been chased away with antibiotics,

but they always seemed to come back worse than before. It was plausible that David's hearing was clogged, our GP agreed. He might have a condition called 'glue ear', where bungs of mucus blocked off the eardrum. That could make him indifferent to sounds and slow to talk. It could also give him a throbbing headache, reason enough to scream day and night.

That appeared to explain all our baby's problems. And glue ear was simple to fix: tiny plug-busters, or grommits, would be inserted into the bungs to clear them, the aural equivalent of Draino.

'How's he sleeping these days?' the GP asked.

We said he was fine, that he liked his eight hours and so did we. It was embarrassing to say much more, because we'd cured David's sleeplessness with a dose of alternative medicine which had looked like utter mumbo-jumbo. It was also astoundingly effective.

After eight months with no more than forty minutes of unbroken sleep at four-hour intervals, Nicky and I were prepared to try anything. We'd discovered there was a name for this sleep pattern: Uberman's polyphase. Geniuses from Leonardo da Vinci to Thomas Edison to Winston Churchill had practised it. By working for 200 minutes and napping for 40, day and night, they packed more greatness into every week. David was a natural genius. He'd probably go on to paint masterpieces and win world wars, or at least start some. But we weren't geniuses, and we were knackered beyond description.

'A real genius,' I complained, 'would realize this might be fine for Leonardo, but to the rest of us it's sleep deprivation torture.'

We tried lavender bags in his cot, we tried changing him

and winding him, we tried leaving him to cry it out, we tried swaddling him, we tried snuggling up to him, we tried pick-up-put-down, we tried dosing him with gripe water, we tried CDs of whale song and womb noise, we tried begging him, we tried screaming back at him, we tried anything, even when it was patent desperation ... like spending £57.50 on a session of brain massage by a 'cranial osteopath'.

The cranial osteo said things like, 'I can feel an unusually active mind here,' as she pressed her fingertips to the back of David's skull. I would have hooted with laughter, if I hadn't been slumped, half asleep, across her spare treatment table.

That night, David slept for eight and a quarter hours. And the next night, and the next.

His 'unusually active mind' was diverted by unusual entertainments. We bought him a playhouse: all he wanted to do was open and shut the door. We let him trundle his own pushchair: he'd wheel it back and forth for an hour over a crack in the pavement. We sat down with him to watch Thomas the Tank Engine on video: he ignored the stories, and ran to press his nose against the screen during each burst of title music. At the zoo, he took no interest in the animals, but the mirrorball at the entrance to the insect house entranced him.

Bristol Zoo is a second home to hundreds of families with toddlers. The walls are high, the gates are guarded, scooters and bicycles are banned and there are no cars. And no dogs – it's the only park in the city where a two-year-old can hop, crawl, stagger, slide and roll across the grass without getting smeared in something unpleasant. It's also the only park with lions and crocodiles, of course, but moderate parental vigilance ought to be enough to ensure no one gets eaten.

Parental vigilance failed, one day just after Christmas.

David was clambering over the climbing frames in the zoo's playground, and I was trying to teach him peek-a-boo. Every time his head appeared between the bars, I'd thrust my face towards his and say, 'Boo!' Other dads can induce breathless excitement in toddlers with a well-timed 'Boo!' but I must have been doing it wrong, because David was ignoring me, the way you'd ignore a reeking drunk on a bus.

A contingent of cub scouts swarmed over the bars, and I stepped back. When they'd gone, so had David.

The first stage of panic hit me instantly. When a child isn't yet two, losing sight of him even for five seconds is too long. I scanned the woodchip under the bars to see if he'd fallen, checked the top of the slide to see if he was stuck, and then cast my eyes around the park. There were two or three other children his size, in similar blue tops, but none of them had blond hair. My panic started to swell.

The worst fear is the most improbable, but so horrific that it's also the first thought, before more likely dangers are even considered: what if a molester, a paedophile, a child murderer, has taken my son?

Stories of children snatched from their gardens, or beaten to death on woodland walks with their parents, are rare, but too nightmarish to be forgotten. Stories of children who died under the wheels of 4x4s and lorries are all too common. My immediate reaction should have been to make certain David was not heading for an exit point where he could stray on to a main road. Instead, I was ready to run through the gardens and grab hold of anyone who might have a toddler concealed under their coat.

I called David's name, once or twice, half-heartedly. I was too scared to care whether strangers thought I was a bad father for losing my child, but I knew there was no point in shouting. He had never come at our call. Never, not once. David wouldn't walk across a room if you bellowed his name. He wouldn't even turn round.

And if he wouldn't come to me, the only thing to do was seek him out.

I checked his favourite places – the insect house, the aquarium, the penguin pool. I ran around the monkey islands, scanning the water. I returned to the playpark, and then repeated my circuit. After twenty minutes, fighting to reassure myself that this was a closed environment and that I'd eventually find David, even if he hid all afternoon, I did what I should have done immediately, and went to the front desk. I reported him missing, checked outside the gates to be certain that he wasn't lying dead on the main road, and asked the shop staff at the exit to keep an extra eye out for him.

The tannoy broadcast an appeal as I worked my way around the gardens again: 'Would David Stevens please go to the information point, where his father is waiting for him?'

I realized then how different David was from what other people expected of a boy his age.

The announcer was right to assume an eighteen-month-old would know his own name and that he was lost. He'd want to hear that his father was waiting. Perhaps he would have found a family, and told them that he couldn't find his dad.

David couldn't do any of that. It was obvious, though I'd managed not to see it until then. He knew no more language than a baby two months old – and that made him easier to find. I wasn't looking for a naughty runaway, or a frightened, lost lamb. David probably hadn't even noticed my absence. He'd be doing the usual David things. It had to be the insect house.

And it was. He was tucked into a corner, where he wouldn't be trampled, lying on his back and gazing at the mirrorball. He showed no sign that he'd missed me, nor that he understood how worried I'd been. I tried to hug him, but he ducked away.

He wouldn't leave the insect house, until a break came in the ambient music. Most children wouldn't even notice it was there, masked by the whirring, chittering recordings of insect sounds. But David would always wait for the last note – and if the room was crowded, and he couldn't push his way out before the tape restarted, he'd have to sit through it again.

I was holding the hood of his anorak – he wouldn't take my hand – as I guided him towards the exit, and thinking that his glue ear couldn't be too bad if he could hear that music, when David lunged forward and disappeared up a woman's skirt.

She wasn't even looking in his direction. I yelled his name, which was pointless, and the woman screamed, exactly the way you'd guess a woman would scream if a strange child with cold hands bolted up her skirt.

'Sorry!' I said. 'Sorry, he thinks you're his mum.' I had no idea if this was true, but we'd had a similar encounter at a playgroup, a few weeks earlier, when David's hand had disappeared into a cleavage. The way that woman had yelped made me think David knew what he was looking for, and had found it.

The woman at the zoo was jerking her leg and shouting,

'Stop it! Stop it!' at the squirming form. She slid a hand down her waistband to dislodge him, but it was obvious David had taken firm hold of something. I could only hope it was a thigh.

'Shall I, umm?' I said, and crouched to grab David's ankles. I didn't know if I should reach inside her skirt. It might seem too forward: I'm still not sure about the etiquette in that situation.

David was beaming when he emerged. Since no apology or explanation would be enough, I simply dragged him away, while his victim gaped after us.

'How was the zoo?' Nicky asked later.

'David had fun,' I said.

The following week, we went to the children's hospital. That wasn't fun. The waiting room had a sliding door, and everything went wrong from there.

This was the plan: the specialists were going to change David's life. They would bore holes through his glued-up deafness and drain away the pain, and he'd start talking and stop screaming, and we could all relax.

We rolled up at the children's hospital twenty minutes early. Nicky usually cares more about punctuality than I do, but I'd dreamt, the night before, that we'd lost the appointment by arriving thirty seconds late. In my dream the hospital receptionist was a bullish woman, more like a police sergeant behind her desk, who gloated that David would be deaf all his life because I couldn't be bothered to get out of bed.

The real receptionist was small and smiling, with a Jamaican accent mixed up in her Bristol burr. I liked her instantly for greeting David instead of Nicky and me: 'Hello, little fellow, how are you today?'

She asked our names and checked our appointment, and added to David: 'I love your wonderful curly hair.'

'It's better now I've washed the Weetabix out of it,' Nicky admitted.

'Oh, ho – messy eater, are you? Do you like sweeties?' She reached under the counter and offered an open bag of wine gums. David ignored it.

I picked out a red one and pressed it into his hand. 'Go on,' I said, 'sweetie. Yum yum!'

David sniffed it, and dropped it.

The receptionist managed not to look hurt. 'Don't like the red ones? Choose another! No? Well, you need to go up the stairs at the end of the corridor through the doors, along the corridor on the second floor, up the stairs at the end, and then you go past the sensory room ...'

Inevitably, we got lost. David let out occasional yells, though nothing to make the walls quake, as we stumbled around the maze. By the time we found the waiting room, we were all on edge.

A bright, furry Fimble was lying across one of the plastic chairs. As I sat down, I nuzzled David's face with it.

The screams were awful. It was as if I'd pushed a live rat at him. Every other child in the room, and there were eight or nine, started crying, though all of them together were not half as loud as David, who arched his body and ripped himself out of my arms to the floor. He stood up and threw himself down, stood up again and hurled himself sideways at the chairs, cracking his head across the edge of a seat. I tried to hold him, but he pulled free, stumbling towards the sliding door.

'I didn't mean to ...' I gasped to Nicky. 'I was trying to ...'

David seized the stainless steel door handle in both fists and bellowed as he hauled the door shut. Then he head-butted the plywood, shrieked again and slammed the door back along its runners.

Nicky crouched to inspect the livid marks under David's curls. His head jerked away, and the door hurtled shut with a bang and a scream.

I tried to pry his fingers off the handle, but the shrieking intensified. I backed off.

The door hammered open, rammed shut, smashed open, crashed shut. And when it flew wide again, a man in a tweed suit stepped in and held it open. He was tall, in his mid thirties, with a peninsula of brown hair from the crown of his head, and he pointed at David with the end of a fat fountain pen: David tugged at the handle, and flung himself howling at the man's feet.

'Who's he here to see?'

He was asking me, but Nicky answered: she knew that I wouldn't remember my own name at that point, much less the hearing specialist's. 'Miss Jackson,' she said.

The man raised his eyebrows, and his forehead puckered all the way to the vanished hairline. Evidently, David was not typical of Miss Jackson's patients.

'It might have been the sight of that door that set him off,' I put in. 'He's got a bit of a thing about doors lately.'

'A bit of a thing,' he repeated. 'An obsession, would you say?'

'No! Obsession? No, no. He's a bit young for getting obsessed about anything.'

The man in the tweed suit just tapped his chest with his pen and watched David thrash on the floor. With his free hand he pinned the door back.

'What's his name?' he asked suddenly, with the air of a man who has allowed himself to waste too much time on a distraction. 'I'll ask Miss Jackson to fit him in as soon as she can. In the meantime, the best thing, if he wants to play with the door, is to let him do it.'

David scrambled up, and emphatically shut the door on him.

'That was Dr Howe,' one of the other mothers told us, with a note of reverence that I'd thought existed only in Australian hospital soap operas.

David calmed down when he got the door rolling into a rhythm. I had half hoped that Dr Howe's word would catapult us to the front of the queue, but others in the waiting room were called, and each of them stepped past David with a polite, 'Excuse me,' and an anxious, sidelong look.

Ten minutes passed to the rumble-thud, scrape-thud of the sliding door. Parents talked in low voices, and the other children played with the scattered dolls and trains and Lego, and another ten minutes went by, until one father finally lost his patience and barked at me: 'Does he really have to do that?'

My first instinct, when David was being antisocial, had always been to apologize, but something about the doctor's reaction made me weigh my reply now. 'Did you like the alternative?' I asked him after a few seconds.

'I suppose he gets to do whatever he likes at home,' said the woman beside him.

I turned away. A boy of three or four pottered across to inspect me. He was wearing a clear plastic contraption around one ear. I didn't know exactly what it was, but for the first time I had doubts about the earaches. Whatever that object was on the side of the boy's head, it looked medical and uncomfortable, and he wasn't screaming. He wasn't obsessed with the door.

Obsession – what kind of word was that to use about my own son? And what kind of place had we dragged him to? Didn't he have enough problems, that we had to drum up more for him?

'I've had enough of this,' I muttered to Nicky, and I had already stood up, when David swept back the door to reveal the tweed-clad doctor and a woman in a sapphire jacket and skirt. They made a natty couple against the chipped green enamel of the corridor walls, like wealthy Westerners slumming it in the Eastern Bloc.

'David Stevens?' asked the woman, looking around the adults, though it was obvious the child was right beside her, struggling against Dr Howe's foot to shut the door.

I held out my hand.

'I'm Andi Jackson,' she said. 'Dr Howe is the consultant paedio – he tells me David was getting a bit bored with waiting.'

David let me scoop him up, but when we took one step into the corridor, he started screaming.

'Got to leave the door now,' Dr Howe told him loudly.

'It isn't the door,' I said, as David broke off his howl to suck air in. 'I think he expected ... to leave, he wants ... to go the other way!'

By the time I'd been able to cram that sentence into the gaps, we had reached Miss Jackson's room, and Dr Howe parted company with us. He might have had half an idea of sitting in on the examination – if so, he'd thought better of it.

The room was a windowless office lined with speckled

plasterboard. The speckles were holes, as small as grape seeds, and they seemed to deaden even David's shrillest yells.

'No good bellowing in here,' I told him. 'The world can't hear you.'

Miss Jackson looked harassed. I guessed a hearing specialist needed sensitive ears. David was probably endangering her career.

'I can't examine him like this,' she said, and rummaging through a toy box found a plastic clock, shaped like a house. The cover of its attic window slid back; behind it was a green cuckoo. Holding it up to David's face, she pulled back the little door with a fingertip and clicked it shut.

David scowled. He didn't want to pay the clock any attention, but it had a sliding door. Snatching the toy with a roar, he wrenched at the plastic cover. It was sturdier than it looked: he could slide it, he could waggle it, but he couldn't snap it. Simmering with pique so intense I could almost see it steaming off him, he quietened down.

'I have a feeling,' Miss Jackson said, 'that I'll need to be quick about this.' She lifted a pair of headphones, like the cans on a seventies hi-fi. David shook his head vigorously as soon as the cushioned earpieces touched his skin.

'Hang on,' I said, 'he likes this.' I cupped my palms over his ears and pressed them flat. 'This chills him out sometimes,' I explained, peeling my hands back and pushing them flat again. 'OK, now try the headphones.'

He wasn't having it: one jerk of his chin sent the headset tumbling.

Miss Jackson tried holding just one earpiece to the side of David's head. He leaned away so much that he almost rolled off the seat. 'Is there anything you can do,' Miss Jackson asked hopefully, 'to make him understand that we do need him to put these on? Just for a minute? The headphones play sounds at varying volumes and pitches, and I want him to tell us when he can hear them. We could make it a game.'

'That's probably too ambitious.'

'He doesn't communicate at that level?' Miss Jackson prompted. 'So how does he communicate? Does he ask for things by name? Does he point? Does he try to drag you or push you in the direction he wants?'

'Oh yes,' I said, glad to hear a question I could answer positively. 'He's very assertive with the dragging. A good shove and a scream, we soon get the message.'

'But he doesn't point, for instance?'

'Too busy screaming,' I said. 'And also, if his ears are blocked and they're hurting, he has trouble hearing, and he gets frustrated, so he screams, and he can't think of anything else when he's screaming.'

I was labouring this point, intent on making Miss Jackson understand what verdict we expected her to deliver.

'You think it might be a vicious circle?' she asked, gingerly probing David's lugs with a flashlight.

'He's playing with that clock,' I pointed out. 'Now, the other day, at a toddler group, I spent about ten minutes trying to get him to say "clock". There was a big wind-up alarm clock that played a tune, and he loved it, so I kept telling him, "Clock, clock, clock," over and over. Eventually some woman said, half joking, "Yes, I think he's learned that word by now." But I'm not so sure. I think his poor old ears must be so horrendously gummed up that he can't hear any words distinctly enough to mimic them.'

Nicky poked my arm, a gesture that implied I ought to have an 'off' switch.

Miss Jackson put the flashlight down. 'I can't see any blockages in the ear canals,' she said. 'It appears he can hear sounds, but I can't say how clearly.'

'Music, mainly,' I insisted, playing my last defence. 'David responds to music, but I don't think he can distinguish verbal sounds: they're too muddy. Isn't that the problem?'

Miss Jackson hesitated. She gave David a look, somewhere between worry and pity. 'Possibly,' she said at last, with a weak emphasis that suggested it was barely possible at all.

Three

We bumped into two of our neighbours as we returned from the ear clinic. I can't remember why we told them that David had been having tests at the hospital – perhaps they could see bad news all over our faces. The husband, a man in his sixties, nodded: 'We've always said that baby had something wrong with him,' he remarked.

As revenge for all the nights they had been woken by David's screams, his comment was cruel enough. Other people were less rude, but they gawked when David shrieked in shops or parks. At playgroups, they either moved away from us or they glared. The city farm had a barn full of padded bales, where David sometimes liked to play; he let off a few howls in there one afternoon with me, and for the rest of the session, a heavy-set woman followed us, staring silently and contemptuously, clearly convinced I would hurt David if she turned her back.

The idea of admitting people like that might be right was unthinkable. There could not be anything wrong with David, or with our parenting. We devoted all our time and energy to our children. I had left the local newspaper, to be a sub-editor on *The Observer*: that job took me to London every weekend, but left me free to work from home during the weekday evenings. My days were spent helping Nicky with the children. To admit even to myself that David's behaviour was worrying would be a betrayal of everyone I loved.

I hid behind my optimism. My raucous son would sort himself out in his own good time.

Nicky was braver. When David was still not talking after Christmas, she started to search books and websites for information on speech and language delays. There were many causes, she discovered: the rarest and most devastating was autism. So she began with that.

One webpage featured stick-man drawings, which illustrated typical autistic behaviour in children. All of David's mannerisms that seemed so cute were there: a stick-man twirling on the spot, a stick-man flapping his stick arms like a penguin trying to fly, a stick-man examining his twiggy fingers.

Some of the less cute behaviours were there too – the rug-chewing tantrums, the incessant way he crashed his head against the slats of his cot.

Nicky showed me the page, and I was scathing. If we were going to diagnose our child with a catastrophic disability, on the basis of some doodles on the Internet, then we might as well believe in alien abduction and pyramid selling.

Nicky went back to the net, searching for stronger evidence, and found the *Diagnostic and Statistical Manual of Mental Disorders, DSM IV*. It catalogued the formal criteria for autism: David would have to match at least six of them, from a list of twelve.

We worked our way down the page, trying to translate

the medical jargon into layman's language. When we had finished, there was a tick beside almost every point.

I tried to shrug it off. 'It's like a *Cosmo* questionnaire. Mark your answers, tot up your points and turn to page 43 for our sensational personality assessment. If you scored six or more, see a specialist. If you scored 0–3, congratulations! You're normal!'

But *DSM IV* is the official handbook for mental-health professionals in America. It listed the three key areas of disability in autism: social behaviour, language and imagination. David matched point after point – though we were desperate to make excuses and give him the benefit of the doubt wherever we could, he looked like a textbook case.

He never held our gaze and rarely made eye contact, his face revealed his feelings only when he was screaming, and he didn't use simple gestures like waving, nodding or pointing (that's 'marked impairments in multiple non-verbal behaviours').

He ignored dogs, cats and his brother ('failure to develop peer relationships').

If he'd ever brought a toy to show us, we couldn't think when ('lack of spontaneous seeking to share enjoyment').

He was oblivious to our attempts to play games like peep-bo or chase, and he didn't make up games or copy other children ('lack of social reciprocity and appropriate play').

He couldn't talk, and showed no sign of understanding anything we said ('lack of development of language').

He watched the same videos repeatedly, spent whole hours stepping back and forth across bumps in the path, and was fixated on opening and slamming doors ('abnormally intense and focused preoccupations').

He shrieked if we turned left instead of right when we stepped outside the door ('inflexible adherence to specific routines').

He fluttered his hands in front of him when he was agitated ('repetitive motor movements').

Though he never made his toy cars drive or crash, he'd always chew their tyres off ('persistent preoccupation with parts of objects').

It didn't look good. David had achieved top marks on the Diagnostic Criteria for Autistic Disorder. The only points he'd failed to net were on questions where he didn't even have the ability to be disabled ('repetitive or idiosyncratic language; impaired capacity to sustain a conversation').

I made a last attempt to laugh it all off, by underlining fragments of the criteria which could apply to me. 'I've got dodgy social skills,' I said. 'I like to be solitary. I've got a million rituals. He's not autistic, he'll just grow up to be a journalist.'

Nicky pointed to the last sentence in the *DSM* extract. It warned that the only other condition which accounted for David's behaviours was Childhood Disintegrative Disorder, and neither of us was anxious to know what that meant. 'Stop trying to make a joke of it,' she told me. 'We need to talk to a doctor.'

David was in a sunny mood for his visit to the surgery. He sat on the carpet, ignoring the toys and the doctor, and giggled to himself.

The GP was a relaxed, amiable man. 'He looks right as rain,' he remarked. 'Certainly cheerful enough. Yes, he doesn't seem to take much notice of us, but why should he? We're pretty boring. I'm not a specialist, and I think you ought to see one, just to discuss your concerns, but I can tell you that autism is incredibly rare. In this whole practice, there isn't one autistic child. Yes, *DSM IV* is the standard manual, but it's written for professionals. Don't go poking about the Internet, looking for symptoms: it's a hypochondriac's playground.'

I liked that doctor. I still admire his optimism. My own optimism borders on delusion and shining-eyed denial, most of the time.

Nicky, fortunately, is more realistic. The significant outcome of David's trip to the GP was a referral to a consultant paediatrician at the children's hospital. But when our appointment date came through, it was for December, nine months away.

Everything Nicky had read about autism emphasized that 'early intervention' was essential to effective treatment. The sooner treatment started, the better David would progress.

And nine months was nearly half his little life.

Determined to face whatever problem David had, Nicky insisted we book a private consultation with a paediatrician. The BUPA hospital on the edge of Bristol's Downs gave us an appointment in April, only three weeks away.

I couldn't grasp the enormity of what was happening to our family. When it stared me in the face, I closed my eyes. Left to me, David wouldn't have seen any specialist till Christmas, so he'd have been officially 'right as rain' for the whole of the year.

He couldn't understand a word we said. His bouts of screaming were, incredibly, getting worse. We struggled to endure till the next moment of calm: during the songs in *Teletubbies*; when the theme music to *EastEnders* chimed up; while his favourite CD was playing. But strangely, I could blank my emotions out of each day. The thought that David might be like this for the rest of his life, and mine, was so much more abysmal than anything I could comprehend that I simply skated over it.

If the daily battering couldn't hurt me, the details could. I was shocked when the city library sent a note asking me to collect a book ordered in my name, an autobiography by an autistic woman. At first, I thought it was a bizarre hoax; then I discovered I really had ordered the book, more than six months earlier, even before we thought David might have an ear problem. I vaguely remembered reading a newspaper extract from the book, but the idea that my subconscious had been taking an interest in autism back in September horrified me.

I was outraged, too, by a six-line tabloid story that a child in the Philippines thought she was a bird after her parents forced her to live with the chickens in a hen house. The girl couldn't talk, and she flapped her arms. That made me boil: she had classic signs of autism. What kind of paper reported stories of child abuse as if it was funny?

I could diagnose autism half the world away, from a single paragraph. But I couldn't see it in my own son.

The BUPA appointment fell on my thirty-fourth birthday. We knew it wouldn't go well: David was calm as we drove to the hospital, but for the past ten days he'd been screaming whenever we took him into a building, any building, that wasn't his home. He'd let us trundle him up the street, but as his pushchair rolled through a doorway into a shop or a friend's house, he'd erupt. It was a frightening noise. Nobody joked about it – that scream was full of terror and pain, and it was weeks since anyone had quipped, 'Good pair of lungs!' or 'Somebody's not happy!'

The screaming wouldn't cease until we left the building. I knew David would yell all through the consultation. This time, he would not emerge 'right as rain'.

David did scream as we carried him through the sliding doors. His distress became more desperate as we wound through the corridors, and by the time we reached the doctor's office, he was frenzied. He writhed on the floor, howling so hard that the paediatrician couldn't ask his questions: he just pointed to pages on his notes, and we nodded or shook our heads.

David dragged himself across the carpet, seized the bars of a radiator as if he wanted to haul himself to his feet, and then slammed his head against the metal.

He did it again, and again, before I could pull him away. The bars rang as though they had been hit with a hammer.

The doctor gestured for us to leave the room. As soon as we stepped through the doorway, David started to relax. It was as if each step into a building was a torture to him, tightening a band of metal around his brain. Every step we took to leave relieved the pain a little. I knew that, by the time we walked into the car park, his tears would be drying.

The doctor was looking at David with a face of raw pity.

'I can't say whether it's autism,' he told me. 'That will take a full assessment. But your son does have a severe mental disability. I'm sorry.'

I swallowed. It was as though we'd been falling into an abyss, turning slowly through the void, for many weeks. And now we'd hit the ground.

The doctor told us to go back to our GP and insist on seeing a specialist as soon as we could. We weren't being neurotic parents, he said: David's needs were urgent.

I said I'd ask his receptionist to send us his bill.

'There's no fee,' he said. 'I couldn't charge you.'

We'll always be grateful for that gesture of sympathy. It said, more eloquently than words: 'Go back to the National Health Service. Make them take this seriously.'

If this chapter seems to be a succession of appointments with GPs, consultants, nurses, therapists and psychologists, that's how the entire year seemed to us. There were times when we felt we were punishing ourselves for lack of anything better to do. Everything we read about autism emphasized that doctors didn't know what caused it and couldn't make it go away. We weren't going to get answers, or a cure – so why put ourselves through the wringer?

At every medical examination, we'd be asked: 'Is he in good health generally?' And the truth was, his health was better than good, more ox-like than robust; not just a bonny bouncing baby, but a Barnes Wallis bouncing bomb. He could demolish a bowl of pasta as fast as he could scoop it into his mouth with his fingers, though he couldn't use a fork. And now that most of his teeth were through, the run of ear infections seemed to have ended.

He spent a lot of time giggling to himself, and the merriment was catching – he'd be sitting in the hall, watching television through a crack in the sitting-room doorway and chortling, while we laughed in bemusement. 'Inappropriate laughter' was a common autistic behaviour, the Internet told us, but a case of the giggles seemed a harmless kind of medical complaint.

Other parents complained to us that their toddlers were

boring. They asked the same questions, watched the same videos, went to the same places, day after day. 'Basically,' one colleague told me, 'I see far too much of my kids and I can't wait to get to work.'

David wasn't dull, ever. Take his habit of watching *Teletubbies* through a doorway – why did that entertain him so much more than viewing it with us on the sofa? He seemed perpetually amazed that the show kept playing when he was in a different room, as though by going through the doorway he'd entered another universe without completely leaving the old one behind.

Nicky and I puzzled over that, smiling at his bouts of laughter – but not daring to turn our backs, in case the trembling switch in his head flicked from giggles to screeches. We had to stay within a few steps of him, ready to restrain him if he started smashing his head on the floor. It wasn't enough just to keep an ear open, because the rages could start while he was still laughing: there'd be chuckles, and the hollow 'thock' that can only be made by a toddler's skull hitting floorboards, and then more chuckles, and a howl.

Half an hour of *Watch with Mother* felt like a full emotional workout. It was exhausting, frustrating, bewildering, frightening, rewarding. It wasn't boring.

Because David couldn't talk, we still thought of him as a baby. He drank hot milk through a plastic teat from a bottle, and outside the house he never walked but always rode in a buggy. He was three feet tall, but he was a baby.

Except, of course, he wasn't. There was nothing physical to prevent him from using a cup, or holding our hands and going for a walk: it was just that he wouldn't. He could, but he wouldn't.

Nicky and I had never been creatures of routine, but David seemed to expect it. He was happiest doing things he'd done before, and we were happy to do anything that made life easier. So we fell into routines – on Mondays, for instance, Nicky would walk to work, but on Tuesdays we'd take her in the car. On foot, her office was a mile away; by road, it was three miles of one-way systems and congested detours round pedestrianized streets. Traffic doesn't flow in Bristol, it oozes. After dropping Nicky off, we'd struggle across town and James would run in to his nursery. Other parents came and went, but we couldn't leave at once – David would scream if I tried to drive away before he'd sat and listened to three pieces of music on Classic FM. Adverts didn't count. Traffic bulletins didn't count. He wanted excerpts from symphonies and operas, and when he'd heard three, we could go. If he'd been obsessed with Radio 3, which plays the classics in full, we could have been stuck outside the nursery all day.

For Nicky and me, all this was guesswork. David couldn't tell us what he wanted – he could only react when we guessed wrong. We were feeling our way through a maze of corridors, with traps behind almost every door: all we could do was open each door a crack, and slam it shut when a scream burst out.

When we got home from the nursery, David would choose a video, always *Postman Pat*, and I would take a shower. That was living dangerously, to leave David unattended for five minutes. Call me crazy, say I'm addicted to risk, but I did like to have a shower.

And it wasn't as if he could get out of the house. He was just a baby.

So when I stepped out of the shower one Tuesday and

realized I could hear cars and people in the street outside, and I peered down the stairs to see the front door was wide open, I didn't believe David could have escaped. I thought Nicky had come home, or that I'd left the door open myself, or that possibly we were being burgled.

Barefoot and dripping, in a ragged towelling robe, I called out as I walked down the stairs: 'Nicky, is that you? Are you back?' She didn't answer. I could hear *Postman Pat*, though; if we were being burgled, the thieves hadn't got to the TV yet. I stuck my head into the sitting room.

David wasn't there.

Calling to him was pointless. I did it anyway, as I trotted out to the pavement, hopping from one foot to the other with grit under my toes. I doubled the robe across me – it didn't have a belt, and I was vaguely conscious that I wasn't wearing anything else. I also had an idea that I should put shoes on my feet, and that I should check the kitchen and the garden before dashing out of the house, and that I ought at least to grab some keys and shut the front door.

None of those thoughts made much impact. My brain was too busy processing the concept that David was on the loose. On foot. Unaccompanied. It was hard to imagine what that looked like, let alone why he'd made his break. This wasn't part of our Tuesday routine.

I trod awkwardly between the parked cars, scanning the street. There were a few people near the corner of the next street – no one I knew, but at least they weren't shouting or standing frozen, the way they would if a child had been knocked down.

With my arms folded across my chest and doing that high-stepping trot which only barefoot adults on stony tarmac can achieve, I tried to guess where David would go. The park and the corner shop were my best bets, and they lay in the same direction. As I rounded the corner, I caught sight of David: he was marching with a purpose to the grocery shop.

I grinned. It was a relief to know he was safe, and I admired his cheekiness. In years to come, there would be more escapes – one or two that scared us so badly that I still dream of them at night and wake up sick with fear. But this first jaunt wasn't really an escape, just an escapade.

I could hear Vince, the shopkeeper, lecturing David as I reached the doorway. Vince and his family were part of Bristol's Sicilian community and, with the 1998 football World Cup only weeks away, they had festooned the shop with bunting. Vince's accent was as Italian as the flags.

'Hi! Excuse me, little fellow! You want sweeties? You have to give me money, yes? No money, no sweeties. You give to me.'

And then there was a shriek, so blood-chilling that Vince must have thought he'd accidentally hurt the little shoplifter … maimed him, in fact, because no ordinary injury could provoke a sound like that.

'He's with me,' I shouted, and tried to give Vince a thumbs up as I scooped David off the floor and kept my robe shut at the same time.

Vince pressed the sweets into David's hand, a free gift. The screaming didn't stop, even though David crammed a couple straight down his throat.

They were Rolos. David had done what he normally did – grab a packet, rip it open, start eating. He had no idea that they didn't belong to him, or that anything belonged to anyone except him. He had no idea that usually, while he was scoffing Rolos, his dad and the shopkeeper would be sorting out a payment. He had no idea that this excursion had gone so painfully wrong because he'd tackled it on his own.

All he knew was that he'd been mugged for his Rolos. He wasn't pleased. He bellowed all the way home, and the women on the corner scowled at me. They probably thought I'd given my child a hiding for his naughtiness. Or perhaps they thought I hadn't whacked him hard enough.

We have never smacked our children. We wouldn't hit each other, and hitting a child seems even worse. To David, it would have been meaningless. He had no idea he'd done anything wrong: he'd simply done what he wanted. How could I punish him, unless I explained why he was being punished – and how could I do that, if he didn't understand a word anyone said?

I sat David by the telly with the last of his Rolos, and hid in the kitchen. Sure enough, he was back at the front door within moments, stretching to undo the latch and slide the chain free. He'd worked that out on his own – no one had shown him what to do. And he'd done it without any vocabulary. David had no words for 'lock' or 'turn' or 'door' or 'house'. He was incapable of telling me that he wanted to go out, or of understanding when I told him he mustn't. But he was able to observe, interpret and remember.

He wasn't stupid.

We were at pains to stress this fact to the NHS paediatric specialist when he visited our home, the day before David's second birthday. David wasn't daft. He was smart. A bit slow to talk, it was true, occasionally uncooperative, louder than your average toddler, but a bright lad.

The consultant – we'll call him Dr Smith – was a pleasant chap. He saw a very different child from the one who had smashed his head on the radiator at the BUPA hospital, a few weeks earlier. David was quiet, and distant. Nicky and I were talkative, and emphatic: we accepted that our son had learning difficulties, but we refused to ignore all his abilities. Dr Smith tentatively diagnosed a communication disorder, and promised that David would have a full assessment as soon as possible.

James started primary school that September. Six days later, David's assessment began, at the Tyndall's Park Children's Clinic, just around the corner from Bristol University and the BBC buildings: he was having his bumps examined in a select part of town.

We parked under a chestnut tree. Wood pigeons perched in the heavy branches and cooed at us; a squirrel was on the wall, watching. As we sat and steeled ourselves to go into the clinic, David showed us his new trick – he could unbuckle the belt of his car seat.

'It took me a week to work that out,' I said, 'and I had the instructions.'

'Let's get you assessed while we're here,' Nicky said.

We felt like frauds as we led David into the clinic. He was grinning and bouncing. There were two other children in the waiting room, and they were both in wheelchairs. One little girl was bald, with dark rings around her eyes. She looked exhausted. The other might have been a boy or a girl – thick curls, a round face, a clear bag on a stick which fed a liquid through a tube under the child's jumper.

I smiled at the mother. 'Who's this?' I asked.

She just stared at me. 'Kayley,' she said at last.

'Hello Kayley. You've got lovely hair.'

The child's head lolled from side to side. The mother reached over to wipe her mouth.

'This is David,' I said. 'He's two. How old are you?'

Kayley's head turned away. Her eyes were rolled up. 'She's deaf,' said her mother, 'and blind. She can't move on her own. She has to be fed through a tube in her belly.'

She said each fact like an accusation. Whatever was the matter with our child, it was insignificant compared to everything inflicted on her daughter.

I wanted to tell her it wasn't my fault. I wanted to gather all the teddies from the shelves around the room and press them into Kayley's arms. I wanted to take her home and care for her and nurse her till a miracle happened and she could see.

And she was a stranger's child. I couldn't begin to imagine how I'd feel if she was my own little girl.

More than anything, I wanted to take my child away. He didn't belong here. He was healthy and clever, and I was dragging him into a place where he would be labelled as sick. One look at Kayley told you that this was the last place any parent would want to bring their child – but we'd campaigned to be here. We'd demanded an assessment.

Kayley's mum was watching me. I looked away, and tried to catch the bald girl's eye, and gave her a desperate smile and a thumbs up. She looked like she was having chemotherapy for cancer. There was nothing I could do to help her or Kayley. Even the teddies were a symbol of impotence, donated by well-meaning businesses who wanted to make life better for children like these and had no idea how. Here was a little girl who was too weak to hold a teddy, and another who couldn't move her arms by herself to hug it – and my own son, who didn't know what teddies were for and didn't care. But soft toys were stacked all round the room, like a mockery.

There was nothing keeping us there. No law said David must be assessed. We had marched to the brink of a dark hole in the ground, but we could still step back.

'Let's go home,' I whispered to Nicky. 'We don't have to put him through this.'

'You're not making this any easier,' she hissed back.

I felt ashamed. There was nothing useful I could do in this waiting room, except make things a little more bearable for my wife. Instead, I was indulging in self-pity.

David started to whinge. Then he wailed. Then he yelled. Then he let rip. I looked at Nicky, and I could see she shared my relief: David was showing our credentials. We had a right to be at the clinic.

A nurse showed us into a hall, with a child-sized dining table and beanbags and plastic crates of toys. 'Fine healthy lungs,' she commented.

'Just warming up,' we said.

Other parents arrived. All the children in David's group were there to be assessed, over the next six weeks, for suspected autism. David's howls set everyone off. He was the youngest, and almost certainly the loudest, but a couple of his competitors had developed techniques which went beyond mere volume. One child, the only girl in the room, could hit a high note and hold it, without wavering, for minutes on end. It was like a finger running round the rim of a glass, right inside your eardrum.

There were three boys, all older than our son and just as robust. There were also twin brothers, aged three, and the girl, who was about five: she could talk, but she had, as one of the therapists remarked, some 'idiosyncratic behaviours'.

She liked to wear her clothes back to front, for instance. I couldn't see much harm in that, but the girl had an older autistic brother and the GP was concerned about a genetic link.

The twins had an autistic brother too, and a sister with a wasting disease. The brother lived at a residential school in the Midlands. Nicky, who was braver than me with her reading, already knew autism could sometimes be so bad that a child would be unable to keep living at home.

I hadn't realized that.

A parade of medical types examined David during the following weeks. I lost track of them, but I know that one day a white-haired consultant came and stood in the cramped room where the parents spent each morning. He watched the children through a one-way mirror, and I asked him if he'd always specialized in autism.

'Not really,' he said. 'You hardly used to see it, years ago. If you did, the child would go into an institution by the age of five, and nature would take its course. I sometimes think that's still the kindest option – for the family, as well as the child.'

'When you say nature would take its course ...'

'Well, there was a lot more TB around in those days,' he remarked.

Those six weeks were hard. The other parents were emotional, and there's nothing like the tears of strangers to let you know you've arrived at a bad place. But the attitude of the therapists and nurses was tougher to bear. They'd seen all this before; they were used to the story; they knew the ending. We didn't – this was the first time a child of ours had been diagnosed with a disability, and we refused to submit without a struggle.

Looking back, it's clear the nurses had the right attitude. Almost all the other parents, like us, had convinced themselves their children could not be autistic. One father would cut off the discussion if the word was even mentioned. Others, like us, had stacked the facts precariously, so that the child's problems, when viewed from a certain angle, seemed ambiguous. We kept emphasizing that David couldn't talk. He was smart, he was bright, he could work out buckles and locks and gadgets, so he didn't have 'learning difficulties' – he just couldn't talk. It would hold anybody back. Once that was sorted out, he'd be flying.

No one ever quite said: 'Face facts. Get real. You're only fooling yourselves.'

They didn't have to. The looks and gestures, the sighs and tuts, said enough. And if we ever conceded any small criticism of David's behaviour, we were eagerly encouraged – at the worst moments, it felt like we were being urged to inform against our own child. An administrator sat with us as we went through every question on the forty-three pages of the application forms, spread across three sections, for his Disability Living Allowance (DLA) award. We were asked to describe 'things the child does because of their mental health problems' and 'why the child needs someone awake with them during the night' and 'roughly how many times a day the child needs help'.

We gave up on that set of forms, twice. We didn't want the money, and we didn't want social workers and civil servants to know our private family business – how often we were woken at night, for instance.

But without the DLA, it would be harder to obtain a statement of David's educational needs from the city council, and without a statement he wouldn't get extra help at school. And it was plain that David wasn't going to fit straight into the local primary. So we answered the questions.

Roughly how many times a day did he need help? '*Constantly.*'

Roughly how long did it take each time? '*Constant.*'

Did he have a delay in the development of learning skills? '*Does not comprehend or respond to speech; cannot understand instructions or make requests; cannot use coherent gestures; cannot distinguish between people (e.g. confuses other adults with his parents); gives no facial clue to what he is thinking; shrieks, screams, bites himself, smashes his head on walls, etc., when he cannot make himself understood (i.e. continually).*'

We felt as if we were signing his committal papers.

David found the assessment just as distressing. He hated the clamour of the other children and the fuss the staff made of him. My temper frayed as I watched one nurse try repeatedly to perch a straw hat on his head while she sang 'The Sun Has Got His Hat On'. David was livid, and I couldn't understand why she didn't see how angry she was making him. I realize now that was the point: a boy of two and a half ought to be enjoying a song and a game with a cheerful lady. He couldn't talk, and he couldn't understand instructions, and the staff were carrying out their assessment in the only possible way.

One morning, a woman with mournful eyes came and gazed at the parents. She watched with muted sighs as I boiled the clinic's two-cup kettle again and again for the seven adults, and she offered a hopeless little smile whenever I turned in her direction. Other people seemed to know her, so I assumed she was a relative or one of the staff.

'I'm Mary,' she said, suddenly holding out her hand to me. 'From social services.'

I goggled at her. 'We haven't asked for a social worker.'

'But when you do,' she said, with another of her hopeless little smiles, 'it'll be me.'

'Why? David's very well cared for. Surely the doctors haven't told you any different?'

'It's routine,' said Mary. 'David has special needs, so obviously a social worker has to be available.'

'We don't want that!'

The social worker shrugged, and simpered. 'It's routine,' she repeated.

'Are all disabled children treated as social-work cases in Bristol?'

'If they're serious enough.'

'But it's insulting! And it's a waste of money. He's still being assessed – we don't even know what's the matter with him.'

'It must be serious,' Mary said, 'or he wouldn't be here. And we believe in early intervention. It's best for the child.'

Nicky was meeting the speech therapist. I urgently needed her with me. Through her work as a careers adviser, she had professional experience of social workers. I knew them only from news stories, as bureaucratic sadists who accused ordinary parents of devil worship, and who barred cigarette smokers from adopting babies. After ten years of personal dealings with social workers, of course, I now know they're much worse than that.

'What sort of intervention?' I asked Mary.

'You might want David to have respite care, or to have him fostered for short periods.'

'David lives with his family,' I said, my voice shaking, 'and we're all coping very well.'

'That might change,' she said.

It was like blundering into an East European sitcom – 'One Foot in the Kafka', or 'Are You Being Absurd?' Her talk of respite and fostering sounded like a threat, but the way she shrugged off my indignation was even more frightening. She clearly had no doubt that Nicky and I had failed to be adequate parents. That was self-evident: our child was disabled.

It was so sinister that what followed sounds like a bad gag from the Kafka sitcom. I didn't see Mary again, because she moved jobs a few weeks later, but Nicky subsequently met her at the Tyndall's Park Christmas party. The gaunt clinical psychologist donned a cotton-wool beard to play Father Christmas, and gave the children bottles of bubbles. David wasn't interested. Nicky blew streams of bubbles for him, and he screamed when they touched his skin, so she stopped. She put the bottle on a table.

Just before the end of the party, she watched Mary slide David's bottle of bubbles into her bag, without looking at it.

Nicky couldn't challenge her. 'The whole party was so upsetting, and that just summed our year up,' she later said to me. 'The social worker stole David's Christmas present.'

There was one high point during the six-week assessment, one moment that made the experience worthwhile for David. Another boy knocked a glass full of brushes off the painting table, and it smashed. David was agog. He'd had no idea that things could shatter.

He grabbed a doll and threw it, but it bounced.

He hurled a toy car at the floor, but it rolled into a corner.

He picked up a chair, and got a good telling-off, which meant the square root of nothing at all.

He swept a coffee mug on to the floor, and it exploded. Joy.

That evening, he threw Nicky's glass of orange juice at the wall. Then he flipped her dinner on to the floor. When we'd cleared up, he whisked a plate out of the dishwasher and skimmed it like a frisbee down the kitchen.

David had discovered a purpose in life.

We sort of forgot to mention this to the staff at Tyndall's, the following morning, but they found out. For the rest of the assessment, they had their tea out of paper cups.

We'd expected to see Dr Smith, the consultant who had visited David at home, during the six weeks, but he was on a sabbatical. He returned in time to discuss the team's initial findings with us: on the last day, the parents were called into his office in turn.

We were there to learn the truth about our son's disability: whether he would ever marry, get a job, live independently ... all these hopes depended on the doctor's findings. But we exchanged the usual English pleasantries first – 'You're very tanned, have you been somewhere nice? Warmer than Bristol, obviously!'

Dr Smith explained he'd spent his break in central Africa, working with refugees. He was diffident, earnest, impossible to dislike. And he was anxious to put David's problems into context.

'Autism isn't just one thing,' he said. 'We call it a spectrum disorder, because it covers a wide range of needs and behaviours, some of them slight and some of them severe. The spectrum of light progresses from the palest colours to dark blues that are so intense the eye can barely see them. And that's what autism is like: one child might be in the yellows and greens, and that's what we call 'high-functioning'. At the other extreme, there's profound autism where, really and practically, there's no ability to function at all.'

Nicky and I were both leaning forward, literally on the edge of our seats.

'And where's David on this spectrum?' Nicky asked. 'Is he more … high-functioning?'

The doctor sighed. And then he smiled.

'Yes. High-functioning. If he's even on the spectrum at all, David is certainly no worse than mildly autistic.'

Four

We made the doctor say it again. We couldn't quite believe it, even when it was what we desperately wanted to hear: 'Your son is probably not autistic, or only mildly so. He has a communication disorder, and that has to be addressed. But my opinion is that he's outside the autistic spectrum.'

This was straightforward headline news, as far as I was concerned. 'NIGHTMARE OVER ... Screaming Boy of Bristol is Not a Fruitloop, Say Medics.'

Nicky was less trusting. She wanted to see the written report. That came two weeks later, by post: it described David's 'significant difficulties' with communication, his 'unusual patterns' of behaviour and his way of treating others 'more as objects than people'.

'All these aspects quite clearly put David within the autistic spectrum of difficulties,' the report concluded.

We read it over and over. The report's most devastating findings were contained in a single paragraph, and I found it impossible to read more than a few words before my brain blanked out. I had to chisel the meaning out of those sentences, inch by inch.

Dr Smith had the grace to visit us and apologize. He admitted he had based his conclusions on his brief inspection of David six months earlier, in our kitchen. He hadn't looked at the stack of reports from the assessment before seeing us, fresh from his African trip. Now he revised his diagnosis: David was moderately to severely autistic.

Moderate to severe: he didn't like to be more specific than that.

By the time the Tyndall's Park specialists called us to a meeting, the final stage of the report, David's diagnosis had been revised upward again. He was now 'profoundly autistic'. That was as bad as Autistic Spectrum Disorder (ASD) could be, off the scale in the invisible colours. David's autism was ultraviolet.

'What about other learning difficulties?' Nicky asked. 'We've read that about 80 per cent of severely autistic children have general learning difficulties, as well as the specific ASD issues.'

The clinical psychologist waved a hand. 'I shouldn't get too hung up about that,' he said. There was impatience in his tone, the way a scientist would dismiss worries about a hosepipe ban after an announcement that the Earth was about to plunge into the Sun.

David was officially 'disabled'. We realized for the first time how broad that word was. It superceded all other characteristics. Most single-word summaries of people are trite, at best, and usually offensive, racist, sexist, contemptuous. But medical opinion seemed to be that one word was good enough for David now: he was disabled. And Nicky and I no longer had 'young kids' – we were 'parents of a disabled child'.

The nurses kept urging us to take David to the NHS

playgroup for disabled preschoolers. We'd meet 'other parents like us' and David might feel more relaxed with other 'disabled kids'.

We resisted the idea. It felt like the lid of another box was closing. The nurses, of course, expected us to resist: 'parents like us' always went through 'denial'. We tried to turn the argument upside down – David was 'disabled' because he was 'profoundly autistic', which meant he regarded other children as 'objects'. He wouldn't care if he was with a group of 'disabled' toddlers or a squad of teenage gymnasts training for the Olympics. Either way, he'd ignore them.

The nurses nodded sympathetically. It was good when 'parents like us' moved from 'denial' into 'anger'. That was part of the acceptance process.

In the end, the easiest option was to do what they wanted us to do. We took David to the playgroup.

All five of the other children there had Down's syndrome. I knew as much about Down's as I'd known about autism twelve months earlier, which was next to nothing. I didn't know obvious things: that Down's children were frequently small and delicate for their age, or that the condition ranged, like autism, from mild to severe.

And no one thought to mention it. The nurses had been urging us to visit this playgroup for weeks, but no one had said, 'Watch out for the Down's babies. They're fragile.'

David arrived at that playgroup like Godzilla crashing the Teddy Bears' Picnic. He screamed for ten minutes, and then he found a door to slam. The other parents stared at him, aghast. They probably didn't know anything about autism, and perhaps they all had other children who had been healthy toddlers: David must have seemed like the worst behaved preschooler on the planet. The other children all buried their faces against their mothers.

We were used to meeting parents who were alarmed by David. I'd never seen children who were quite so frightened of him. One of them was a doll-sized girl in a red dress, with bows in her hair. She looked very sweet, and very scared. 'She's gorgeous,' I told her mum. 'What is she, about a year old?'

The woman stared at me and burst into tears. Her daughter, I discovered, was four.

The nurse in charge was laying out biscuits and beakers of orange squash for the children. She didn't believe me when I said David wouldn't be interested – he must have looked like a boy whose whole diet consisted of sugary treats. But he ignored the custard creams, tipped the squash on the floor, and grabbed bottles of formula milk from the mouths of two children. Then he threw the bottles aside, because he liked his milk scalding hot, and went back to banging the cupboard door. If he really thumped it, the door facing it would swing open, and he could smash that shut too.

He'd got quite a rhythm going, when the nurse asked us to leave. 'I've got a headache,' she said, 'and he's making it worse.'

'We'd better go before he starts getting noisy,' I said.

It's more infuriating to be unwelcome at a place you didn't want to go to than it is to find yourself rejected by friends. I felt about four years old again, and it took all my self-control to keep from stopping at the door and stamping my foot and yelling, 'Fine! I never wanted to come to your stinky playgroup anyway!' David was sorry to leave, though. He shrieked all the way home. I should have taken him back, sat him next to the nurse with the headache, and said, 'You've hurt his feelings now.'

That was our only visit to the NHS playgroup, but we went back to the clinic at Tyndall's Park every Tuesday at 2 p.m., as if we were on probation. We'd let ourselves into the main room, and someone would call out, 'David's here!' – the way U-boat captains used to shout, 'Dive, dive! *Schnell, schnell!*' Everyone would make a grab for their coffee mug, and usually someone would be too slow.

It baffled us that David understood so clearly the science of smashing china, yet he couldn't seem to grasp that smashing his skull against the floor was a stupid thing to do. Every time he did it, it hurt – and every time, he seemed convinced that this was the only way to make the world better. Experience had taught him how to break mugs, and experience must have been warning him that banging his head would hurt, but something was overriding experience. This was a compulsion. He had to obey the urge. When we held him and prevented him from harming himself, he struggled and fought and never tired. The desire to beat his head against something hard would not abate or be diluted even if we restrained him for hours. We always weakened first – he'd wrench a hand free and punch himself in the eyes and the nose, or he would find a bone in our legs or faces to pound with his head.

We tried to understand him. Maybe, during a split second of pain, he felt relief from the confusion and terror. He was surrounded by much bigger creatures, and he couldn't understand their language or their motives, or even tell them apart. No sci-fi nightmare could be more horrific. Perhaps the pain blocked that out, and he was desperate for those instants of oblivion, the way a crack addict will give anything for a high that is ended almost before it has begun.

Perhaps he couldn't accept that his own actions were causing him pain. We all blame bad luck and the world in general for problems we've brought on ourselves – what if David was taking this to an extreme? When he punched his own face, he might be attacking the pain, as if it was something separate from him, something the world had imposed.

Or perhaps he couldn't connect cause and effect. If he saw a flame – a candle on a birthday cake, for instance – he'd reach out and try to hold it. He'd burn himself … and then he'd try to do it again.

Slowly, we realized this was what the psychologists meant when they insisted autism was an impairment of the imagination. That wasn't just an inability to make up games or stories. David couldn't imagine how any series of events would unfold, even if he'd experienced them hundreds of times. He couldn't see the consequences.

When we changed his nappy, for example, he fought us. We'd show him the packet of Pampers and the wet wipes, we'd lay out the changing mat, we'd unfold a fresh paper diaper. We'd say, 'New nappy, let's get clean,' in the soothing tone you'd use to coax a cat out of a tree. David never could see where this was going.

When we lifted him on to the changing mat, he would scream. He'd kick and lash out. He couldn't see what was going on, and he was scared. By the time he was two, we had to pin him by the shoulders and change him one-handed. At an age when most toddlers are using a potty, David couldn't imagine what would happen next when the nappies came out.

David was never going to learn to think like us, so we had to try to understand what was going on in his head. The idea of an imagination breakdown helped, but the metaphor that worked best for me turned up by chance on a radio discussion. The show was Radio 4's *Start the Week*, which was broadcast on a Monday morning when David was sometimes too busy eating to be screaming. I tuned in one week to catch a physicist explaining his theory that continuity was an illusion. The universe didn't have to be unfolding second by second, he said – our brains just interpreted it that way. Maths and physics worked equally well if every event in the ten-billion-year history of the cosmos had, in fact, occurred simultaneously … or if the ten seconds in a boxer's knockout count were separated by thousands of millennia. Nothing really happened in sequence: it was a trick of consciousness, to thread events together in a daisy chain.

David's brain might not be able to do that trick, I realized. Whether the physicist was spouting waffle was irrelevant: the point was, could our son perceive events in sequence? Or did everything hit his senses in a souped-up jumble?

It was a bizarre notion. I tried it out on a couple of people, and got strange looks. But Nicky understood why we needed to explore weird ideas – David's mind was very different to ours, or to any ordinary child's. His perspectives were going to make us dizzy. Maybe that was why he liked spinning round in circles until he crashed into the furniture – dizziness only makes sense when the rest of the world is spinning.

David liked round objects, especially coins and the wheels on his toys. He ran his fingertips around their edges, enjoying the way they never ended or changed. Just before his third birthday, he'd started dipping into our pockets to find coins. He sorted them into different denominations and clutched them in tight fists. If we prised his fingers open, he screamed.

We discouraged him from pickpocketing strangers, but if he wanted to go through my jacket or Nicky's handbag in search of money, that seemed harmless.

We still attended the Tyndall's Park clinic every Tuesday at 2 p.m. I needed to fortify myself with a strong coffee before we turned up. One week, because David had smashed our cafetière, I had to take a detour via a sandwich shop for a large Americano. That coffee saved David's life.

I'd buckled him into his car seat twenty minutes earlier, to drive him across Bristol, and as I harnessed him, I spotted he was clutching a 10p coin. He wouldn't give it up.

David was quiet on the journey through town. I glanced over my shoulder once or twice, to convince myself I'd remembered to bring him. When he wasn't howling or kicking, he would sit so still in the car that it was easy to imagine his seat was empty. He didn't share his presence, the way any other child would. He kept all his thoughts and fidgets locked inside himself.

'We're in no rush,' I told him as I negotiated Clifton's backstreets to find a parking spot near the Full Stop Sandwich Shop. It didn't matter that he couldn't understand anything I was saying, or even distinguish a laid-back tone from an angry shout: I wanted to tell him what we were doing. 'Let's get a takeaway from that shop. Coffee for Daddy, biscuit for David.'

I pulled on the handbrake and looked around. 'OK?'

But David was not OK.

His face was dark red. His eyes bulged. His hands lay still in his lap, and he was rigid in his seat. Even as I stared at him in horror, a bluish tinge spread around his mouth.

My son was not breathing.

A slow-moving calm came over me, the opposite of panic. I twisted between the seats and pressed down on his chin with my thumb, to open his mouth. For a moment his eyes focused on me, and then they rolled up.

I could see he had not swallowed his tongue. If this was some kind of fit, it was nothing like seizures I had witnessed in other people. And then I caught a dark glitter at the back of his throat. With my forefinger, I probed over his tongue. My fingernail touched metal. The 10p coin was lodged in his windpipe.

I tried to pick it free, but at this angle, leaning around the driver's seat, I could barely see what I was doing. I undid my belt, threw back the driver's door, swung my legs out and tugged David's door open. All this used up vital seconds. There was a rising bubble of panic in my chest now, a fear that I was wasting my time by manouevring while my child choked to death, but a solid, calm weight pressed the panic down. I knew I had to get this right, first time.

I tried to push my finger under the coin's edge, with my right eye as close to his mouth as I could get it without blocking all the light. I could feel a swollen ridge of flesh all the way round the coin. There was no sliver of a gap, even for a fingernail, and by prodding I was wedging the coin deeper in his throat.

Snapping open the buckle, I lifted David out of his seat.

Instead of wriggling and kicking as he generally did, he hung like a stuffed doll in my hands.

I propped him against my knee and slapped his back, three or four times. Another probe with my finger showed the coin hadn't moved. I turned his back to me, put my right fist under his ribs and curled my left hand around it. A first-aid teacher had told me this was a sure-fire technique for clearing the windpipe – but he'd also warned against doing it on small children. 'It's easy to break the ribs,' he had said.

Scared of hurting my son, and more scared of letting him die, I jerked my hands into his stomach. Nothing happened.

I did it again, harder. Nothing happened.

David was flopping forward. His whole face was blue and he seemed to be losing consciousness.

I thumped my fist under his ribs a third time, as hard as I could force myself to squeeze. Even when I knew my child would suffocate within seconds, I couldn't make my fist punch him with enough force to hurt him. My arm just would not obey.

Turning him upside down, I slapped him wildly on the back. The acid bubble of panic had almost burned through the layers of calm. Setting him back on his feet, I battered the heel of my hand between his shoulder blades. No one had shown me this manouevre. I was just trying anything I could. I wasn't thinking rationally now. My left arm was crooked around his stomach, my right hand thrashing his back, instinctively.

A dribble of vomit escaped David's lips, and then a brief gush. The 10p coin tinkled on the pavement.

He hauled himself upright and took a deep breath. As I

squatted on the flagstones, hugging him and hugging him, he ducked down to seize the coin again in his fist.

'I thought I was going to lose you,' I told him. But he couldn't understand what I was saying, or have any concept that he had almost died. All he had been aware of was some physical discomfort, but that was over. He had no idea either that I was shivering with shock. But he did know that he'd dropped his coin, and he wasn't going to leave it lying there.

Any child might choke on a coin. What was different about David was his absolute absence of fear. He couldn't be scared, because he had not known he was dying. And eight years later, nothing has changed: he cannot imagine what death means. He cannot imagine growing up either. He's David, the only little boy in the world, and he always will be. He lives with his mum and dad, his brother and his dog and cat – and he believes with total faith that he always will do.

I could imagine, very easily, how David might have died. I thought of the ambulance at the roadside, and the phone call to Nicky at work, and what we would say to James, and the saccharine bitterness of the lies we would have to tell when he asked if David was still autistic, now that he was in heaven.

I thought of how people would try to reassure us that, in some ways, David's death was 'for the best'. How many times would I be able to stand that before I screamed at someone or lashed out? I didn't want to know how many people secretly thought death was the kindest thing that could happen to my little boy. They were the ones who saw his disability as half a life – the thoughtlessly awful things they could say to us at the funeral, and the terrible words we'd fling back, all rushed into my head.

That incident with the coin focused all the tension which had been building up since the beginning of David's assessment. We walked into the Tyndall's Park clinic, and I felt we were a pair of ghosts. I looked at David and could not believe he was still alive. I looked at myself, and heard the greetings and small talk I was mouthing, and I could barely accept that the nightmare had slipped past us. I didn't have to talk to paramedics and police, or break the worst news possible to my wife. I could go on ignoring the people who thought David would be better off dead, because he wasn't.

As the shock subsided, I drew confidence from the strength of my reaction. I came so close to losing David, that afternoon, that it felt for a few hours as if he'd died. And I've never forgotten the grief and the shock of it. I started to see the experience as a privilege: it helped me reject the idea that our son was inferior to other children. Even when David's tantrums were at their most ferocious and most pitiful, I knew beyond doubt that we loved him as much as we could love any child. The sad-sigh-and-shake-of-the-head brigade could carry on giving David doe-eyed stares and rueful smiles: if they thought he was worth less than other toddlers, they were wrong.

As far as David was concerned, he was perfectly normal. The rest of the world was odd, but that was its problem. We were going to treat him as an ordinary child. If anyone was bewildered by that, they could work it out in their own time.

An encounter in the playpark, a couple of days later, put the seal of approval on our new approach. It was a sunny schoolday, so the sandpit was churning with under-fours and the wall around it was dotted with indulgent adults. I wasn't the only father there: a guy with a Harley-Davidson T-shirt and a designer jacket slung over one shoulder was watching a bruising boy stomp his authority all over the park. He was hurling plastic buckets, careering through sandcastles, clambering up slides and roaring like a motorbike. That was the boy, of course – the dad looked like he'd join in, except he might get sand in his mobile phone.

David was astride a wooden elephant on a spring. He'd been rocking on it and chortling for ten minutes, when the motorbike boy seized the elephant's ears and leapt aboard, shoving David aside. One or two of the mothers tutted.

The Harley dad gave me a sideways grin. 'Survival of the fittest in this place,' he said.

David marched to the front of the elephant. He leaned into the boy's face. The boy ignored him. David shrieked.

It was a noise like a tomcat being scalded by the blast from a steam whistle. David opened up at full volume and the shriek didn't waver until the bigger boy had scrambled backwards off the elephant and run to his dad. Then David closed his mouth, climbed back on to the ride, and continued to rock and chortle.

I winked at the Harley dad. 'David's highly evolved,' I said.

I was treated to the scalded cat/steam whistle too when we left. David let me steer him to the gate of the park, but as soon as we stepped outside, he threw himself backwards on to the path and assaulted it with his head. I slung him over my shoulder and carried him screaming to the car.

As soon as he saw his car seat, David calmed down. We'd driven to the park as we always did; we'd parked where we always parked, but the sight of our green Volvo seemed to be a merciful surprise to David. The transition

from playpark to car was indescribably strange and frightening for him, like a settler on Mars who has to cross a
tract of space-desert to reach his spaceship. The unknown
terrors of that desert were infinite – between sandpit and
Volvo, David was a lonely speck in a vast and malevolent
galaxy.

He stayed calm all the way home, apart from once when
I had to back up a few feet to let a bin lorry squeeze past.
David couldn't cope with reverse gear. Cars were supposed
to travel forwards: that was the point of them. Reversing
was unnatural, like time running backwards. He screamed,
and he kept screaming till we restored order to the
universe by edging forwards again.

David's melodramatic attitude to transitions made
house-hunting difficult. We'd decided to move – house
prices were finally picking themselves up off the floor, and
we wanted to buy a place with a garden while we could
afford one. We scoured the estate agents' windows on the
other side of the city, beyond the rolling downs which
bounded the Avon Gorge. The air on those heights was
clean, while our terraced house lay at the bottom of a bowl
which filled with engine fumes every summer. On a sunny
day, we could stand at the middle of Brunel's suspension
bridge and pick out our rooftop amid the brick rows,
under a smarting haze of gases. A quarter of children in
central Bristol carried asthma inhalers. We didn't fancy our
chances of teaching David to use one, when he couldn't
even drink from a cup. Better to move, while he still had
his much-admired 'good set of lungs'.

But when we carried him through the front door of the
first property on our list, he went spare. The agent gritted
her teeth and tried to keep her sales pitch upbeat, but she

must have known that first impressions are crucial and most buyers don't regard a child's hysterical breakdown as any sort of a good omen. She probably couldn't imagine us sitting down with the printed details over a coffee and saying, 'I liked that first one – you know, where David tried to rip up the patio with his teeth.'

We developed a relay system: when James had gone to school, I'd take a look round a house while Nicky sat in the car with David, listening to nursery-rhyme cassettes. If a property looked promising, we'd reverse our roles. David let us know when he was bored by unbuckling his car seat, crawling over the handbrake, ejecting the cassette and unspooling 200 yards of tape with a twitch of his finger. He could do that in a blur, in less time than it took to say, 'David, don't …' His instinct for destruction was breathtaking – while we were bringing boxes down from our attic, getting ready for the move, David found a hoard of C-90 cassettes that I'd laboriously pirated in my teens from friends' LPs and library recordings. In three minutes, the time it had taken to boil a kettle, he carpeted our bedroom with brown magnetic ribbon.

The strain of house-hunting helped us ignore the implications of David's diagnosis. We couldn't think about the rest of our lives until we had sorted out somewhere to live. These were major problems we had to ignore – would David ever learn to communicate, where would he live when he was grown up, and who would take care of him if we died? Most of our friends collaborated with us by making the tiniest of small talk: the louder David screamed, the more interested they would be in James's paintings on the fridge. One or two took the opposite tack, and asked the most direct questions they could: 'What's going to happen to him when he's an adult?' one friend demanded, in a tone that warned I hadn't thought properly about this whole autism business.

To make sure we kept from thinking about it, we inspected about forty houses, made offers on seven, got outbid four times, put in three mortgage applications, had two refused on surveyors' reports, got gazumped once, and lost two buyers. The houses within our range were being fought over by buy-to-let investors as well as couples with families, and average prices were rising by a few thousand every week. Unless we got lucky quickly, we were going to end up mortgaged to the backs of our teeth. So we asked ourselves, 'What happens if we go straight for those mortgage molars? What kind of house do we find now?'

The answer, and the price, made us whimper. We looked round a semi-D on a leafy street close to Redland Green, with views across the city to the hills round Bath, with gardens front and back, fruit trees and light, airy rooms. The vendors were retiring to live abroad, and had already dropped their price by £20,000 for a quick sale. The decor was putting buyers off – 'It's a bit grim,' I warned Nicky, as she went inside and I took custody of David and the nursery-rhyme tapes. 'Grim' meant every wooden surface was painted battleship grey, the threadbare carpets were burgundy, the built-in cupboards were made from buckling plywood, and the kitchen was coated in grease – when I pulled a dangling length of string above the breakfast table, to switch on a fly-crusted neon light, it left a treacly line across my palm.

'Needs some work,' admitted the estate agent. 'You'd have to be the sort of people who can see hidden potential.'

Nicky was. She saw stripped floorboards, conversions in the kitchen and the bathroom, a treehouse and, for James, the best bedroom a boy could dream of. We made a low offer which was accepted without haggling, got a mortgage that defied gravity, and moved in at the beginning of spring 1999. It felt like some sort of cosmic refund from the department store of the gods: 'Dear Mr and Mrs Stevens, please accept our apologies for the ongoing difficulties with your order for progeny, which we understand does not fully match your specifications. In compensation, we enclose an improbably generous gift voucher.'

My parents came down to help us with the move. They had, of course, been deeply upset by David's diagnosis. 'We'll have a proper conversation one day, mate,' my dad insisted to his grandson. 'A conversation, you and me.'

Mum had probably been expecting to spend the day making cups of sugary tea for the removals team, but David found her something better to do. For three hours, she stood in the street, opening the passenger door of our car for David to slam. Volvo doors are heavy, and when they're closed with sufficient force, they make a noise like a muffled gunshot. Do that a couple of hundred times and you'll have a headache, but you'll hardly feel it, because the effort of opening the door will be tearing your shoulders out of their sockets and setting your wrists on fire. As we trooped from the house to the van, Dad and I called out encouragement to Mum – 'You're doing a great job' and 'He's enjoying that' and 'Don't worry, the men are making their own tea.'

Our great fear was that David would be frightened of the new house. He'd miss his old home, and there was no way to help him understand he'd never be going back to it. We couldn't change that, but we thought constantly about how to help him accept the new place. If he refused to go inside, there was every chance we'd end up living on the drive in the car.

We bought a beachball, a plastic fire engine, a tricycle and a four-pack of Rolos. I drove with David across Bristol the roundabout way, via the airport, to give Nicky time to unpack the kettle and break out the baby bottles. When David arrived at his new home, his mum was waiting on the doorstep with a tube of Rolos and a bottle of hot milk. David knew a good thing when he saw it – he strolled inside like a millionaire tourist returning to a favourite hotel. Before his luggage arrived, he checked out for a visit to the zoo. The shouting and barging of the removals men would have scared him, and we couldn't risk that on his first afternoon, so I spent two hours with David in the foyer of the insect house, watching the mirrorball. That summed up how hard it had become for Nicky and me to do anything together, even something as basic and important as moving home. One of us always had to be looking after David.

All but the essential boxes were stacked in the garage. We decided to leave them till we had some energy to spare, and it was five years before we finished unpacking.

Five

If I could tell just one anecdote that summed up autism, one story that revealed how David's mind worked and explained why we were dropping dead from fright even as we killed ourselves laughing, I'd tell this one.

We went to the seaside. The beach at Aberdovey, in mid Wales, was probably the prettiest stretch of sand in Britain until the council built a car park on it, a couple of years ago. It sloped down to a tidal estuary where dozens of sailing boats were moored and children fished off the jetty for crabs. In the lee of the cliff, Victorian houses were painted in a ribbon of individual colours, like bunting. When the tide went out, it exposed acres of the softest sand. Even on breezy days the waves were no more than ripples, and the shallow water was warmer than the sea: it was perfect for toddlers to paddle in.

A few weeks after his third birthday, David was a stocky boy. Any amateur astrologer, confronted by our sons in their bathing trunks, would have no trouble divining which one was Taurus the Bull. For a child who'd sworn off hot food the previous autumn, and who had refused to eat fruit or vegetables since he'd grown too big for his high chair, David was an ox of a boy.

An astrologer who was half awake would have spotted James for Pisces the Fish: he was straight across the sands and into the water. David didn't try to follow. The idea of copying his brother would never occur to him. Imagine a family who took their cat to the beach, and when the children flew a kite, the cat wanted to hold the string, and when they built sandcastles, the cat helped to fill the buckets. The idea is ridiculous: even a cat that thought it was human wouldn't want to join in all the human games. David didn't suspect he was human, and he certainly wasn't tempted to imitate James.

But there was nothing we wanted more. Even if we could only get David's toes into the water, we'd have achieved something normal as a family: we'd have gone paddling at the seaside together.

Picking David up was the first challenge. He wanted to run in circles, whooping like he'd trodden on a jellyfish. Then he wanted to throw sand in his own face. Then he wanted his eyes to stop hurting. Then he wanted to throw sand in his face again. When the fun of blinding himself had started to sag, he let Nicky carry him on her hip while she splashed with James at the water's edge.

Faced with a namby little brother who won't let go of Mummy in the sea, a healthy five-year-old can't restrain himself for ever. James managed ninety seconds, and repressing such a basic urge for any longer might have left him with psychological scars. Two-handed, he sloshed a pint of seawater straight at David's face.

There's a split-second of tension, before the worst of David's screams, that feels like a cable snapping taut, from the base of my skull to the small of my back. It runs down the inside of my spine and, when it pulls tight, headache and nausea strike at the same time. I saw Nicky wince with the same pain, and we braced for a shriek that would freeze the whole beach like a panoramic photo.

But David didn't scream. He blinked, and discovered his eyes weren't full of sand any more. Then he chuckled.

Nicky seized her chance and dipped David's legs in the water. He chuckled some more. James and I splashed upstream for a water fight, while David hung round Nicky's neck and kicked his feet in the ripples. At last, she let him down and held his hand, as he stood waist deep in the water.

We cheered as Nicky let go of his fingers.

David sat down.

He disappeared.

Even as his face vanished below the surface, he looked serene. He must have been certain, until he was completely submerged, that the water level would go down as he sat – and the full truth didn't hit him for a couple of seconds more. Nicky was trying to grab his arm, while his blond hair floated like strands of seaweed. Then he lurched to his feet and, with an air of middle-aged outrage, he strode out of the water. For the rest of the afternoon, he refused to go near the edge. He wasn't frightened of the sea, he was simply disgusted at its behaviour. If the water didn't have the sense to remain waist-high, David was having nothing to do with it.

Years later, I was watching James play a video game and I realized that, although the cartoon hero seemed to be leaping and ducking and running, he really remained dead centre of the screen all the time. The landscape jumped and flowed around him. His movement was an illusion: we expected to see the man move, not the world, because that's how life is.

Not David's life, though. He is always dead centre of the screen. The world flows round him. He is stationary, and everything is relative to his position. When physics breaks down, and he sinks while the water level stays unchanged, he's shocked.

Nicky and I laughed till we hurt that afternoon, but David never saw the funny side. He refused to be carried on to Aberdovey beach ever again. Eight years later, he won't even get out of the car there.

Every day of that holiday, we spent an hour on the phone to the council offices in Bristol. Mobile-phone coverage was patchy by the sea, and non-existent in the hills, and it was impossible to use the pay phone at the chalet park because, although David would consent to squeeze into the kiosk with me, he quickly became bored – and I didn't want to be in a soundproofed booth with David when he was feeling loose-endish. So we made our calls from a playpark on the seafront, where David was happy to force his legs into a baby's swing. I pushed him back and forth, and dialled the mobile one-handed.

All toddlers squeal excitedly in playgrounds; David made a noise like a calf being butchered. When he screamed these happy screams, I talked louder on the phone. The council staff on the other end of the line would ignore the bellows once or twice, but eventually they'd have to ask: 'Is everything all right?'

'That's a happy noise,' I'd say.

'Are you sure?'

'You'd know if it wasn't. You wouldn't need the phone to hear it, you could just open your windows.'

David let out another horror-movie bellow.

In a council office 150 miles away, that afternoon's duty officer would be wincing out loud: 'Oooh. It's quite distracting. Could somebody else look after him while we talk?'

'Yes, how about a nursery?'

'Can you take him to one now?'

'No. That's why I'm calling you.'

We'd applied to Bristol council for a statement of David's educational needs in October. They had a statutory requirement to complete the paperwork in six months, but it was now August and the process was getting nowhere. Coincidentally, the council had a legal obligation to provide a school or nursery place for a child with a statement, but not for a three-year-old without the documents.

I'd been calling every day for a month. The staff at the Local Education Authority (LEA) were happy to waste an hour, repeating the same basic questions about David's disability, but they wouldn't fill out the paperwork.

Every now and then, when I could sense another screech building up like steam in a pressure cooker, I'd hold the mobile to David's mouth. Then I'd apologize: 'Sorry about that, David grabbed the phone.'

'Could your wife, perhaps, look after him while we talk, Mr Stevens?'

So I'd explain about that.

David had devised new rules for this holiday: Ladies Only (except for David) at the chalet, during the day. I wasn't allowed in, and Nicky wasn't allowed out. David started each morning by firmly ushering me out of doors. Then James was evicted too.

If my parents dropped by, Nanny was welcome, but Grampa wasn't. My grandparents, both in their eighties at the time, visited one afternoon – they lived just a couple of miles away, but the hill from the car park to the chalet was a steep climb. I've always been close to my mum's parents and to see them wave a greeting to us, as they walked slowly up the steps, was a touching sight.

David glared suspiciously on the threshold as his great-grandmother patted his head. Then he slammed the door on his great-grandfather.

When we tried to open the door, David put his shoulder to it and screamed. My grandfather has a dry sense of humour: 'Don't think I'm welcome,' he said, and smiled.

There was no point in getting angry with David. He couldn't recognize other people's emotions. A telling-off meant nothing to him. And he would learn nothing if we forced him to share the chalet with his family – I could have held him, thrashing and screaming, on my lap, but that would have upset my grandparents much more, and David might easily have refused to go inside the chalet ever again.

He had to get his own way. The alternative, for David, was too terrifying to endure. This wasn't a mere matter of life and death, because he didn't know about death. He just knew he had to impose his rules.

I adopted the same tactic with the LEA. I knew we'd win, because winning mattered much, much more to us than to them. This was their job; it was our life. And until they worked that out, I was going to call them every day.

I wasn't going to ruin James's holiday to do it, though. He was already having a tough time, watching his little brother monopolize his mother. James and I went exploring, scoffing chips in paper cones and collecting starfish. My phone stayed switched off, because I wasn't prepared to ignore James while I ran through the Q&A litany with the education officials for the tenth time.

Then, to give Nicky a chance to leave the chalet, I'd take David to the playpark, where I'd make the daily call. He'd be happy, because he couldn't imagine his mum might sneak out of the chalet while he wasn't watching. It didn't matter, either, that I'd be talking on the phone about David and his disability in front of him, as I pushed his swing – he assumed everything in the whole world was about him.

At every stage in the statementing process, there were arbitrary deadlines for reports from the paediatrician, the clinic's team, the psychologist, the GP, the community nurse and the special needs coordinator. A row of hoops stretched into the distance: we had to jump through them all. If we missed a hoop, or took them in the wrong order, we'd be sent back to the beginning. If we ever lost our tempers and shouted or swore at a council official, the process would halt and the hoops would be removed indefinitely. I was chancing my luck by letting David shriek into the mouthpiece during phone calls, but in the end it didn't matter – we reached the end of the row of hoops, and the LEA suspended the process anyhow.

One of the officials went off sick: she'd amputated a toe while mowing the lawn barefoot. I was just surprised she hadn't chopped her nose off too, looking for her toe. As long as this woman stayed at home, David's case was on hold. We'd dragged him through the diagnosis because the doctors agreed his best long-term hopes lay in 'early inter-vention'; now the council was dodging its responsibility to help him.

We couldn't enrol David as an ordinary preschool pupil, though we knew Bristol had some first-rate nurseries. The Montessori school where James had started to learn letters and numbers offered to take David, if we could pay for a full-time assistant to care for him. We couldn't, unless we chose to stop paying the mortgage.

Then there was the nursery class next to James's primary school, run by a no-nonsense woman who noticed David while we waited at the school gates to pick up his brother. 'Send him to us,' she advised. I explained that David couldn't talk or use the toilet, and the breezy tone became more insistent, the kind of voice that warns a toddler to stop being awkward and start paying attention. 'Send him to us,' she said. So I bumped David's pushchair up the steps, and he looked around the deserted classroom suspiciously. And then he saw a pedal-car. It had a roof, and a door that David could open and slam, and just enough space behind the steering wheel for him to squeeze inside.

'You see, he's settling straight in,' the teacher declared.

I didn't say anything. I knew what happened next.

James came out of school, and we stood in the nursery while he showed me that afternoon's painting. David sat in the car, not moving, not playing, making no sound. The teacher started scraping chair legs and switching the lights off. 'Shall we see you in the morning?' she asked.

'Depends on whether we can get David to leave tonight,' I thought.

In the end, it took the pair of us ten minutes to prise him out of the car. The teacher gripped the axles and I held David under the arms, and we pulled – but he writhed and fought and clung to the steering wheel and braced his body against the roof and hooked his legs under the doors, and I started to think we'd have to cut the car apart before he finally emerged.

And then he screamed. It was rage, and terror, and frustration, all on top of a standard toddler tantrum. The classroom door burst open as the school head rushed to see what awful injury had occurred to a child on her premises. David got louder. We'd been asked to leave the Tyndall's Park clinic a couple of weeks earlier, at the height of a head-splitting shriek-fest, but this one pipped it. It was the kind of scream that would make Mötorhead lay down their guitars and appeal for someone to 'take that f*****g kid outside, he's damaging our ears'.

'Shall I bring him back tomorrow?' I shouted, as David let go of the car and started smashing his head against my shoulder. The teacher just shook her head.

I hadn't played fair. The woman couldn't have guessed, by looking at David, that he'd behave like that. He looked such a sweet little chap. But the way she'd brushed aside my warnings, as though anyone could see that indulgent parents were David's only problem, had nettled me.

David treated the incident as unfinished business. Whenever we passed the nursery, he struggled to get through the door and back in that car.

It was obvious what sorts of nurseries wouldn't suit David; that didn't help us to know where he might fit in. He couldn't understand words, gestures or consequences. What teacher could possibly overcome that?

A charity called MusicSpace, based at the community centre just round the corner from our old house, offered us a term's worth of weekly half-hour sessions. Music therapy lessons should have cost £15 or £20 each, but these were coming out of the Tyndall's Park budget. After the disaster of David's diagnosis, it was a thoughtful gesture: we weren't the only ones racking our brains for ways to communicate.

The sessions were booked for Tuesday mornings, when Nicky was at work. I didn't have high hopes as I took him to the first – in fact, I had no hopes above getting through the next thirty minutes.

David grumbled when he arrived at the door. He 'eeek'ed, like a submarine's pinging sonar, in the entrance hall. And he went into a frenzy in the windowless music room. The teacher was a calm, reserved woman called Jane. Patiently, she showed David the piano, the xylophone, the drum, the whistles: he drowned them all out. After fifteen minutes, Jane took us back into the foyer and David eased off a little.

'Thanks for trying, anyway,' I said.

'That was a good start,' Jane replied. 'See you next week.'

Seriously? That was good? What counted as bad?

'I've had much worse. Instruments flying round … David's nothing like that. There's no aggression in him, he wasn't trying to intimidate me. More importantly, I can see he likes music. We'll make lots of progress together.'

And Jane was right. Within four sessions, David was sitting on the piano stool, watching as she picked out notes. By the middle of the term, he was touching the guitar strings as she strummed, and he tried to join in a song – he was sitting on my lap as Jane sang, 'Row, row, row your boat,' and when she paused before the third line, he chimed in warily: 'Mehr, mehr.'

'Merrily, merrily!' sang Jane, and we laughed and

cheered. The following week, he anticipated us – when it was time to sing 'Row Your Boat', he started Jane off with, 'Mehr, mehr!'

At the end of the first term, I was driving David home from MusicSpace when the nursery-rhyme tape ended. Before I could flick it over, a clear, high voice sang, 'In the bad, bad lands of Australia!'

I almost drove into the river.

My first thought was that another child had climbed into the car with us. I gawped at David in the rear-view mirror: he was smiling out of the window, and he was alone. Then I thought that we'd passed through a miracle beam, and that David was cured, and could talk to me now. 'Was that you singing?' I asked. But David kept smiling and ignored me.

I turned over the tape. The first song was a silly tune called 'My Boomerang Won't Come Back'. Its first line was: 'In the bad, bad lands of Australia.'

David had anticipated it, just as he had with 'Row Your Boat'. But he'd done it with perfectly formed words. He didn't know what they meant – nobody, in fact, knows what 'My Boomerang Won't Come Back' is about, nor 'Tie Me Kangaroo Down, Sport' for that matter. They're nonsense songs, and that doesn't stop people singing them. It hadn't stopped David, either.

I was hopping with excitement as I called Nicky at the office. I'd just heard our son's first words. Some little boys say 'Dada' … David had launched into a music-hall number about a faulty boomerang.

The music teacher wasn't surprised. We use different parts of our brains for music and communication, she pointed out. David's profound autism had paralyzed some of his thought processes, but it had left many more untouched, just as a bad stroke can leave one side of the body unaffected. He had perfect coordination, good vision ... why wouldn't he have musical intelligence?

I remembered a school friend, Richard, the cleverest boy in my year. A fluent essayist with an effortless memory, he strolled into Oxbridge: he only had to sit down in an exam to score top grades. We walked to school together for years, Richard lugging his cello every Tuesday and Thursday. He practised diligently. But he was tone-deaf and with the first eight bars of a Bach cello suite, he could clear the assembly hall.

I also thought of my dad's father, who had died when I was a boy. He was an oboist, a professional musician, and so talented that, in the early 1930s, he was offered a post with the Berlin Philharmonic. Then, as now, it was one of the most respected orchestras in the world. He and my gran already had several children, and perhaps they didn't want to run the risk of bringing them up in a country devastated by economic collapse, where extremist politics were on the rise, as they didn't take up the opportunity. I'm glad they didn't: my father would have been born German, and I wouldn't have been born at all.

David could have inherited some of my grandad's musical talent. And, like Richard, perhaps his musical mind was unconnected to his brain's word processor. If that was true, then David probably heard lyrics as part of the melody. A line like 'In the bad, bad lands of Australia' would be musically different to 'Do you know the way to San José?' even when those words were sung to the same tune. Most people would spot the different meanings; David heard a subtly altered melody. It was the only way I could find to explain how he'd been able to imitate the sounds of the words, without knowing what they meant ... without even knowing they were 'words'.

That gave us the first real hope of communicating with David.

'Sing him songs,' Jane suggested. 'Whatever you're doing, give it a theme song. Getting him dressed, coming to MusicSpace, anything and everything: a simple tune, with words that explain what's happening.' She started singing, to the tune of 'London's Burning': 'David's clothes on, David's clothes on / Put your clothes on, put your clothes on / Clothes on! Clothes on!'

She didn't get any further than that, because I was laughing too hard. But I wasn't ridiculing the idea – I thought it was brilliant, and practical, and irresistible.

'Be consistent,' Jane said. 'Always use the same song. Before long, as soon as you start singing, David ought to know what's happening next. He's a bright little boy – he just needs to use a working part of his brain for communication.'

'He might even learn to ask for things,' I said, goggling at the concept. 'If there's a song that means "bottle of hot milk", he could sing it when he's thirsty. That's so much better than dragging us into the kitchen and smashing his head against the fridge door.'

'Even David might think so,' Jane agreed.

A growl and a squawk silenced us. I recognized the noise as a threat – not that David was warning us to stop talking, because he had no idea that he could send us signals; it was simply a throat-clearing sound, a kind of vocal exercise to prepare the larynx before the lungs vented. Chattering adults seemed to bother David more than they once had. I hoped that meant he was starting to suspect our talk signified something. He couldn't fathom it, but he might be wondering about it.

Or our voices might just be irritating, like the clatter of a pneumatic drill up the street.

Either way, I was glad to identify a warning noise. I was learning to think like a vulcanologist instead of a parent: the signals that preceded a volcanic eruption weren't intended as a message to us poor puny humans, about to be engulfed by rivers of molten rock, but it was handy if we could read the omens.

And then David provided the clearest sign yet that he wanted the session to be over: he picked up Jane's guitar and pushed it at her.

The guitar only came out for one song, the one that went 'Goodbye, David, goodbye'. Clearly, he wanted to go – and that couldn't happen till the right song was sung.

His gesture couldn't be called communication: it was more of a hopeful attempt to get a machine working, like Homer Simpson thumping a television and shouting, 'Stoopid TV!'

But it made two clear indications inside one minute: David was starting to make himself understood, and it was all happening in the context of his music lessons.

I wanted to introduce a library of action songs immediately. We'd have tunes for every aspect of David's life: he wouldn't be able to blink without musical accompaniment (to the tune of the Alleluia Chorus: 'Day-vid's blinking! Day-vid's blinking! David's blinking! David's blinking! Day-ay-ay-vid's blinking!')

Nicky, probably horrified at the prospect that I'd be in full voice from breakfast to bedtime, had a better plan. We'd assign songs to four essential actions – changing a nappy, getting in the car, having a bath and going to bed. When David showed he understood that the songs had meaning, we could introduce more.

I was a little crestfallen. My vision of family life as a stage musical, with children whose shoes and faces were polished to a warm glow, had resurfaced briefly. I wanted to spend every day fitting songs to incidents: 'You Can't Always Get What You Want' when David was demanding Rolos … 'You Win Again' when he got them … 'Take That Look Off Your Face' as I wiped chocolate off his chin.

We chose a Woody Guthrie song, 'Riding In My Car', for outings, and I sang it four times in the next two days as we buckled David into his car seat. The fifth time, we were in a playpark, and David didn't want to leave – I kept reaching for his arm, and he kept dropping to the ground like a broken puppet. Crouching over him, I started to croon the car song: 'David's riding in the green car, David's riding in …'

He jumped up and ran to the gate. I had to hare to catch up with him. When we reached the car, he looked up and uttered a terrified squeak. Suddenly, he didn't know what had possessed him. Why had he run to the car? What happened now? I started the song again, and he almost fell over with relief. So did I. That was the first time in his life he'd been able to understand that anyone had told him something. If it felt like a breakthrough to me, it's hard to imagine how important it must have been for David. After a lifetime in a shapeless maze, he'd found a signpost.

I wanted to sing to him that he was a clever boy, that we

loved him and we were proud of him. But those things, as we discovered over the coming months, were harder to convey. It didn't matter that nearly every pop song we knew was about love, or longing. 'Riding In My Car' worked a treat, but it meant less than nothing to David when we sang 'I Love You Love Me Love'.

David was three and a quarter, old enough to be at a nursery, and if we could have enrolled him as a full-time pupil at MusicSpace, we would have. Instead, we took him to look at two Bristol schools with special units for autistic children. David still didn't have a statement from the LEA, and without that he wouldn't be going to any school or nursery, but we had to discover what provision was available. The first of the two units upset us so badly that we seriously thought David would have to be taken right out of state education: we'd teach him at home, even if that meant giving up work and losing our house. Nothing could have forced us to send our child to that place.

I won't name it, because there have been many changes in the past eight years, and we know other parents of autistic children who are happy with it. But I won't gloss over what we saw, either. The unit was part of a mainstream primary school. To stop the autistic children from escaping on to the rest of the site, their section of the playground was segregated.

Eight-foot iron bars, like the perimeter of a brutal zoo, cut the playground in two. The other children could peer through the bars at the autistics. But they were as different as humans and aliens, and they were kept apart.

Nicky couldn't speak when she saw it. Her hand was over her mouth and her eyes were full of tears. I didn't trust myself to say a word, either – I was furious. The teacher who was showing us round bridled at the looks on our faces.

'The bars are there,' she said, 'to keep the autistic children where they're safe. Otherwise, they could escape into the road. And they have to be high – these children are climbers.'

Nicky took a deep breath. 'What does it teach the other pupils,' she asked, 'when they see the children with special needs are behind bars?'

'It isn't like that,' the teacher said, icily. She showed us into a small room with no furniture, only cushions, and a thick carpet. 'This is where we bring them when their tantrums get too much to control.'

It was a padded cell. Only, perhaps because of budget considerations, there was no padding. Just cushions.

We drove home, and David started screaming. He went through phases when left turns would set him off. We planned our trips along spirals, so that wherever possible we could take three right turns instead of a single left. But driving across Bristol on a route we hadn't taken before, left turns were inevitable. So were the screams.

The noise stoked our tension. What made it worse was the frustration: we were unable to make ourselves heard over it, though we were desperate to talk about what we'd seen at the school. When Nicky pointed out that we'd missed our junction, I lost my temper, and began yelling too. I wasn't just snappish or sarky. I bellowed, and I kept bellowing and punching the steering wheel until Nicky started shouting back. I've no idea what we were yelling – it was probably 'Don't blame me/ Oh, so it's my fault, is it?'

I do remember it ended when Nicky told me, 'Shut up! You're upsetting David!'

I glanced in the mirror, and saw that David was sitting in bemused silence. His mouth was hanging open, and no sound was coming out. He'd had no idea his parents could make such a racket – we'd never shouted at him, nor at each other in front of him.

We were too drained to laugh about it. We simply drove home in grateful silence. 'At least we know how to make him belt up,' I said later. 'Outscream him. I'll try it next time he throws a tantrum in Tesco's.'

Two days later, we visited another autism unit, at Briarwood special school. The head teacher, Ms Reynolds, was leaving at the end of that term, so she wouldn't be working with David, but she made a point of introducing herself in the front foyer and apologizing for the security set-up. 'All the doors and windows are locked, and visitors have to be buzzed in by the secretary – we daren't risk an escape. All our children have severe learning difficulties, and many of them have physical disabilities too. But our autistic children are pretty fast on their feet. Some of them would be off and out of that door like Olympic sprinters. We have to keep them safe.'

'Not behind bars, though,' I said.

The head looked horrified. 'Bars? Like a prison? That would be awful. These are our children, their school is a second home.' She showed us into the playground, a wide lawn with climbing frames and woodchip. A wooden fence, backed with bushes, ran around the perimeter.

'Come and meet Claire,' the head said. 'She teaches our youngest autistic group. We used to teach mixed classes, but the children with autism tended to dominate. When you've got four little people sitting quietly in wheelchairs, and the fifth is swinging from the lights, guess who gets all the attention?'

'How many pupils per teacher?' we asked.

'In Claire's class, it's two to one. Six children, one teacher, two assistants. We work on the basis that you can't control more autistic pupils than you have hands.'

'We've got one autistic, and four hands,' I said, 'and even then we struggle.'

Ms Reynolds nodded gravely. 'Before I take you into Claire's classroom,' she said, 'let me be sure we won't disrupt anything. Sometimes autistic children are upset if strangers appear.'

And that clinched it for us. We wanted David to go to a school where he was respected. Briarwood promised that.

When we stepped through the door, one boy detached himself from the table and, beaming, leapt at me. His arms went round my neck, and his legs locked round my waist. He had to be unpeeled like a banana. 'Eric likes you, anyway,' commented Claire.

The head left us watching the lesson, and I chatted to Andy, one of the assistants. 'David loves being tickled,' I said. 'That'll distract him before a tantrum can achieve terminal velocity. Also, he loves feeling stubbly beards.'

'Good excuse not to shave,' said Andy.

'And the biting game – you hold his hand, and chew on his arm. With sound effects.'

'Fantastic! A child I can bite, instead of one who bites me!'

The head then took us to her office, on the pretence of collecting a copy of the Ofsted report. Her real purpose, I think, was to introduce us to a little girl called Sharia, who was curled up sideways on a wheelchair. Her legs were no thicker than two of my fingers, and bolsters gripped her head to keep it from slipping. Her hands were curled back to her arms, but with a teacher's help she had managed to hold a brush and draw a boat.

'Sharia,' said the head, 'well done. Won't your mum be pleased with you!'

The little girl couldn't answer. She couldn't even nod. But she was exuding hell-raising cheekiness without moving a muscle.

'Sharia,' I said, leaning forward to see her face. 'Are you a mischief-maker at home?'

Sheer delight sparkled in her brown eyes.

'Do you wind your mummy up?'

I only met Sharia that one time, and she couldn't speak a word. But I understood the look on her face completely. Her eyes said, 'You wouldn't tell me off! You'd laugh! I like being naughty, it's fun!'

Ms Reynolds was laughing: 'You see, Sharia, we can see right through you.'

I'm sure the head wanted us to see this tiny child, who was eight years old and half David's size, to remind us gently how much there was to be grateful for. It worked: I was grateful then and I still am. But I realized something else – David's lack of words was a symptom, not a cause, of his inability to speak. Sharia couldn't talk because she was physically unable to work her lungs and her throat and her tongue. Her eyes had their own language.

But David couldn't talk because he had no language anywhere. His eyes were as silent as his mouth.

'Those staff are brilliant,' Nicky said as we drove home.

'If I was a teacher, I'd want to work with people like that. They could really help David.'

'Thank God we've found somewhere,' I said. 'That's another obstacle gone.'

But the obstacle that came up in its place was a jaw-dropper.

Six

We got fed up of calling our case officer, and her team leader, and his line manager, and her department head. We got tired of sending emails that weren't answered and leaving messages that weren't acknowledged. We were cheesed off by standard thank-you-and-go-away letters from our MP, the minister for disabilities and the education secretary. Frustrated and angry, I decided to phone the LEA's director.

He wasn't going to pick up the phone to an irate parent, of course. But there was a way to make him talk to me. It meant pulling a stunt that would make most journalists screw up their eyes and grind their teeth. Frankly, I was past caring.

I left a message with the director's secretary, with my phone number and the name of my newspaper. I explained I'd been discussing a case with our education correspondent about a little boy in Bristol who, because he was disabled, couldn't get a place at school. I didn't explain that the boy was my son.

The director called back within ten minutes. He'd guessed which child I was talking about – the LEA offices were probably papered with Post-It notes from the calls we'd made. He had the notes in front of him, but he hadn't made the connection that David and I shared a surname.

'Is *The Observer* planning to run a story?' the director wanted to know. 'Because I don't think you've got all the facts.'

'What am I missing?'

'The LEA recognizes this child does have special needs. His parents want him to go to a special school, but there aren't any spare places. We are prepared to fund a one-to-one carer for David at a mainstream school instead.'

He was right: that was news to me. 'Why not a one-to-one carer at the special school?' I asked.

'We're not diverting any extra funds into special schools. That's policy, and that's not changing, no matter how much fuss Mr Stevens wants to …'

There was an audible clunk as the penny dropped.

'Are you David Stevens's father?'

'Certainly am, and I'm delighted to learn there's money to provide a carer for him. But why send him to a school where he doesn't understand anything, where he'll disrupt the lessons with uncontrollable tantrums, where his screaming fits will frighten other children … what's the point?'

'You,' the director retorted, 'have to consider why you are wedded to the concept of special schooling.'

The Observer couldn't run a story about David. Newspapers don't exist to sort out their staff's personal problems. But now that we'd prised the LEA off their fence, we did have a real news story about our son: their pledge to provide a full-time assistant for a disabled child, but only if he attended a mainstream school, was textbook controversy for a local paper.

I called the *Bristol Evening Post*'s education reporter, Kate Hinder. She grasped the issue in one phone conversation – after months of calls to the council, I'd forgotten how easy it could be to make people understand David's problem when they wanted to.

'Little David Stevens,' she wrote, 'has acute behavioural problems, no sense of danger, and requires constant supervision to prevent him hurting himself ... [His] parents say he is being denied an education because his problems are so severe ... Council policy is to provide at least a part-time quality education place for three-year-olds. The authority confirmed the money is available for a classroom assistant in a mainstream school, but not a special school, as the number of children requiring places in special schools had exceeded their forecasts.'

That summed it up, in under a hundred words. The *Evening Post* sent a photographer, and I ruthlessly tickled David into a state of abject giggles: when the story appeared, his picture filled half a page. The reporter added a comment from me – I'd phoned her back after our interview, because I was afraid I'd painted too bleak and depressing a picture of David's behaviour. 'Anybody who didn't know David,' I told her, 'might think he was a child from hell. He isn't: he's a lovely little boy who deserves all the help he can get.'

That story ran on Wednesday 20 October 1999, under the headline 'Please Give David A Chance'.

On Thursday 21 October, the department head from the LEA rang. A nursery place had been found for David. He could go every day, for up to three hours, and a full-time assistant would be provided to care for him; he could stay there until a place became available at Briarwood's autism unit.

The department head, usually an urbane man, was talking as if his jaw had been wired shut. 'Don't think this is happening because you managed to get your face in the paper,' he told me.

'Heaven forfend,' I said.

David liked the Red House nursery. Once initial misunderstandings had been cleared up, about the sanctity of zips and the undesirability of shampooing with poster paint, he settled in happily. Rosemary, David's new carer, was eager to learn about autism: he gave her a crash course. Within a couple of sessions, it was clear David couldn't share a room with the other children. He wasn't a danger to them – David wouldn't think of trying to hurt anyone, not least because he has no conception that other people can feel pain. But he did react badly to their noise and bustle. It would take only one shout from a strident two-year-old, and David would start howling. Once he got going, everyone would be crying. He could turn story time into a tableau from the Pits of Despond.

He was also devoted to destruction. David could assess a room's vulnerable points – the loosely stacked books, the free-standing clock, the hatstand, the crockery, the potential projectiles – at one glance, and then wait weeks for his opportunity. It was useless to warn him, 'Leave that alone.' It was hopeless to shout, 'No, David, don't!' He didn't understand, and he wouldn't have cared if he did.

The only ways to stop him were to hide everything breakable or to stand within six inches of him at all times. Neither of these tactics worked at Red House. The nursery was supposed to look like a friendly home, not an earthquake zone, so the ornaments and chinaware had to stay out ... at least until they were swept up with a dustpan.

And Rosemary, though she was proving herself an alert and resourceful carer, couldn't outstrip David in a crowded playroom. As he lunged for a defenceless teacup, he was happy to trample toddlers in his path. Rosemary couldn't do that, so the contest was never a fair one.

An upstairs room was designated the David Place. It had a piano, a tape recorder and a box of tractors and cars. Rosemary devised new games to attract David's attention every day, and watched over him in the playground whenever the other children were indoors. His favourite game was bowling an old car tyre. Within weeks, he'd grown to love his nursery, and he'd run to the front door after lunch every weekday, singing the 'Red House' tune. But to the other children there he was a ghostly presence, the boy they saw through the window or heard through the walls.

One little boy came to inspect us at going-home time. 'I'd like David to be my friend,' he announced.

'We'd like that too,' Nicky said. I couldn't say anything. What could we say to help a three-year-old understand?

What could we say, either, to a six-year-old who was starting to see that no one else had a brother like David? James had always accepted our vague assurances – we couldn't tell him lies, but we hated to burden him with our worries, so mostly we provided distractions: 'Yes, isn't David being a bit of a noisebucket today ... hey, I can stand on one leg like a flamingo, can you?' When pressed, we'd say David was having trouble learning to talk, so he used Scream-language, and that a bit of his brain wasn't working properly, which was why he kept seeing the doctor.

James was always willing to play with his brother. He'd

kick a ball; the ball would roll past David's legs. He'd flap round in a Batman costume; David would look through him. If ever James found himself in the path of a David game, he was happy to stand there, pretending to be part of it.

'What's he doing?' James would ask, as David ran screaming in circles round him on the lawn.

'He's a Red Indian and you're a totem pole,' we'd say. James would roll his eyes and stick out his tongue, trying to look totemic, and David would whoop and ululate. The truth was that David had no idea about make-believe, or war dances – he was just running round screaming because it passed the time. James, like most boys, couldn't have done that. Games had to mean something. He had imagination.

James was not an integral part of the game, then, on an evening when David started emptying his toy box into the bath. Big brother just happened to be in the water at the time, that was all. And he loved the lunacy of it.

'No, David!' he was yelling. 'Trains can't swim! Not your teddy! Aargh, books mustn't get wet, you big twit!' By the time the toy box was empty, James was laughing so hard that bubbles were squirting out of his nose, and Nicky and I were curled up to see our boys having fun together.

All three of us yelled, at the same moment: 'No, David, not the cat!' And none of us could stop him. Even the cat didn't quite believe what was happening.

She's a gentle animal. She's never scratched, never scrammed and never caught a mouse. But faced with a mid-air choice of landing in a bath of bubbles or staying dry, she stuck her claws out and sank them into James's bare shoulder. For a fur-bristling moment, she quivered there, like a pirate's parrot, and then she bolted up the shower curtain.

James looked like his shoulder had been used for a dartboard. David bounded away to find something even better than a cat to dunk. He's an ambitious lad, and though he was doubled over with laughter, he was back in ten seconds, dragging the vacuum cleaner. When I took it away from him, he screamed himself blue.

'Why did he throw the cat at me?' James sobbed. It was the cruellest trick he could imagine, and he was as upset for Peggy the cat as he was for himself.

'He doesn't understand,' we said. 'He didn't know she'd hurt you. He thought you'd enjoy it as much as he did. If he's happy, you must be happy too, that's how he thinks. David doesn't know you've got different feelings.'

We were proud of James, because he never tried to retaliate. He accepted David didn't mean to hurt him or Peggy. But he didn't try to share his brother's games for a long time after that – and he wouldn't take a bath until David was out of the house.

David liked cats. Dogs were like children: they meant nothing. But cats were soft and silent, and if they approached him, it was always at a saunter, never a run. Peggy had arrived in our family three days after a puppy called Copper, who was tiny, small enough for James to hold in his hands. Copper was lonely without the rest of his litter, and we couldn't bear to hear him cry, so we bought him a kitten. James, who had been having riding lessons, named her after his favourite horse, and so Peggy settled in to be a puppy's soft toy.

She was much smarter than Copper, a miniature

pinscher who has never really mastered the 'sit' command. She was also too trusting for her own good. If anyone picked her up, she accepted it as the penalty for being adorable. When David grasped her round the throat and marched through the house with her, she bore it with dignity and the pink tip of her tongue poking between her teeth. I'd never seen anyone carry a cat by the larynx before, but it didn't seem to bother Peggy: she was purring like a V8 engine.

We didn't let David out of our sight, though – there was the constant danger that he'd pop his new favourite toy somewhere for safe keeping. The spin dryer and the outside drain were notable hiding places.

Red House gave David a new obsession. He wanted to ride every bike and trike in the world. The collection of three-wheelers in the nursery shed had ignited his inner Jeremy Clarkson. His best-loved toy was a trundler, a slug-shaped vehicle we'd bought for James as a baby: it was low to the ground, and ideal for a toddler's wobbly legs. But it was also as tough as a Land Rover. The plastic shell was half an inch thick. The wheels were like tractor tyres, and the steel axles could double as crowbars. The steering had broken: David had thrown it down the stairs once too often. But he loved to propel himself round the house and garden, skidding into corners and bouncing off walls. He loved it so much that he was prepared to take the ultimate risk – and ride it through the mean city streets.

David wouldn't walk anywhere. He had to be carried from the front door to the car. If we tried to make him stand, he'd 'flop and drop' – an autistic instinct, where his body became boneless and he fell to the ground. It's hard to know why so many autistic children use this 'rag doll' defence: maybe it's a clue to a common genetic heritage. Maybe it's just an effective response, a technique that many autistics discover because it works so well. Either way, when you're holding 50lb of preschooler who suddenly becomes a dead weight, you're liable to dislocate your shoulder.

Because he wouldn't walk, we still used his pushchair. If I needed to walk up the street to get milk or stamps, for instance, it was impractical to take the car – we'd end up parking further from the corner shop than we'd started. But David was too big for a toddler buggy. He dragged his feet under the wheels, and no matter how often I stopped to disentangle his legs from the undercarriage, he kept doing it. When we took the car for its MOT, he wore out the toes of a day-old pair of shoes, during the mile-long journey home. On the way back to the garage, he trailed his feet till they bled.

As an experiment one Sunday, I tied a length of washing line to the nose of David's trundler, and towed him up and down the kitchen. Then we trundled out of the back gate, into the lane beside the house. David kept rolling. After a few canters, he realized he didn't have to propel himself – the Dad-thing was doing the work. He tucked his knees under his chin and let me get on with it.

With reckless daring, I chuntered David past next-door's garden. Then we ventured further still, to the house two doors up. We carried on going … all the way to the lamppost. My nerve gave out there, and we turned back, but David was smiling dreamily. I kept expecting to see him throw himself backwards on to the tarmac. That didn't happen. Aboard his beloved trundler, he seemed to feel less exposed, less lost, than when he had to walk.

Perhaps, on a trundler or in a pushchair, it seemed as if the world was flowing round him while he stayed still – or perhaps he felt safer to be bringing part of his world with him. The reason was less important than the result: the trundler gave us freedom.

We went to the park. It was a hilly ride, at least a quarter of a mile, and David was happy to be towed all the way. The washing line was starting to bite into my hand and turn my fingers white, so I tied it to my belt. We had to stop beside every drain grating: they fascinated David, though he liked manhole covers even better. When I was loading him into the car he'd wriggle free, if I turned my back, and hurl himself face first on to the round metal lid in the middle of the road. There's nothing in the Green Cross Code to cover behaviour like that.

At one drain, David leaned so far out of the saddle that his nose was touching the metal. I tried to sit him upright, but he held on to the grating with both fists. A woman stared down her nose at us as she walked by. I thought that, if she wanted to disapprove of us, I ought to give her plenty to work with, so I scolded David loudly: 'Don't lick the drain. Yuck! That's not hygienic.'

I heard an 'Eurgghoo', the involuntary noise made by a woman regretting her fried breakfast. Most children, I thought, couldn't provide their parents with so much innocent fun. I ruffled David's hair and let him stare into the drain as long as he wanted. Then we went to the park.

On a sunny Sunday, just after Christmas, there were sets of wheels everywhere. No one under seven had arrived on foot. There were Action Man bikes, Pokemon trikes, Star Wars skateboards, Spice Girls scooters, little pink bicycles with Cinderella stabilizers and big red mountain bikes with Ferrari decals. And David wanted to ride them all.

This wasn't Red House, though. All these bikes belonged to families. Most of them were waxed and polished objects of infant prestige – and if the children weren't aware of it, their parents certainly were. Into this top-of-the-range kids' showroom rode my son, on a scarred blue battering ram that looked like a reject from a stock-car rally.

David stood up with the trundler wedged between his knees. He waddled to a skateboard, sat down and frowned. This wasn't really working. He didn't want to be detached from his toy – it'd be like stepping outside the Jeep on a lion safari. But he wasn't in the open now: he was safely inside the playpark. He let go of the trundler. The world didn't end. He leapt on to a bicycle.

I was looking round, guiltily trying to spot whose wheels we had bike-jacked, when a woman shouted: 'Excuse me! Ask before you borrow, please!'

'Sorry,' I said, with a cheesy smile. 'David can't talk. Is it OK if he has a quick ride?'

The woman's beetle-browed child grasped the handlebars. 'This is my bike,' he said.

'Do you mind if David has a go?'

'I want to ride it.'

I held David around the ribs, planning to swing him 'accidentally' very close to the woman's earhole if he screamed. But he let go happily – there were so many other bikes to be commandeered.

Few were satisfactory, though. Some were too big: David couldn't balance on just two wheels. Some were too small: he couldn't get up a turn of speed. And most were too well guarded: some owners let him have a taste of riding, and others laid a warning hand on the crossbar and glared. Within a few minutes, David's face was starting to crease with frustration. He wanted to play with these toys, and the world didn't seem to understand that.

Blinking, he walked to a pink bicycle with tassled handlebars. He threw a leg over it, and his toes just reached the ground. It was the ideal size. But it was plain that he expected to be hauled straight off it – his shoulders were hunched and his jaw was jutting. I looked around, pleadingly.

'He can ride it if he likes,' said a child's voice. A girl with red hair, maybe a year older than David, was pushing a friend on the swing. 'He can play on it as long as he likes. There are plenty of other things for me to do here.'

She must have seen David was different from the other children. How a girl of five could recognize that, when most of the adults were blind to it, I can't say. I told her she was a very kind person, and meant it.

David gave the bike a trial scoot. He beamed. He was like Goldilocks – he'd tried rides that were too slow, too flimsy, too difficult, and now this one was Just Right. He set off at a rapid lope between clusters of children, head low, wild-eyed and grinning. He might as well have been wearing a T-shirt that said, 'Mad as a fish and very, very happy.'

'He's really enjoying it,' said the red-haired girl. 'I'm glad.'

Some people are born nice. It's that simple.

The girl and her family live not far from us, and I think of that afternoon whenever I see them. I'm sure she doesn't remember lending her bicycle to David, any more than I'll forget it. It was just an afternoon at the park for her, after all; for me, it was a day of intense and conflicting emotions – including embarrassment, probably the most memorable emotion of all.

Anger passes, sadness becomes dulled, shock fades. But embarrassment always retains its power to make us cringe. Every time, for instance, that I walk past College Green, in front of Bristol Cathedral, I wince and remember a sunny spring day when David was nearly four: he threw his milk bottle into the ornamental fountain. While I was retrieving it, he unbuckled the straps of his pushchair, which we still used frequently. He'd been planning this – the business with the bottle was just to get me out of the way.

A man was lounging on the grass with a group of friends. They were a youngish bunch, office workers perhaps, and the guy in David's sights was completely bald. One or two of the women smiled to see a golden-curled child running towards them with a bright face. The bald man didn't see him, though. He had his back turned.

David smacked him across his bare scalp. He didn't even break stride, just brought his open hand down with a whiplash crack. Then he ran back to me.

There's no apology good enough to undo that, so I didn't even try. I just called out, 'Sorry about that,' as if it was scarcely worth mentioning, and hurried David away. The bald guy sat stone still. He kept his dignity. A red palm-print glowed on the top of his head.

What put that idea in David's brain, we can't guess. He is never slapped; he never sees anyone being slapped. None of his videos feature a slap on the head for a bald bloke. Perhaps all of us have a primal urge to give a resounding whack to anyone without hair, and David simply lacks inhibition.

Hitting a bald man gives instant satisfaction. That's how David liked his pleasures. Delayed gratification meant nothing to him: he wanted to be gratified immediately, or not at all. That was the attraction of smashing crockery – instant result, instant reaction. And it must have been part of the pleasure of coin-operated rides. He put 50p in the slot, he pressed the 'start' button, he sat in an undulating toy as a favourite TV tune played, and then he wandered off to find something else to do.

David knew the location of every ride in the city centre. If we pushed his chair through the Broadmead plaza, David could steer us by jamming his feet in the wheels of his buggy. He didn't point, or shout out: that counted as communication. He just steered, and we ended up in Debenhams or the Galleries, feeding money into Noddy's taxi and Budgie the Little Helicopter.

When a sprawling complex of shops started to mushroom beside the M5, Nicky investigated it for rides. She found two in the foyer of Asda, and one at Mothercare in the main mall, which warranted a day out for David. He might enjoy his excursion enough to sit still while we had a coffee – it wasn't likely, but we had to hope.

As we carried him across the car park, I gave David a £1 coin and sang him the Thomas theme. David took the hint. He scrambled out of my arms and ran through the revolving doors. We didn't have to show him the way – instinct led David to rides. Perhaps he could hear their motors or their snatches of tunes through the hubbub of shoppers.

But he never reached Thomas the Tank Engine. A distraction stopped him. The mall's centrepiece was a wide pool, sprinkled with water-jets and lined with coins.

Shoppers were encouraged to throw pennies in for charity and make a wish.

I thought, as he raced towards it, that David was going to throw his pound in, but he gripped it tightly. He wasn't letting his coin go, even as he hurdled the wall of the pool, waded across it and dived face first into the water.

I was surprised how few shoppers noticed. When they're on a spree, not much else registers. We dredged David out by the straps of his dungarees, pulled off his shoes and emptied them, and lifted him screaming back to the revolving doors. We couldn't let him squelch into Mothercare and sit, sopping wet, in a ride – he could have been electrocuted. So we took him home. His tantrum lasted all night.

He was back the next morning, of course, with my hand on the neck of his jumper as we quick marched up the mall. He gave the fountain a yearning glance, but a tank engine was drawing him on. Once he'd had his ride, David relaxed. He was like a drinker who needed a stiff double to take the edge off – he'd be tetchy, unpredictable, dangerous until he got what he needed. Afterwards, he could be sweet charm itself.

In that mood, he consented to explore the mall with us. He rode on the escalator, and poked his nose into the bookshop. He found a wooden train set in a toyshop, and tried a chocolate biscuit. When we heard children laughing, we followed the sound to a creche. David gazed in wary fascination at the climbing apparatus, with its colourful slides and ball pit.

'Would he like to join in?' asked the woman at the desk.

'Hard to know,' I said.

Many parents seem afraid of autism. They don't want to

hear about it – perhaps they're scared their own children will somehow be infected. But good teachers, from nursery carers to school heads, want to know more. It helped that David's problems could be defined in concrete terms. We didn't have to say, 'He's a bit like this,' or 'It's more that sort of thing.' David left no one guessing. We'd been reluctant to have him labelled, but a clear-cut diagnosis was far more useful than a shapeless collection of symptoms.

The creche manager, Marion, and her deputy, Jacqui, made no apologies: they got more satisfaction from helping a boy like David than from keeping an eye on a roomful of ordinary children whose mothers were doing a bit of shopping. On his first visit to Time Zone, David stayed for five minutes and never let go of the rug – it was as if he thought he'd float away if he wasn't holding on to the ground. On his second visit, he stayed ten minutes and watched the television between his legs, upside down. We dropped in three times a week after that, with a ride on Thomas before and after every session. Within a month, David was able to last an hour, and Marion or Jacqui sat with him the whole time. I'd wait by the desk, out of sight, with a book, in case David needed to be whisked away quickly – if he was left to get into a strop, he'd remember on his next visit and pick up his tantrum where he left off.

He wasn't exactly playing with the other children. He didn't copy them or join in their games, and nobody else could choose a video while David was there. But he wasn't playing apart from them either.

I had to replace the Time Zone teacups occasionally. Wherever they hid the china, David rooted it out. Perhaps, with so many children throwing themselves around, he could hear it rattling in the backs of the cupboards.

Our mall visits became an important part of our routine, the trips and rituals that enabled all of us to cope. While David was in the creche, I could pick up a few essentials from Marks and Sparks, or find presents in the toyshops for James to take to birthday parties. Nicky gave me lists, since David wouldn't let her join us if he was going to the creche: he was happy to leave her at home, but he couldn't have been parted from her outside the house. We both suspected he was a natural-born chauvinist – a woman's place was at the sink, not swanning around the shops.

As the weather got warmer, we started parking at the back of the mall, where there was an outdoor playground. David was fearless on the climbing frames, but that was all right, because I did quite enough fearing for the two of us. When James had been a toddler, I'd stood underneath the ladders and slides, ready to catch him if he slipped. Now David was four, and I was still standing there, in case anybody else's toddler was thrown overboard. David accepted other children on the equipment; he even seemed to regard them as part of the apparatus. But if they got in the way, he'd move them, just as he'd open a gate if it was closed. A baby at the top of a slide, gathering the nerve to make its first descent as Mummy and Daddy stood with their arms outstretched, was liable to be shunted forward, usually with a toecap, as David took his place.

Nicky and I discussed the best ways to explain David's behaviour to indignant parents, and I had a collection of scripted apologies: the matter-of-fact, 'Sorry about that, he's autistic'; the cryptic, 'Sorry, he doesn't understand'; the heartbreaking, 'Sorry, he wants to play, but he doesn't know how'; the smack-between-the-eyes, 'Sorry, David can't talk'; and the less-than-serious, 'Sorry, he doesn't do queues.'

Nicky's vote went to the wording of the National Autistic Society's card: 'This child is autistic. Thank you for your tolerance.' (Instant win – anyone who kicks up a fuss is officially intolerant.) But I wanted David to have a T-shirt that said, 'Usual rules and conditions do not apply.' Or, 'Mad, bad and dangerous to know.'

To reach Thomas the Tank Engine from the outdoor playpark, we passed through Boots, usually at a trot. I liked to keep David moving: he paused, once, by a make-up counter and gazed at a plastic pyramid, some kind of display ornament. It was studded with round glass jewels, and when he touched it with a fingertip, it revolved.

He patted it gently. It twirled. He patted it again. I could see us standing there for half an hour, playing Turn the Pyramid.

David took one corner and spun it hard. The pyramid whirled, and all the plastic jewels flew off. They went skittering across the stone floor, smashing and bursting open. I had a short, wincing headache, as if I'd stubbed my brain – the pyramid wasn't an ornament, and the jewels weren't decorations. They were powder compacts. That was a display case for about £400 worth of French make-up, which was now powdering the floor of Boots.

David ran. I followed him. None of my scripted excuses was sufficient for this.

Apart from consumer vandalism, the chief risk on a trip to the mall was that another child would be riding on Thomas when we arrived. David could share a climbing frame, but he couldn't wait while someone else finished their ride. He'd run into the store and erupt in screams.

Some parents would ignore him, others would offer to let him share the ride – sharing wasn't what David wanted, so I'd tell them, 'Thank you, but he has to learn.'

One mother whipped her child off the ride and snapped, 'Oh, Thank You Very Much!' David, of course, stopped crying instantly and hopped aboard. The woman hovered, open-mouthed, not knowing which of us she wanted to slap harder. I prised the pound out of David's hand and gave it to her, and she went away – when the ride ended, a minute later, I realized she must have put in 50p. Obviously, she thought she'd come out of that encounter the winner.

A woman in beautiful West African robes approached me one afternoon as I was trying to muffle David's screams against my chest. 'Is there something the matter?' she asked. I explained that David wasn't good at waiting his turn. 'But does he have anything wrong with him?' she persisted.

'He's autistic,' I said.

'Oh!' It was a sound from deep inside her, a cry of fear and horror.

I looked at her. Her eyes welled over.

'My grandson,' she said. 'He is like this.'

I watched her while David had his rides. She was queuing at the till, with a jumper and a pair of trousers for a two-year-old boy, and tears were rolling down her face.

Seven

The family who lived in the semi-D across the road from us had two boys. Their younger son was James's age. James and Elliott became firm friends, but we saw less of Elliott's older brother: he was autistic.

Jordan occupied a different place on the autistic spectrum from David – he could talk, and he'd started school at the local primary. I'd love to report that he and David grew to be best friends too; they're sublimely ignorant of each other's existence, of course. Two boys, avid fans of the same videos and TV shows, obsessive hoarders of cassettes and CDs, with nothing in common. While their brothers charged back and forth between the gardens and rode their bikes in the lane, David and Jordan were oblivious to each other, living parallel lives. They might as well have lived on opposite sides of the city, instead of in houses that faced one other across a suburban street.

Nicky and Jordan's mum, Vanda, became very good friends. Nicky was glad to know someone who didn't need explanations, who was struggling through the same problems herself, and who never announced that she'd seen some news item or TV drama on autism which talked about a cure, and were we going to try it? Other friends and family sent us cuttings and webpage links, to highlight diets and drugs and therapies which had all produced dramatic results for one family or another with an autistic child – the upshot of every 'cure' was always that the child had unexpectedly declared, 'I love you,' to the bewildered parents. These stories were like fifteen different excuses from a liar – each one sounded convincing on its own, yet contradicted all the others.

I got chatting in the playpark to a dad whose son was a year younger than David. John wasn't talking yet, and if he wasn't allowed to switch on all the lights in the house, he threw volcanic tantrums. The diagnosis was autism. John lived in a house across the road at the back of us; years later, his parents discovered his sister was also on the autistic spectrum.

The little boy four doors up the street had been born premature. He had multiple disabilities; his parents thought autism explained some of them. Six doors in the other direction, the young man who lived with his family was also autistic; Sue, the lady in the house at the back of our garden, worked at the nearby residential Steiner school, where most of the teenage boarders were autistic; we had arrived, as if by appointment, at Autism Central.

This might be a statistical cluster, of course: improbable coincidences are an unavoidable feature of statistics. Or it might be the hand of fate, drawing Bristol's autistic community together by serendipity and synchronicity. Or it might be simpler than that – perhaps autism is much more common than the textbooks say. Perhaps it doesn't affect just one child in 10,000, as we were told at first ... perhaps the figures from the Office of National Statistics in Britain, and the Centers for Disease Control in the US, are more accurate.

They say one child in every hundred, in parts of the UK and America, is autistic. Because the condition is much more prevalent among boys than girls, this means a newborn boy has about a one-in-sixty-five chance of being autistic.

One in ten thousand, or one in a hundred. From David's perspective, the difference is meaningless – he is 100 per cent autistic. He's the one, the one-in-whatever. If life was fair, disability would be shared out equally and every boy in Britain would be 1/65th autistic. We'd all get it, like a tax credit.

From another perspective, the statistics are all-important. David appears to be the victim of a transatlantic trend that has multiplied the number of autistic children a hundredfold in a single generation. The cause must be found – because even if boys like David can't be cured, we need safeguards to make sure that the next generation isn't equally afflicted.

And from a less lofty, more irritable perspective ... this is my son we're talking about. Autism shapes his personality, but so do a great many other factors: that's why you won't find another child exactly like him. He's a boy, as real and individual as all the others. I bridle when analysts define him by his disability, as if he lives on a slice in a pie chart, as if he's One-in-Sixty-Five like a *Star Trek* clone.

Some people, when I explain that my son is autistic, see me as a statistical challenge. They want to refute me. There are various techniques for this. The abrasive: 'I hope you're not blaming the MMR triple vaccine.' (People who work in universities favour this one.) And the trying-to-sound-clued-up: 'But I thought they proved it was nothing to do with the MRSA jab?' (These people have jobs in television.) And there's the thoughtful: 'How much of the rise is down to better diagnosis?'

David had the vaccination for measles, mumps and rubella. He didn't enjoy it, but it can't have made him autistic, because he already was. He also had numerous courses of antibiotics for ear infections, which fits a pattern commonly reported by parents of children with autism. One school of thought says these medicines can introduce high levels of mercury to the bloodstream, and that some children are unable to excrete the metal naturally, for example as their hair grows. A report in the *International Journal of Toxicology* in 2003 found much lower levels of mercury in locks of hair from babies who were later diagnosed with autism, than in hair from unaffected babies: the implication was that mercury stayed inside the autistic children's systems, poisoning them.

It sounds plausible ... but then, I know nothing about the toxic effects of mercury, nothing about the mercury content of medicines, nothing about measuring toxins in baby hair and nothing about how the human body rids itself of poisonous metals. There's a detox treatment, called chelation. It's one of many 'autism treatments' on offer.

'David was born autistic,' we tell people who want to know if we blame vaccines or any other external factors. 'And better diagnosis might account for some autism cases, but you don't have to be Sigmund Freud to spot that this boy has a couple of screws loose.'

Most people are content with the short answers. They don't want hours of hectoring, lecturing, theorizing rant.

Sometimes they get it regardless, of course – serves them right for asking. Dropping a casual question about autism to me is like remarking to the Ancient Mariner, 'Bet you've seen a few things, eh?'

The short answers are wordplay, verbal tarpaulins to cover up the facts and fears. David was born autistic – but that doesn't explain what caused his condition, whether it's entirely genetic or the result of some outside factor such as toxins or a virus, and whether anything has happened since his birth to make the autism worse. And Freud wouldn't have diagnosed David with autism: he was dead by the time the first cases were identified.

I sometimes remember, with a shudder, that comment by an older doctor at Tyndall's Park: 'Years ago ... the child would go into an institution by the age of five, and nature would take its course.'

The term 'early infantile autism' was coined by Dr Leo Kanner, a psychiatrist and physician who emigrated to the US from Austria in 1924 and became the country's first child psychiatrist. He wrote the first textbook in English to address psychiatric problems in children, and in 1943 he published a paper titled 'Autistic Disturbances of Affective Contact'.

'Since 1938,' the paper began, 'there have come to our attention a number of children whose condition differs so markedly and uniquely from anything reported so far, that each case merits ... a detailed consideration of its fascinating peculiarities.'

Kanner described eleven children, all aged ten or under, and noted that while writing the paper, he had heard of two more cases. Three could not talk, or could only parrot words. All of them found communication difficult. Kanner described how seven-year-old Elaine from Boston was placed in an institution for three weeks of observation: 'her expression was blank, though not unintelligent, and there were no communicative gestures,' he wrote. She replied to questions by echoing them, and burst out with repetitive phrases: 'Dinosaurs don't cry ... Seals and salamanders ... Needle head ...'

Kanner commented that Elaine became intensely anxious during her stay, fleeing from the playground to hide in her room, and unable to sit on the toilet. He doesn't, however, wonder what three weeks of questions in an alien hospital must have been like to a girl of seven who couldn't talk.

Elaine's story had a happy ending: her parents placed her in a private school, where within four years she learned to talk and hold a conversation, and developed a wide general knowledge and an 'almost infallible' memory. 'She is a tall, husky girl with clear eyes that have long since lost any trace of that animal wildness,' her father wrote to Kanner, while adding, 'It is obvious that Elaine is not "normal".'

Kanner's paper was written in a clear, elegant style. Like the classic case histories of Jung and Freud, it's worth reading simply as literature: he describes and analyzes the children's personalities with a novelist's eye for character. In all his cases, he says, 'there is ... an extreme autistic aloneness that, whenever possible, disregards, ignores, shuts out anything that comes to the child from the outside. Direct physical contact or such motion or noise as threatens to disrupt the aloneness is either treated "as if it weren't there" or, if this is no longer sufficient, resented painfully ...'

'Resented painfully': it's a phrase to stand beside Nicky's favourite, 'exceedingly vexed'. Ask me if David was cross when his Thomas the Tank Engine ride was removed from the mall, and I'll tell you, 'he resented it painfully'.

Kanner's paper ended on a disastrous note: his children were alone from the beginning of their lives, he said, partly because their families were not warm-hearted. The mothers, fathers and grandparents were 'strongly preoccupied' with science or the arts, and 'limited in genuine interest in people'. Some parents were happily married, though they were 'rather cold and formal affairs'; other marriages were 'dismal failures'.

Six years later, Kanner identified autism with a 'genuine lack of maternal warmth'. Psychologists started to talk about 'refrigerator mothers'. In a 1960 interview with *Time* magazine, Kanner claimed autistic children were born when a cold-hearted woman 'just happen[ed] to defrost enough to produce a child'. Professor Bruno Bettelheim, another Austrian-born child psychologist and a survivor of Dachau, likened autistic children to the mental wrecks created by concentration camps.

There's a whole new psychology paper to be written here, on mamaphobia, the irrational loathing of mothers. The psychiatrists' implied disgust for children with autism is equally repellent. It's hard to understand what motivated psychiatrists such as Kanner and Bettelheim to do their work, unless it was sadistic contempt for people whose lives were not like their own.

And it's easy to imagine how autistic children in the fifties and sixties could be taken away from their parents, who had supposedly caused their condition, and placed in institutions. That in turn explains why there are comparatively few people my age or older with autism: they didn't survive childhood.

By 1965, a new generation of researchers was putting forward a less hysterical theory. Autism, they said, was not caused by emotional experiences, and was not a psychiatric illness; it was a neurological condition, something hard-wired into the brain.

This thinking was pioneered by Dr Bernard Rimland, a psychologist from California and the father of an autistic son, Mark. He took the simple and logical view that, since most autistic children had siblings who were not disabled, their parents could not be responsible for the condition – and he was quite certain that he and his wife, Gloria, weren't refrigerators, or any other kind of household appliance. 'From the moment Mark was born, everyone noticed he was different,' Rimland told an interviewer in 2002, four years before his death. 'He was always screaming at the top of his lungs and nothing would placate him.'

Leo Kanner renounced the 'refrigerator mother' theory in 1969, and it's now dismissed by most European and US psychologists. A 2007 report in *The Guardian*, though, suggested that child psychiatrists in South Korea, where autism is thought to affect one child in 10,000, are still blaming mothers: the women fail to adapt to cultural change, so the theory goes.

Psychiatry, neurology, politics: a lot of people were taking notice of autism, and for a long time, nobody had a good word to say about it. The ingenuity, the intelligence and the innocence of autistic children didn't get a mention.

Yet as Kanner was publishing his initial findings,

another Austrian child psychologist was studying similar cases at the University of Vienna and coining the term 'autistic psychopathy' in 1944. (For those keeping count, that's three Austrian child psychs, two groundbreaking papers in the mid forties, and two men coining the word 'autistic', on two continents.) Dr Hans Asperger's work was barely noticed till the early eighties, after his death: his papers were not translated into English, and his name wasn't widely known until, in 1981, the writer Lorna Wing used 'Asperger's syndrome' to describe people on the high-functioning parts of the autism spectrum.

Asperger's approach was positive. He saw abilities and rare qualities that balanced the children's difficulties. Many had excellent vocabularies, innate patience and problem-solving skills, musical talents and eidetic memories. If they found social etiquette difficult to grasp, that was hardly anything to be ashamed of – Asperger wasn't exactly a party animal himself. He called the children his 'little professors'.

Because Asperger found so much to praise, and Kanner so much to criticize, it is generally assumed now that the two psychiatrists were examining very different groups of children. In fact, most of Kanner's case notes feature children who matched the Asperger profile and used their idiosyncratic intelligence to fit the world around their needs. The more devastating type of autism, beyond communication and comprehension, is not discussed; ironically, it's now labelled Kanner's syndrome.

Autism, as a medical condition, was identified in the forties; the question is whether it existed before then. Kanner, after all, was America's first child psychiatrist – there was no one before him to observe children like these and write papers on them. Psychiatry was a primitive practice, grasping at lobotomy and electroconvulsive therapy as tools to treat mental illness. You could argue that, since autism was noticed so early, it must have been a blindingly obvious problem.

But Kanner clearly saw his eleven cases as extraordinary. He calls them 'unique from anything reported so far', and describes them as though his audience of medics will have seen nothing like this before. Tellingly, he catalogues the eccentricities among the children's families – one grandmother is 'a dyed-in-the-wool missionary if ever there was one', a mother is 'hypomanic', one father 'does not get along well with people', another is 'mostly living within himself, at times alcoholic' – but never once does he report that the families have seen children like this before. No one ever says: 'The child's uncle was just like this, as a little boy.'

A scattering of similar cases was documented prior to 1943. One of the most convincing describes Victor, a boy of about twelve, who was discovered living wild in the woods of Aveyron, near Toulouse in France, in 1800. He was taken in by a young medical student, Jean Itard, who tried, and failed, to teach Victor to talk. The boy had perhaps been abandoned by his parents; he certainly had autistic behaviours, such as treating people as tools. When he wanted to ride in a wheelbarrow, he would grab Itard by the wrist, drag him across the garden, press his fingers around the handles, and then climb into the barrow. Victor knew what he wanted from his doctor, and it wasn't language lessons.

More famous was Blind Tom, a musical savant who could barely talk, but who could imitate any sound, learn three melodies simultaneously and identify all the notes in a twenty-finger discord. Mark Twain, writing his newspaper column in the *San Francisco Alta California* in 1869, recounts how he first saw Tom on an Illinois train. He was rocking wildly in his seat and imitating the noises of the express: 'Clattering, hissing, whistling, blowing off gauge-cocks, ringing his bell, thundering over bridges with a row and a racket like everything going to pieces, whooping through tunnels, running over cows ... for three dreadful hours he kept it up.'

Two months later, Twain sat entranced for three consecutive nights at Blind Tom's piano recitals. The perfection of the nineteen-year-old's playing delighted the writer, but what really fascinated him was Tom's behaviour – when he listened to others at the piano, the blind boy stood on one leg and, bent double, hopped in circles as he clapped his hands. And then he reproduced the music, even duets, note for note and tempo for tempo. When the audience applauded, 'this happy innocent joined in'.

It's a bravura piece of writing, and it deserves a prominent place in any anthology of literature about autism. But that would be a thin volume, with large type, and almost all its characters would be savants – people with inexplicable gifts. Unlike geniuses, the Michelangelos and Leonardos, who have brilliant and wide-ranging minds, a savant is exceptional across a narrow range. Extraordinary feats of mathematics and memory don't spill over into other areas: some savants are ordinary people, with a quirk of the brain that enables them to know without calculating that 23 May 1471 was a Thursday. Others are on the autistic spectrum, such as the British artist Stephen Wilshire, who can reproduce every detail of a cityscape at a glance, and the writer Daniel Tammet, who has recited pi to 22,514 places.

Autistics are more likely to be savants than the rest of the population, perhaps because they're less inhibited – without embarrassment, self-consciousness or an instinct to conform, they're free to explore their minds. And perhaps because people who can't communicate through language must rely on other brain functions for survival, they develop extraordinary musical or artistic or mathematical skills: parts of the brain which most of us hardly use are dragooned into constant action.

But the majority of autistics aren't savants. They haven't been run through by slivers of genius. They are not, as Mark Twain described Blind Tom, archangels trapped in human form.

It isn't surprising that Twain, the connoisseur of eccentricity, would be so interested by both Tom's savant and autistic sides. The real mystery is that same oddity which marked Kanner's paper: why hadn't these professional observers of human nature ever encountered autism before?

Tom's innocence, his echolalia, his hopping and spinning and clapping and flapping, even his violent rocking – they're familiar to most parents of autistic children. And if I can look across the street, and up the street, and down the street, and behind my house, and see the homes of people with autism who are similar in lots of ways to my own son ... why was Blind Tom so extraordinary to Mark Twain?

Imagine that anthology of autism. We'll put Dickens in there, for his portrait of the sweet and simple Barnaby Rudge; we'll include a short story, 'Bartleby the Scrivener', by Herman Melville, about a tragic clerk who has autistic mannerisms. We'll cite the obsessions and eccentricities of Sherlock Holmes, regarded by many as a figurehead for Asperger's syndrome. We'll stretch the point till it twangs, and add Mr Darcy from *Pride and Prejudice* – not because we think he's autistic, but because one writer, Phyllis Ferguson Bottomley, has published an imaginative analysis of 'autistic traits' in Jane Austen's best-loved book.

It's fun, but it's a long way from the bewildered, wordless children at Tyndall's Park and Briarwood school. Where are they in literature? A century before autism was identified by psychiatrists, great writers were attempting to catalogue all human nature. But you can search Balzac, and Trollope, and Eliot, and Tolstoy, and Zola, and Dostoevsky, and you won't find anyone like my son. You can even turn to the sensation writers, who painted a world of privilege and injected it with horror – Wilkie Collins, and Mary Elizabeth Braddon – but there are no portraits of autistic children.

Many of these writers had big families. Tolstoy had thirteen children, Dickens had ten, Braddon had six of her own and six stepchildren. The characters, adventures, illnesses and tragedies of those children are reflected in their parents' books. But there's not a glimpse of autism.

The conclusion is unavoidable: autism is much more common today than it was 150 years ago.

If we knew what caused it, we might know why it's spreading. Numerous theories exist to explain the condition: it's a genetic disorder linked to chromosome abnormalities; it's a neurological problem where the brain mishandles sensory input; it's the misfiring of 'mirror neurons' in the brain; it's a toxic reaction; it's a digestive dysfunction, in which enzymes leak through the gut into the bloodstream; it's caused by vaccines, or mercury from coal-fired power plants, or pesticides, or petrol additives, or too much television. All these theories have their champions, though most agree autism must be caused by a combination of factors.

Because it appears far, far more prevalent than it was when I was born, I'm tempted to speculate that autism is triggered by an unknown virus which has become widespread. There's no evidence for this at all.

A search of *The Guardian*'s online archive shows that the paper first used the word 'autistic' in a news story in February 1964, two months before I was born. The Society for Autistic Children, which later became the National Autistic Society (NAS), had issued a warning that the number of children with autism in the UK differed wildly from what statistics would predict.

What makes this story different from anything you'll read today is that the real number of autistics was far lower than the prediction. And the prediction seems low – the Society thought there must be 5,000 children with autism in Britain.

Yet it knew of only 2,000.

The implication was that in 1964, 3,000 families across Britain could have been struggling to care for an autistic child, without the benefit of a diagnosis, medical intervention or educational aid. Since the popular view was that cold-hearted parents froze the condition into their children, it isn't surprising that thousands of families may have chosen to hide the problem.

It is surprising, though, that in 1964 there were just 2,000 known cases of childhood autism ... but by 2007 the NAS was reporting that 133,000 children in Britain had the condition, with 392,000 autistic adults known to them. Anyone who thinks that more than half a million cases of autism have appeared because of 'better diagnosis' will have to explain why the best efforts of the Society for Autistic Children could not uncover more than 2,000 in 1964.

It isn't as though autism's primary characteristic, the absence of communication, is easily ignored. Most people expect everyone to be able to communicate. Some scientists claim that's what makes us human: we have, in Professor Steven Pinker's phrase, a 'language instinct'. Pinker is a dazzlingly brilliant psychologist and writer, and I'm not, but I do feel that in a head-on debate I could trounce him on this one. My son's lineage, on both sides of the family, is wholly human. Go back as far as you like, and we've traced one branch back to the English Civil War – you won't find anything except human beings (that seventeenth-century ancestor was French, but I can't really see this weakens my argument).

David has no language instinct, but he's human. When people treat him as anything less, they emphasize his autism. They magnify it.

In the months following his diagnosis, Nicky and I were desperate to treat David's problem. We tried to accept that he would never be cured, because his autism was pervasive – it coloured everything he did and thought. Taking away the colour would be like stripping the paint off a canvas. But we wanted to tone it down, and we were ready to consider any treatment.

There were two main contenders: behaviour and diet. Through the local branch of the National Autistic Society, we heard about 'applied behavioural analysis', sometimes called the Lovaas technique after the doctor who developed it. His method involved intensive therapy, where a parent or teacher spent thirty to forty hours each week with the child, mirroring every gesture and sound. I didn't fancy spending all day, every day, punching myself in the face and howling, and I wasn't sure this was quite what Dr Lovaas intended, but I went to an NAS lecture on the treatment anyway.

The speaker was a woman with an autistic son a couple of years older than David. She got the talk off to a bad start: 'All men are a bit autistic,' she said.

'That's rubbish,' I muttered. She just cocked an eyebrow at me. I should have walked out – I would have done, if the remark had been racist, and anything that mocks my son's disability is as bad as racism. But I was the only man in the room, and I didn't want to seem like an over-sensitive dad.

In the end, I did leave. There wasn't any one trigger – it was a cumulation of sneers and put-downs. In a room filled with the parents of autistic children, she described the behaviours and obsessions of autism with a thin contempt. She could spot autistics from fifty yards, she said: their sidelong looks, the way they held their heads, their gait, their noises. Nothing about them was *normal* and everything *stood out*. The more she talked, the more I thought: 'I love my son. I like the way he is. It's you I can't stand.'

By the time she came to describe her own son and the treatment he'd been through, I was rooting for the boy. I wanted him to defy all her efforts to train him and turn him into a performing pet. He didn't, of course – but the child she triumphantly described sounded cowed and lost. He sounded like a canvas with the paint scraped off.

We didn't want to bully David into conformity, especially if he couldn't understand why he needed to conform. We didn't want to make him invisible. He was blissfully happy when he had what he wanted.

What we wanted was a miracle. We wanted the son we had, and the one we'd hoped for. We wanted David to learn to talk. And I did pray for a miracle. As a teenager, I'd thought I must be an atheist, because I couldn't believe in a God who stage-managed human events. Later, I realized I did believe in God, but not a God with a human personality, not one who chose whether or not to intervene in our lives. After David's diagnosis, I would have been delighted to admit how wrong I'd been. A plague of frogs and the spontaneous combustion of every bush in our garden would have been very welcome.

I searched the Internet for news stories of modern miracles, and read about a girl in Massachusetts who had been in a coma since falling into a swimming pool, aged three, in 1986. Her name was Audrey Santo, and her family were convinced that, though she couldn't speak or move, she could work miracles. Her room was filled with the scent of roses, and oil wept from religious icons and paintings around the walls. A phial of this oil could be obtained in exchange for a donation.

I made a donation. Nicky told me I was being ridiculous, but not in the way she would when I experimented with Fairy Liquid in the dishwasher or got lost in backstreets to avoid the roadworks. I knew I was being ridiculous: it didn't matter.

I managed to dab the oil on David's head. It wasn't

possible to do this during a 'quiet and meditative moment' as the Santo family recommended: we didn't have those. The only definite effect was that David's hair became, for an hour or two, more oily. *The Washington Post* tested a phial of Audrey's oil in 1998, and concluded it was 80 per cent soybean extract and 20 per cent chicken fat. I've put worse things on my hair, and paid more for them.

When I dabbed the oil on my son's head, I prayed. And I kept praying. When I asked for a miracle, we didn't get one. There were no frogs, either. But when I prayed for strength, it came from somewhere.

By the time he was four, David's diet was so restricted that we couldn't understand how he was growing. He drank full-fat milk, diluted with boiling water, from a baby bottle. And he ate dry Weetabix. End of diet sheet.

He wouldn't eat Weetabix soaked in milk, or supermarket own-brand wheat biscuits, or drink milk with vitamin drops in it. If we ran out of full-fat milk – because, for instance, David had emptied four pints across the kitchen floor – he wouldn't accept semi-skimmed as a substitute. He loved eggs, but only because he could smash them and bodysurf across the raw omelette: he wouldn't dream of eating them, or anything hot, or anything sweet, or anything green, or anything at all except hot milk and dry Weetabix.

We tried every day to broaden his diet. Chocolate, pineapple, buttered bread, Sugar Puffs ... David could have been living like a spoiled prince in a fairy story, if he'd wanted. He could have eaten ice cream for breakfast, custard creams for lunch and clotted cream for tea – we were ready to try anything. He rejected everything. All he wanted to eat was Weetabix, and he munched through a packet of twelve most days.

He was growing. He had good teeth, strong bones and limitless energy. He knew when he was hungry, and he dragged us to the kettle and the cupboard as often as he had to. There was a ruthless self-sufficiency about his appetite – some children are like goats, who will eat everything they can find, without stopping, until it makes them ill. David was no goat: he was like a lion, who'll accept nothing but fresh, raw meat and who eats only till he's full. (That analogy sounds sentimental, until you look at four-year-olds consuming cheeseburgers, fries, jellybeans and cola every teatime – now tell me which child has the healthier instincts.)

We were anxious about his eating habits, though, because every diet that promised breakthroughs with autism had two basic rules: no wheat (gluten) and no milk (casein). Some practitioners made wilder claims than others, some promised cures and some hoped for improvements, but all of them promoted a gluten-free, casein-free regime.

If we banned wheat and milk from David's diet, he'd starve. And he'd be very cross about it too. We talked the diets over with his paediatrician and our GP; they suggested we could try oat flakes instead of Weetabix, and ewe's milk instead of cow's. We might as well have offered him foix gras and rocket salad with a chilled Chablis – David knew what he liked and it didn't involve oats or sheep. So the paediatrician and the GP pointed out that there was no medical evidence to back up claims of a dietary cure for autism; diet changes were an alternative therapy, and a conventional doctor couldn't condone any alternative medicine which caused a child distress and harm. In other words: it probably won't work, and it'll cause a lot of misery, so don't do it.

We would have risked the misery, if we could have found a convincing medical reason. It was worrying to know that David's two staple foods were the two cited as causes of autism on so many Internet sites. We had to remind ourselves that when David lived on breast milk, he'd been autistic; and when he graduated to fruit purée and egg custard, he'd stayed autistic. If anyone had offered a cogent medical explanation of how wheat and milk robbed our son of speech and filled him with an urge to headbutt bathroom tiles, we would have paid attention.

Then we heard about leaky gut syndrome.

I read about it first in *New Scientist* magazine, which was better than a stray web link. The theory was backed by research from a British university. It explained why wheat and milk were danger foods. It suggested a convincing reason why David wouldn't touch anything else. And it offered hope of real improvements for his autism.

It was still alternative medicine, but it had clear ambitions to commandeer the mainstream. Leaky guts, said the theory, failed to keep food in the digestive system. They let 'macromolecules' of harmful allergins, such as wheat and milk, leak into the blood. This happened because mucus lining the intestines had been stripped away, for example by toxins in antibiotics or by stress. When the macromolecules hit the brain, they damaged it – but the brain could recover, if the allergins were banned from the diet.

That sounded plausible. There were big holes – how, for instance, do macromolecules wreck communication functions while leaving musical intelligence untouched? But we were ready to be convinced.

Then one of the theory's leading proponents, a

researcher who claimed to have pioneered the treatment, arrived in Bristol to deliver a lecture.

It was more like a travelling medicine show. The speaker opened with a short fantasy about who was going to play him in the Hollywood movie of his life, *The Man Who Cured Autism*. I think he settled on Brad Pitt. He explained the 'leaky gut' theory, and warned us that breaking our children's 'addiction' to wheat and milk was like weaning them off hard drugs – their blood was hooked on macro-molecules, he said, and an autistic tantrum was no different from a heroin high.

He wasn't, luckily, a charismatic speaker. Most of the people in the hall were looking for a way to help their children. They didn't need a guru. There was a steady scrape of chairs, as people left. I kept waiting to hear how macro-molecules targeted some brain cells and not others, and why they were addictive, but the talk ended and the speaker invited questions from the floor.

One woman raised her hand and said, hesitatingly, that she'd been to one of these lectures six months earlier. Since then, her son had been permitted nothing with milk and nothing with wheat in it.

The speaker nodded approvingly. 'Congratulations,' he said. 'How's he doing?'

'He's very thin. He's not eating. And his autism's no better,' said the woman. 'He was very upset when we stopped his milk and Weetabix.'

'He would be. He was an addict.'

'But he hasn't replaced them with anything else. It's all we can do to get a sip of water into him. He just refuses.'

'You're doing the right thing,' the speaker insisted.

'All I really want to know,' the woman pleaded, 'is when

it's all right to give up. He's just as autistic as ever. Does your method fail sometimes?'

'Not if you're doing it right,' the man snapped. 'Now, you've asked more than your share of questions – let's hear from someone else.'

Nicky and I didn't need to talk it over, after that. We couldn't do anything that put David's health at risk. Something had caused his autism – logically, there must be some way to ease it, even to change it. But we were never going to permit anything that hurt him.

We told our GP about the lecture. 'If only his rages *were* like drug trips,' I said. 'At least he'd be enjoying them. Still, that campaign to legalize cannabis is picking up momentum. It won't be long before we can chill out David's tantrums by rolling him a spliff and sticking some Bob Marley on.'

'Interesting idea,' said our GP, with a smile. 'Next time you're smoking a joint, try puffing the smoke in his face and see what effect it has.'

We don't smoke dope. Nicky's never even tried a ciga-rette. It's a shame, really ... we could be helplessly stoned every night, on doctor's orders.

Eight

That September, David was offered a place at Briarwood school, in the youngest of the autistic unit's three classes. It meant a fifty-minute bus ride every morning and afternoon – the school was only five miles away, but the bus had to journey across Bristol, collecting other children. We were pretty confident David was going to enjoy it all. We were almost certain. But just in case we were launching into an eternity of screaming rages, we thought we'd have a holiday.

We booked a cottage in Lympstone, on the Exe estuary in Devon. From the upstairs windows, we could see a castle, and the Plymouth express hurtling along the far shoreline. Turning round, we could see a blond wrecking ball, bouncing across the beds and on to the wardrobe, where we'd concealed the breakables.

Whether it was a cottage, a cafe or a waiting room, wherever we took David our first job was to gather up the glassware and the ornaments, and hide them. David's first job was to search them out and destroy them. Most of that holiday was spent replacing lampshades, flowerpots, books and mugs, and finding new hiding places for the survivors.

David relished the excitement of the first day; expected to go back to Bristol on the second; banished James and me from the cottage as a safety measure on the third; and set off home on his own on the fourth. James spotted him – 'David's escaping to Quay Cove,' he said, as he and I explored the cliffs south of the cottage at low tide. And there was his brother, breaking out of our barred-and-bolted cottage via a porthole window that a cat couldn't get through. A second too late, Nicky's hand appeared and made a grab for him.

By the time we'd clambered down to the beach, David had wriggled under a fence into the next-door garden and was marching through their vegetable patch, trailing lettuces. I didn't like to break into private property to corner him – if he threw a blazing tantrum, explanations could be awkward. As long as he was a danger only to the cauliflowers and tripods of runner beans, and wasn't at risk himself, we'd stay outside the fencing, yelling at him and pretending that was going to do any good.

He climbed a shed and vaulted over the far fence. There are not many children who can affect a nonchalant swagger as they drop into half an acre of stinking river mud, but David did it like a movie star. By the time we dragged him off the estuary bank, he was Swamp Thing. Buckets of water sluiced the worst off, and we scrubbed him down in the yard behind the kitchen – he looked triumphant, as if he'd made a daring discovery.

And he had. David had found out that, when he was with his mum or dad, they put a brake on his fun ... but when he went by a different exit, leaving them behind, he could get all the excitement he craved. Climbing fences and sliding in the mud was just the start – the world held everything a boy wanted. New houses to explore, for instance.

But because he wasn't talking, he didn't share that discovery with us. We were left to work it out.

A day or two after our holiday, when Nicky was back at work and James was playing at a friend's house, I lost David. He was pottering sweetly in our garden, singing to himself, when the phone rang. I took the call indoors. As long as I could hear his voice, I knew he was safe … unless the whole of north Bristol could hear his voice, in which case something was irking him.

A couple of minutes later, as I put the phone down, I realized David had gone quiet. That meant nothing – he was so absorbed in his own world that he sometimes seemed scarcely to exist in ours. But he wasn't on his swing, or in the shed, or stretched out on the flower beds. He must have slipped into the house while I was on the phone. If he'd gone upstairs, I would have seen him, so he had to be in the kitchen or the sitting room … only, he wasn't.

David liked to squeeze himself into cubbyholes, so I checked behind the sofa, under the stairs, inside the blanket box, even in the kitchen cupboards. Then I looked under the bushes, inside the wheelie bin … he wasn't anywhere. But he couldn't have broken out of the garden – the gate was triple-locked and the lowest fence was taller than him, with no wriggle-room below it.

Even though I knew he wasn't upstairs, I looked under the beds. The alternative was to leave the house and search the streets – and that would be dangerous, because I knew logically that David must be somewhere in the house. I simply hadn't looked in the right place. I hadn't looked hard enough.

I lose things every day. My first reaction is to ask Nicky: 'Have you seen my wallet? Any idea where I put the keys?' But I couldn't call her at work and say, 'David seems to have disappeared … where d'you reckon he'd be?'

Anyhow, Nicky's usual response is to throw the question back at me: 'Where was it the last time you saw it?'

The last time I'd seen David, he'd been in the garden.

I stood on the lawn, staring round helplessly, as the sickening feeling grew that he could have been gone for ten minutes. And that might be the first ten minutes of the rest of our lives.

That's when I heard him – or rather, I heard the sound his silence makes. In the lane beyond our garden, a woman was talking with a mixture of humour and exasperation to someone who wasn't answering: 'Well, if you won't tell me where you live, can you point to your house?'

I wrenched back the bolts on the gate as David marched past, magnificently ignoring the woman in his wake. I think that he was heading for our front door, but when he saw a short cut appear, he barged past me and went back to sitting and singing on his swing.

'You found him, then?' I said weakly.

The woman folded her arms. 'Oh, he's been turning our house upside down for the past five minutes,' she said, and indicated the roof behind our back wall: 'We live there.'

I explained that David was autistic, that he couldn't talk, that I'd been searching for him, but that I hadn't believed he could escape. 'Has he done much damage?' I asked.

'Mess, yes. Damage, I don't suppose so. He's been sitting in front of our telly, putting every one of our videos in the player for ten seconds and taking it out again. My partner found him – he said, "There's a child watching television in the lounge," and I said, "So?" and he said, "I don't think he's one of ours." I couldn't persuade your son even to look up from the television until he'd tried every video on the shelf.'

'You don't have any *Postman Pat*?'

'My lot are a bit old for that.'

'Good job. David wouldn't have budged all morning. Ah – that's how he does it!'

I'd been edging behind the shed, out of David's sight-line, hoping he'd have another shot at freedom if he thought he was unpoliced. Sliding off his swing, he'd climbed on to the compost bin, which gave him the boost he needed to scramble over the fence. For form's sake, I shouted, 'David! No! Don't you dare! Come back!' But before I could cross the garden, he was gone.

I craned over the fence and saw the low place in next-door's wall, which led to the garden behind. This time, David ignored it, and wriggled through a gap in the far fence. He was looking for other video collections, in other houses.

There was no way I could chase him down by vaulting the fences. Instead, I ran back into the lane, around the front, down the street and into our neighbours' garden two doors up. David was on the point of giving up on their window locks and trying the next house. He accepted arrest as calmly as any old lag. After all, he was going back to an open prison – he could escape whenever he fancied.

We dismantled the compost bin and doubled the defences. I wanted to run barbed wire along the fence-top. We settled for wicker battlements – Nicky didn't mind if the garden looked like a play fort, but she drew the line at Colditz.

All our windows, even on the hottest days, were shut and bolted when David was at home, and I insisted on deadlocking the front door. One Saturday, I left for London and the newspaper at 6.30 a.m., carefully locking the door behind me, without thinking that, because I had both sets of car keys, I had also walked off with the spare deadlock key. And since I was the only one who had memorized the number of the new combination lock on the back gate, I'd effectively barricaded my family into the house for the whole day. When James went out to play, he had to climb through a window.

That's when our social worker came round.

Sometimes life is like a bad West End farce: just as your trousers fall down, the vicar sticks his head round the scenery.

We weren't on bad terms with social services at the time. One of its departments, the Community Care Team, had employed a young worker named Kate, who dropped by twice a week to take David for an outing in her Morris Traveller. David thought Kate was heaven-sent. So did we. She let him ride in the passenger seat and investigate all her music cassettes, and she took him to playparks with ponds where he could feed the ducks, and when he hurled himself into the water or stole toddlers' trikes, she didn't panic. She wasn't upset by the snides and tirades from other children's parents. She just got on with it, and she never once missed an appointment. When the summer came, Kate went off to India – the last time we had a post-card from her, she was working at an orphanage in Cambodia.

Kate was David's ideal 'big sister'. Even now, if he sees an old, half-timbered Morris van, he'll try to climb in.

It was a long time before we found anyone to replace her. The next carer, an agency worker with no experience of autism, lasted one session: she took David out, he started howling, and she gave up. We'd told her we were going out for half an hour, taking James to a friend's house, but the woman brought David back anyhow.

When he discovered the house was empty, David went wild. He probably thought we'd gone away for ever – he couldn't imagine, after all, that we would be coming back. One of us had always, always been at home, and now we weren't. He lay on the drive and tried to beat himself unconscious against the tarmac, while the carer stood against the wall in shock.

David's screams brought our neighbours out of their houses. James's friend Elliott and his dad brought a ladder to climb into our garden, hoping they could find a way into the house and get David inside. They couldn't – instead, we came home to find neighbours camped on the drive and trapped in our high-security garden, and David shrieking fit to shatter the windows.

All we'd done was take our other son to tea with a schoolmate. We felt like the sort of parents who go for an all-nighter at the pub, leaving the children with a pit bull terrier and a Zippo to play with.

The daily pressure would have been unbearable, without the support first from Rosemary and Red House, and then from David's school. We'd seen within weeks of his start at nursery that David was willing to learn new behaviour in new places. The first proper game he ever played with Nicky and me was one that Rosemary taught him – he mimed filling a teacup from a plastic teapot, and served us with tea. He was imitating the actions Rosemary had shown him, which were probably meaningless to him: he couldn't imagine there was invisible tea in the pot. And he had to be Mother: the game didn't work if we poured tea for David. But it was two-way play, and more followed.

He spent a whole Saturday filling saucepans with tap water and carrying them to the kitchen to fill a bucket for Nicky. She had to supply constant praise and encouragement: if she let go of the bucket, David lost interest. But as long as she played the game, he obeyed the rules and didn't slop the water or chuck the saucepan at the wall. I could hardly believe this, till I saw it for myself – a week earlier, David had been trying to smash everything he could lay his hands on. Tin cans, rolling pins, weighing scales, place mats, oven trays, kettles, bags of sugar, packets of macaroni ... some broke, some shattered, some made a mess, and all of them delighted him.

We learned not to catch the things he threw. If they were unbreakable, a bounce on the patio wouldn't hurt them; if they were fragile, our hands were even more frangible. We could, and did, buy another casserole dish, but there's no getting round a month with bandaged fingers.

Most toys didn't interest him. Teletubbies and Spidermen are designed to stand tough treatment, so where was the fun in bunging them down the stairs? He did like a pyramid of coloured rings, though, which stacked on a pole. Nicky sat for hours with him as he guided her hand to each ring in turn. She had to say the colour before he'd let her add it to the stack: 'Purple, pink, orange, red ...' One day, she reversed the rules, and refused to stack the ring before David said the colour. She kept touching his lips and repeating the word – 'purple, purple' – until David whispered, 'Burrr.'

That earned him lots of hugs and praise. He was wary whenever we made a fuss of him, but he also liked the attention. The first time David said his colours, 'Burr, bink, o-rin, ridd,' he sparked a media riot: video cameras came out, flashbulbs popped, and the coloured rings clattered on to the stick like casino counters. After that, David was a puppy with a new trick, reciting the colours and cheering himself.

He had no idea what the words meant, though. He was no different from a child with a skipping rope, reciting a nonsense rhyme. We tried showing him other pink and purple objects: cardies, gel pens, plastic ponies, packets of tissues. David stared at them in bafflement. How was he expected to stack those?

His favourite game of all was tickling. Sometimes when we were larking about with James, play-fighting or chasing, David could be persuaded to join in too. He'd lie on the rug, giggling himself breathless as we scurried our fingers up and down his toes and tummy. Then we'd turn to James, crumpled on the floor beside his brother, and tickle him till he pleaded for mercy. That made David sit up with a frown: the look on his face told us more than any child could have put into words.

When we tickled James, David couldn't feel it. This puzzled him. He could hear laughter, he could see the parent-thing wiggling its fingers in a tickly way, but it left him cold. Nicky and I laughed at his bewilderment, and put words in his mouth: 'You're doing it wrong! I'm not ticklish over there!'

David wasn't thinking in words, though. He processed experiences directly – no middleman, no interpreter. And without words, we couldn't explain the obvious facts to him: 'We're tickling your brother. He's not you. You can't feel it. James can feel it. That's why he's laughing and you're not.'

None of that made sense to him. All we could do was start tickling him again.

He tried, though. He really wanted to laugh when James was tickled, and he came up with the clever idea of copying James's actions. It was as if David was trying to jump-start his own sensations. We grabbed at James and he ran away, and David ran too. James fell down, and David tumbled over too. Out came the video cameras again.

We played that game till all of us, except David, were exhausted. We played it again the next day, too, but it was years before David could be persuaded to join in again. It went from being the best game in the world to absolute taboo, and the best explanations we could come up with were wild guesses. Perhaps David got bored, or perhaps he lost the connection in his brain that enabled him to copy James. Perhaps his controller sent a text from his distant star fleet: 'Don't fraternize with the natives, X901. Bad for morale.'

The notion of a lost connection fits a theory from San Diego University in California, which suggests that 'mirror neurons' malfunction in an autistic brain, destroying its ability to copy actions, develop language or feel empathy. But I prefer the idea of orders from an alien commander.

Within six weeks of David starting at Briarwood, we saw more improvements. Rosemary had introduced PECS, the Picture-Exchange System, at Red House, where David could exchange a symbol for an object he wanted: to lay his hands on the ring-stacker, for instance, he had to find the picture of the coloured rings and 'pay' it to Rosemary. He learned to do this as part of the game, though it never occurred to him to initiate it by finding the symbol unbidden. At Briarwood, PECS was used all the time: each child had a board on the wall, laden with symbols. The teacher, Claire, asked us to supply pictures of ourselves, our house and our car, so that David could build up a catalogue of actions for the day: at going-home time, he'd find his PECS card for the school bus, and add it to his family pictures. For the first time in his life, he was using a kind of language: simple, graphical and effective.

At the first parents' evening, Claire was full of excitement about David's potential. 'He's such a bright boy,' she insisted. 'His mind works so quickly – faster than ours, half the time. He's spotted what he wants before we've even looked around. If we can only help him to understand ... It must be so frustrating for him. He sees everything, he takes it all in, but most of the time he can't make sense of it.'

'Do you think he'll ever learn to talk?' Nicky asked.

'He reminds me a lot of another of our autistic boys, George,' said Claire. 'When George started here, he wasn't talking. Now he's copying words clearly. His mum says he loves those rides at supermarkets, just like David, and when he climbs in, he says, "Hold on tight! Super-fast ride!"'

'We'd love to hear David talking,' Nicky said. 'He'll have such a musical voice.'

He was already showing signs of understanding what

we said, instead of sang, to him. When we called his name, he'd turn round, even in another room. And when he wanted a refill of hot milk in his baby bottle, twelve or fifteen times a day, he'd drag us to the fridge and, instead of trying to smash the door off its hinges with his head, he'd say, 'Mi!'

That was an indication of how complex David found words. After months of work, he'd memorized the first half of a syllable for his favourite drink. It was like committing half a symphony to memory – learning the whole thing was just impossible, but he'd managed enough to make it unmistakable.

Even better, he had recognized that parents could be operated with spoken commands as well as manual controls. We'd undergone a serious technological upgrade. 'Mum-thing and Dad-thing – now with awesome audio activation! You talk … they move!'

Understanding and obeying were two very different concepts, however. David knew what the word 'no' meant, but he couldn't say it to us when he wanted to refuse an order. To David, 'no' was the sound of a machine that wouldn't do what he wanted, like a computer that beeps when it processes an illegal command. And since he could usually override the computer, he did.

If David wasn't within an arm's length, it made no difference to tell him 'no'. The word had to be enforced. To most children, 'no' carries the threat of enforcement and they react to it, the way Pavlov's dogs learned to expect food when they heard a bell ring. David didn't care about Russian trick-cyclists and their pets. He knew when he was out of reach: at any range greater than three feet, he was beyond the law. We could say 'no' or *'niet'*, *'nein'*, *'votch'*, '*ez*' or '*nahaniri*' – David could be disobedient in every language on the planet.

And his disobedience wasn't always spontaneous. He'd started to plan ahead. One Sunday morning, as Nicky was tying his shoelaces at the bottom of the stairs before a trip to the zoo, we turned our backs for a few seconds. He seemed calm. There was no glint in his eye. But when we looked away, we heard his feet thumping up the stairs. By the time Nicky had followed him, David had gone. Vanished. He wasn't in his room, our room, my study, the bathroom ... I heard Nicky call out to James, 'Is your brother in your room with you?' but I already knew the answer: James's orderly storeroom of treasures was out-of-bounds to the Crown Prince of Destruction.

Then we heard singing.

David had a song for every occasion. He'd taken the MusicSpace concept of applying tunes to specific activities, and expanded it to include everything he did. In a high, wordless voice that never missed a note, he provided his own soundtrack. We had to supply the translations – he never told us, for instance, that Windy Miller's theme from *Camberwick Green* meant, in David's parallel world: 'It's 3 a.m. and I'm tiptoeing downstairs to find something to break.' (We worked that one out quite quickly.)

Now we could both hear singing from somewhere, and it wasn't a song I'd heard him do before. He was embarking on a novel experience.

We looked into the bathroom again. The shower curtain fluttered. Nicky looked behind it, and he wasn't there. But the window above the bath was open.

The window should never have been opened. It was supposed to be locked at all times. But I'd had a bath the night before, opened it to let the steam out, and forgotten to latch it again afterwards. It was less than two feet across and five feet above the bath, with hinges at the top. David must have dived through it like a human cannonball.

At the back of the house our kitchen sticks out, with a roof that slopes up to a parapet above a concrete path. David was on that parapet, running back and forth, his arms pumping like a steam engine's pistons, chuff-chuffing to the end and peering over and chuntering back.

'David, no!' Nicky said. 'Stop that! Come here!'

He didn't even look at her. Any other child would know they'd been caught – they might defy you, they might shout and plead and argue, but they'd know they weren't getting away with this. David didn't even glance our way, because he knew he hadn't been caught. He was out of reach. And he wasn't expecting anyone to follow him out through the window.

He was right about that – I can barely walk in a straight line on the pavement, let alone keep my balance on a second-storey ridge of tiles no wider than my hand.

I tried singing the zoo song. David responded with his own tune, and prised his shoes off his feet. He flicked them into the next garden and stood on his heels above a sheer drop, wiggling his toes in space.

Nicky summed up the situation calmly. Her child was a slip away from horrible injuries and panicking wasn't going to help him. 'He'll get overexcited if we yell at him,' she said. 'We need Rolos. Bribe him in.'

We offered him a whole tube, with the wrapper ripped off and the gold foil flashing. This wasn't the time to be negotiating with single sweets. David stared sadly at the chocolates. He knew he was beaten. He held out a hand, as if he couldn't see why he shouldn't eat his Rolos on the kitchen roof, but it wasn't a serious stand-off. Boosting his shoulders through the window, he slid head first into the bath, and lay there scoffing chocs.

Six weeks later, it happened again. Somehow, nothing is ever as bad the second time: we looked at him and thought, 'Oh, the old whisker-away-from-death routine. Seen it.' Plus, we were barely awake.

We'd had builders in, and they'd been leaning out of upstairs windows to pass equipment to mates on ladders. We followed them around, locking up, but one of the keys had disappeared. David must have found it and palmed it.

He didn't use it straight away. He waited until dawn on a Sunday morning, when he crept into our bedroom, pulled back a curtain and slipped out.

I woke up, fractionally, when Nicky nudged me. 'We need Rolos again,' she said.

'What? What are you talking about?'

'David's looking through the window. From the wrong side.'

It took several seconds for my brain to catch up. I was gazing at my son, in his pyjamas and bare feet, who was gazing back at me through the double glazing. In an upstairs bedroom. There was no parapet under that window, just a two-inch sill of sloping plastic; below that, rose bushes and tarmac.

He sidled in so promptly when the sweets appeared that I think he staged the whole stunt to earn a bribe. David didn't know how to say, 'I want a Rolo, please,' but he had worked out how to manipulate his parents with suicidal recklessness.

We struggled to make him understand he could hurt

himself, or someone else, but David couldn't even grasp the connection between injuries and pain. As the Christmas decorations went up, we took the risk of lighting candles – blowing them out whenever we weren't in the room, and hiding the matches in a zipped coat pocket in the cupboard under the stairs. David stood and stared at the bright flame, almost hypnotized. He'd reach out to hold it, just as Pinocchio does in the Walt Disney film, which David had watched countless times. Like Pinocchio, he burned his fingertips.

He'd howl for a while; then the fascination of the flame would assert itself again. He simply didn't see that the candle was dangerous.

The only way we could understand this was to assume David lived in the perpetual present tense, a universe where 'now' was all that existed. When he snatched his fingers away from a candle, they kept hurting. The flame was nowhere near, so the flame couldn't be causing the pain. A note from Claire in David's school diary corroborated this: David had a blood test one afternoon, a tiny jab with a needle and a sticking plaster to follow. He hated the plaster. He was furious about it. His logic was clear: his finger hurt, and there was a sticky pink strip on his finger – coincidence? Not likely.

If nothing was hurting, though, he was supremely happy. Outrageous cheerfulness was David's default position. He never brooded, never worried, never sulked, never fretted – he existed in a state of bliss which Indian holy men spend fifty years on a mountaintop to achieve. His needs were simple, and his pleasures were intense. And since there was no way to talk him out of whatever he wanted, Nicky and I agreed to let him have all the fun he could: if it wasn't hurting him, or anyone else, and it wasn't going to bankrupt us, then we let him get on with it.

We had to adapt to survive. Nicky sometimes remarked, as she prised him out of a cupboard and scooped up the debris, 'He's lucky we can accept it, or we might have gone mad.'

One thing he loved especially was water. He could lie all afternoon in the bath, with his nose poking above the surface and his golden hair floating in a halo. We packed the floor with towels and robes, so that the water wouldn't soak through and drip on the fridge, when he started tobogganing from the showerhead to the taps. If he wanted to coat his body with an entire bottle of pearly blue shampoo, we let him – it was cheaper than a day out at Alton Towers, and no child ever enjoyed a rollercoaster more than David loved his slidey baths.

From February to November, we kept an inflatable paddling pool on the lawn and filled it daily from the garden hose. David dived in fully clothed whenever he could, but if we caught him, he'd let us put him into swimming trunks. He seemed oblivious to the cold – one bonfire night, as James stood duffel-coated on the patio with his sparklers, Nicky and I watched David cavorting in pyjamas between his pool and his swing.

On an even colder day in January, in the parklands at Ashton Court on Bristol's outskirts, David ran down a flight of steps and found a burst water main – the underground pipes must have frozen in the night. He was six yards ahead of us, and waist deep in icy water before we could even shout.

He wasn't hurting anyone, it was free entertainment, and we had no choice, so we let him get on with it. There were spare clothes and a towel waiting in the car – most outings with David required at least a change of T-shirt or socks. On such a cold day, we didn't expect him to last more than a minute or two in the flood, but he splashed back and forward, tearing off his shoes, his coat, his trousers and finally even his pants. Nicky and I stamped our feet and tucked our fingers under our arms: we were going blue, but when David emerged at last, he was glowing with happiness and excitement.

If passers-by stared, Nicky sometimes whispered: 'Explain to them. Tell them he's autistic.' But I often didn't feel like expending my energy on a stranger's education. By the time David was five, I knew I'd need a whole book to explain how different my son was from all the other children. To anyone who hadn't lived with autism, the words 'he's autistic' were no explanation at all.

Also, it was more fun to see their scandalized faces.

David committed his outrages with a showman's instinct. He didn't care what anyone thought of him, but he seemed to be daring the world to ignore him. He arrived at the playpark once, after a night of heavy rain, to find a collection of designer-clad preschoolers and a muddy puddle. Tucking his trousers into his wellies, I let him wade in. He started goose-stepping, showering his coat with muddy water and drawing frowns from the mothers and nannies. Then he started jumping and splashing, and the other children were goggling at him. They tugged at the hands of authority: 'I want to! Let me! Won't get dirty! Promise!'

Now David was laughing, a liberated, abandoned whoop of happiness. He leapt in the air and landed on his backside. The children gasped. It looked like more fun than any one boy should decently have. It wasn't fair. David was getting all their fun as well.

Letting the water soak through his cords, David kicked off his wellies, peeled off his coat and started rolling from one end of the puddle to the other, plastered in mud. The other children were open-mouthed. They looked like urchins pressed against a sweetshop window.

With a climactic flourish, David stood up, threw his sopping wet trousers away, and bellyflopped.

One of the mothers couldn't bear it any longer. 'Well!' she snapped at me. 'It's obvious that you won't be the one who has to wash his clothes.'

We took our last holiday as a family foursome that month. It wasn't meant to be the last – all we intended was a long weekend in a caravan in Devon, to celebrate James's seventh birthday. But it was only when we were away from home that we could see how completely David's needs overruled everyone else. It wasn't just the way he monopolized his mother, or his mounting anxiety at sharing a strange space with James and me. It was his tireless determination to get his own way. If he was thwarted twenty times, he'd come back for a twenty-first attempt … a thousand-and-twenty-first attempt, if that's what it took.

That weekend, he was obsessed with throwing things inside the caravan – his milk bottle, James's birthday presents, the contents of the cupboards. After hours of trying to stop him chucking a four-pack of baked beans at the television, I relented and, taking him into a bedroom, gave him a can at a time to throw at the bed. He slipped under my arm, dodged through the door, shut himself in the bathroom and, giving a shriek of triumph, smashed the washbasin. With a can of beans.

We lost our insurance deposit, which was the least of anyone's worries. After the progress he'd made at school, our hopes had been rising. We thought we'd come through the worst. We hadn't.

Nine

David tried to hear every sound as music. He created a cacophonous symphony from the voices and mechanical noises around him, and he sang the score back. We were startled to hear him say words and phrases at appropriate moments – 'keys', for instance, when we were unlocking the car, or 'Briarwood' when he heard a song he'd learned at school.

One evening in bed, he giggled himself helpless, and gasped, 'No, Jack! Jack, don't, stop that!' It was a perfect imitation of his teacher – and we were glad to know that David wasn't the only one who played her up.

He wasn't talking, though. This wasn't communication. David was mimicking the spoken sounds of his symphony. And his growing suspicion that every sound meant something specific, the way his MusicSpace songs did, was driving him wild with frustration.

David's bursts of fury were frightening us now. He was in danger of seriously hurting himself. Nicky and I couldn't always cope with these tantrums together: they were so distressing that we found it easier to face them alone. To see each other trying to control our child's rages could be unbearable. One evening, I was clearing up wreckage in the garden, with the sound of David's thumps and screams echoing along the whole street, as Nicky tried to stop him from beating his skull against the wall. There was a crash, and I heard my wife sobbing. I ran inside: David had smashed his bedroom window, with his head.

He wasn't cut. I don't know how, because I almost bled to death, knocking the glass out. David could shatter a mirror and run across the fragments, or bite his hands until they were ridged with scar tissue, but he almost never cut himself. He bruised, though. He would go to school with purple blotches spreading over his forehead, and black imprints like tattoos on his legs and arms. The school, fortunately, had seen similar injuries, many times before. We tried to keep a note of every injury he did himself and how it had happened.

One afternoon after Easter, he started screaming. We couldn't tell why, whether he was in pain or just frustrated, but nothing we did could make him stop. He didn't want his favourite toys, his videos, his milk: he just lay and smashed his head.

Nothing unusual about that.

But he screamed all night, and all the next morning at school – so violently that we had to bring him home. He screamed all that night, too. And all weekend. And all the following week, and the week after that: without cease, without sleep. Nicky and I took it in turns to sit with him, trying to direct his lunges so his head would crash against us and not the floor or the furniture. I remember one night spent watching a *Clangers* video, with David howling and shrieking through every episode: each time the credits played, he went silent, and when the music died away, he heaved a breath and screamed again. At the end of the tape, he launched into a frenzy that lasted until it had rewound ... and we watched it again. And again. And again.

All that sustained me was the thought that Nicky was getting some sleep. But when she came downstairs to relieve me at 4 a.m., her red eyes told me she'd been lying awake, listening and crying.

Our GP visited David at home, and prescribed a padded helmet. He wouldn't wear it. Even if we pinned his arms and forced the hat on to his head, he'd tear it off. There was no way to tie it which his fingers couldn't unpick. His scalp was like the bottom of an eggbox, bristling with lumps.

The doctor visited again, and was almost in tears when she left. She thought David might have fractured his skull, but his head was such a mass of contusion she couldn't be sure. Nicky and I were desperate for anything that explained the past few weeks, any kind of answer that held out hope. A fear tortured us: that this misery could go on for years, making it impossible to work or spend time with James, preventing us from having any kind of sane family life.

We didn't believe David had a fractured skull – his screaming hadn't started with any great drama. But the GP's concerns meant an X-ray appointment was booked for that same afternoon and, as Nicky helped me strap our shrieking child into the car, I was determined not to leave the hospital without some kind of explanation.

I hoped the medics at Bristol Children's Hospital might be so shocked by David's distress that they'd insist on sedating him and keeping him on a ward till his frenzy had abated. Instead, when I carried him into reception, we were asked to leave the building and wait in the car park – his screams were too upsetting for everyone, the staff and the patients.

I stood in the car park with David in my arms, and stared up at the hospital windows. If we weren't allowed in there, where could we go for help? I pulled out my phone and dialled social services: perhaps there was somebody who could sit with David and hold him for a few hours, even if they had to do it in our own home – we could check into a hotel bedroom, get a night's sleep. I wasn't optimistic; we'd been asking for help all month.

The woman who organized David's rota of carers sounded achingly sympathetic. 'I'm so worried about him! I'd come and help myself,' she assured me between David's howls, 'but my summer holiday starts tomorrow. We've taken a cottage in Anjou – we love France, don't you? Oh, but I do feel awful for you … I'll be sitting in the garden every day, thinking, "Poor Chris and Nicky – they won't be doing this!"'

I switched the phone off, and fantasized about stealing a camper van and strapping David into the front, driving him on to a ferry and down through France, until we erupted into a somnolent Loire village like a nuclear attack – I'd bounce the caravanette across vegetable patches and through fences to park it in a steaming heap beside our social worker's sunlounger. I'd hand her my screaming son, and I'd say, 'There you go, we knew you were worried about him.'

In the hospital car park, a young doctor was eyeing me. I couldn't tell if he was more concerned by David's roars or the manic glint in my eye.

'Mr Stevens? You've brought your son in, I understand. What's the problem?'

'Listen,' I said. 'Can you hear it? That's the problem.'

'You've brought him for an X-ray ... I don't think we can have this conversation while he's screaming like this. Can you persuade him to let us talk?'

'If I could, he wouldn't be here.'

'Well, look, he's bound to get tired soon. Bring him in when he pipes down.'

'I don't think he's going to stop till he's dead. Not much point in X-rays then.' I knew I sounded sarcastic and bitter, but I couldn't keep holding it back.

The doctor looked into David's throat. He was getting a good view and an ear-bashing. 'It's going to be difficult to examine him like this ...' He gave up. 'A nurse will come and collect you when we're ready. Please don't bring him inside till then.'

For years afterwards, I measured all David's rages against that afternoon at the hospital. It represented the gold standard of screaming fits. Whenever people complained about my son's volubility, I'd say that today's grumble was low down the scale, just a five or a six. 'Six out of ten?' they'd say, and I'd blink in surprise: 'Six out of a hundred. David's been thrown out of hospitals for screaming.'

The X-ray showed David had a skull like a tungsten cannonball. Whatever was aggravating him, it wasn't a fracture. And no, the doctors didn't want to keep him in for observation.

I couldn't believe we were going to be sent away without any diagnosis. One student doctor, a woman in her early twenties, took pity and offered to give David a general once-over, a 10,000-mile service. She checked his bruises, his eyes and ears, his lungs, and then she pressed on his stomach.

David's eyes watered. He had the anxiously angelic look of a choirboy who has just realized he won't be able to hit top C without sounding the trumpet at the other end.

'Does he fill his nappy regularly?' the doctor asked. 'He doesn't seem constipated? What sort of consistency do his movements have?'

Nicky and I had struck a bargain when our children were born: she was in charge of imports, I handled exports. Any embarrassment I had about discussing nappies with strangers had long since wafted away.

'He's very liquidy,' I said. 'If he ever produces something solid, I think we'll frame it.'

'That's overflow,' the doctor said. 'The poor fellow's horribly bunged up. Not surprising, with such a limited diet. Give him a course of laxative and, even if it doesn't cure him, he's going to be a lot more comfortable. You can feel, under his ribs – it's like he's swallowed a cricket ball.'

She prescribed Lactulose. Within thirty-six hours, David had stopped screaming, and all of us were asleep.

Any other child could have said, 'My tummy hurts,' or at least pointed to the pain. Only David could be doubled over in agony, surrounded by people who were desperate to help him, and be unable to help himself by the tiniest degree. We'd never been more aware of how lonely David was. He was like a boy stranded on an island, while ships and planes searched all the ocean for him – and he couldn't signal to them, or even understand they'd come to save him.

We reached two decisions during those six gruelling weeks. The first was that we couldn't cope for ever on our own. We needed support, somewhere to turn when we were desperate. That didn't mean rolling up at the hospital when we had nowhere else to go. David had settled into school because it formed part of an unshakeable routine, and any extra support had to fit the same pattern.

That summer, he was offered respite sessions at an NHS children's unit called Church House, a mile from his school. Six months earlier, we would have turned the offer down. We didn't want to admit we needed respite from our own child. It felt like a confession of failure. But now we saw that, if David didn't have the chance to incorporate regular stays at Church House in his routine, he wouldn't be able to adapt when we were forced to seek support. If Nicky or I became ill, or if David went through another marathon of screaming without sleeping, or if we simply wanted to take James to the seaside for a couple of days, we needed a routine answer. David had to feel safe.

Church House was run by nurses who were more devoted than any we had encountered before. Just as the staff at David's school were more dedicated and experienced than other teachers, the carers at Church House were extraordinary. They still are. Perhaps the extreme needs of children like David attract people who thrive on impossible challenges, or perhaps one reward of caring for profoundly difficult youngsters is a deeper and more compassionate understanding. The Church House nurses would sit with David all day and night, and then they'd write detailed notes on his behaviour and call us to discuss, in long and intense conversations, all our worries.

Which is not to say that David settled in easily. He accepted his first few visits, for an hour, and then an hour with lunch, and then an afternoon, as an interesting addition to his hectic social schedule. But when he was invited to stay the night, he was horrified.

A sleepover? What kind of boy did they think he was?

Unable to believe he was expected to tuck up in bed – in his own little room, with a Thomas the Tank Engine bedspread and triple mortice locks on the windows – David sat rigid on the sofa all night. He didn't demand videos, he didn't require food: night-time was the time when nothing happened, and David was prepared to sit right through it, doing nothing but crying. When he came home, his face was sore and red, as if his tears had burned his skin.

He spent every sleepover this way. When, a few months down the line, we decided to attempt a two-night stay, David tried to last sixty hours without shutting his eyes. He reached 2 a.m. on the second night, and passed out. The nurses gently carried him to bed. At 2.45 a.m., his screams rent the night. He was livid. He'd been tricked. He'd been put in a bed, just because he'd nodded off for a moment. He stomped back to the sofa ... and fell asleep again. And was placed in bed again. And woke up again.

This time, he didn't even make it to the sofa. He lay down in the doorway, and resisted all efforts to move him. From then on, David slept at Church House like Long Tall Sally, with his feet in the bedroom and his head in the hall.

He slept that way for five years: not on the bedroom floor, not in the passageway, but stretched between the two. Nicky and I suspect, though David can't confirm it, that he feels safer when he's straddling two worlds. Just as he still likes to watch TV through a crack in the sitting-room door, like a sci-fi astronomer observing a parallel reality, he seems to believe the hall and the bedroom are adjacent universes. It's always been possible, up till now, for him to step from one to the other – but what if their orbits suddenly diverge while he's asleep? He might wake up and look out of his bedroom window on to another planet. It could happen: past results, as the small print says, are no guarantee of future performance.

Much safer to maintain the link between universes by lying across the doorway. For five years, each night he spent at Church House, David would drag his bedding across the room and nest between two realities. When he finally had the confidence to sleep all night in his bed, aged nine and a half, we agreed he'd settled in to his respite unit.

Our other decision seemed less dramatic, but it changed our lives even more. When David started screaming, I'd take him out for walks.

Until then, we'd tried to bring David out of the house only when he was in a sunny mood. If he was lively and happy, we'd take him to the park or the shops. Because he wouldn't ride on his trundler when he was howling, we stayed indoors during his rages. That wasn't fair to James, though, who would hide in his room or shelter under the kitchen table as his brother screamed. (To gauge David's volume, in an effort to make the latest psychologist understand how bad it could be, we once made sure all our windows were shut during one full-tilt tantrum, and Nicky left the house; counting off her paces, she realized she could still hear David, through the double glazing, from a hundred yards away.)

We'd taken delivery of a king-size pushchair, called a wheelchair buggy, from Southmead Hospital. It had an aluminium frame and blue-and-white candy-stripes and a footplate, and a heavy-duty harness. By leaning over the back of the chair and shielding the supports with my forearms, I could push David and thwart his headbanging at the same time. I learned to steer a wide path round lamp-posts, postboxes and anything else he could lean out to nut, and he quickly accepted a compromise: he'd bash his head on his knees and my elbows, but mostly he'd sit back and watch the world. And I could stand up straight to push him.

After our first outing, when we walked a mile or so to a Bob the Builder ride, David treated his buggy journeys as a tantrum truce. We'd found an off switch: he could be in the throes of a Force 10 screaming fit, it might take both of us to pin his arms and legs as we buckled him into the buggy, but by the time I'd pushed him to the corner, he'd be settling down. His fist would be tightly wrapped round as many pound coins as he could find in our pockets, and he was intent on feeding every one of them into Bob's yellow digger. He wouldn't let me prise that money out of his hands for sweets or anything else: it was his ride money. If he found a coin as we trundled home, though, he would wait till we passed a drain grating and throw it away – no point in hoarding it, can't take it with you, root of all evil, etc.

A couple of Sundays later, when Nicky had been up all night with David, I decided to see how long he would consent to stay out. I packed a bag with nappies, a change of clothes, spare shoes and his new dietary staples, which his teachers had persuaded him to try: cartons of Ribena and sandwich bags filled with dry cornflakes. With a purse of £1 coins, we set off for the zoo.

We inspected the enclosures in the approved order, regardless of whether there were any animals in them: flamingos and storks to be serenaded with a burst of 'Look

Out For Mr Stork' from Disney's *Dumbo*; lions to be avoided; cornflakes to be munched and scattered across the cafe floor while I drank a coffee and begged a dustpan from Sharon or Jo or Tracy behind the counter, who week by week for years had watched David growing bigger without growing up; PenguinLand to be circumnavigated, counterclockwise, in disobedience to the large, clear signs requiring visitors to enter only by the entrance and never by the exit; gorilla house to be traversed at speed, without glancing left or right, for fear of seeing a gorilla; adventure playground apparatus to be negotiated in strict progression ... total time elapsed, one hour and thirteen minutes, though this could be trimmed in heavy rain, when the inconvenience of other children was removed from the playground.

In the zoo, David didn't need his buggy. As we left, he'd strap himself back into it and we would head for Bob the Builder. This Sunday, we didn't turn for home when the money was gone – I sang Barney the purple dinosaur's song a couple of times, and David settled back in his chair, ready for a long trip. The Barney ride was far on the other side of town, over the river and past the Bristol City ground, at Sainsbury's. We'd never walked there before so I was able to take any rambling route I fancied, fitting in as many distractions as I chose. As long as the final destination was Barney, David was happy to make stops at playparks, cafes and a couple of museums. On our way home, he pushed his buggy round Ashton Court and then across the Suspension Bridge. We got back at teatime, and I reckoned we'd walked about twelve miles, with David out of his chair for at least half the time. He wasn't even slightly faded.

We took our walks in every kind of weather, almost every day after school. He didn't care if it was cold, and he enjoyed rain – the heavier the better. We dressed him in a padded coat under a PVC cape, and gave him a transparent brolly that covered his head like an astronaut's helmet: he loved to tear strips off the cape and chew them.

We must have become a familiar site to Bristolians along our route, following the same streets at the same time each afternoon. David would stamp on the front wheels if I tried to cross the road at the wrong point or took the wrong junction, though he made exceptions for roadworks and removals lorries blocking the pavement: no one could say he was unreasonable. He was loud, though. Our pact on screaming didn't cover squeaks, grunts, moans, hoots, manic laughter or full-throated singing. He was a one-boy jungle.

It hadn't occurred to me that people might be watching us go by, until we were caught in a cloudburst one afternoon. The sky was clear as we trollied past the filling station, it was turning smoky as we approached the nursery, and by the time we reached the Friends' Meeting House, black clouds were emptying bathtubs over us. David had a half-eaten PacAMac, so he didn't care. But I was sheltering against a yew hedge with rainwater hosing down the back of my shirt.

A woman came hurrying down her garden path with an umbrella over her head and another in her hand. 'There you are,' she said, 'just leave it inside the gate when the rain stops.' And she ran inside again.

Most people would hesitate before they lent an umbrella to a stranger, let alone walk out into a storm to do it. I'd always assumed that people took very little notice of David's noises as we went by, and that I couldn't care less what anyone thought of me. The lady with the umbrella made me realize how touching it was that someone we didn't know cared about us.

By the time we'd worn out our first buggy, or maybe our second, we were trundling twenty-five miles every week – roughly a marathon, across a hilly city, with 50lb of volatile ballast. It cost a small fortune in £1 coins, but it was better than any gym workout.

During the holidays, we travelled even further afield.

There were Postman Pat vans and Teletubbies merry-go-rounds all over England. At shopping malls in Worcester and Exeter, on piers at Burnham-on-Sea and Weston-super-Mare, outside supermarkets in Tewkesbury and Stroud, David crammed himself into plastic seats designed for toddlers, fed his coin into the slot and pressed the red, blue and green buttons solemnly. He regarded a seventy-second joggle in a lump of red plastic that played a TV theme tune to be full recompense for an hour spent grinding up the M5 and around Gloucester's back roads, for example. And he expected a long push in his chair – the journey didn't count unless we parked on the edge of the city centre and trundled a mile to the Tweenies ride at Eastgate market.

The return trip, though, held fewer incentives.

On the way home, David could get bored. He'd listened to his tapes, he'd thrown his shoes at the windscreen, he'd poured Ribena over the seats, he'd ground cornflakes into the mess, he'd put his bag over his head, and now he was bored. That was hard cheese for him, because he was strapped into the middle of the back seat in a Houdini harness and I wasn't pulling off the motorway, no matter how fed up he got. He was five years old: long car journeys were supposed to be tooth-achingly dull. I'd been bored to tears aged five in the back of my mum's Mini, and it hadn't killed me. David had more legroom, and cloth-covered seats – boredom wouldn't kill him, either.

So one afternoon, driving back from Worcester on the M5, he decided to up the stakes and try to kill both of us.

A Houdini harness looks like the webbing on a parachute. It takes both hands and practice to open the buckle at the centre, even when you know the secret (lever, push together, lift). David couldn't wriggle out: on his first trip, he'd thrown himself around so violently that he'd loosened the straps that fastened the harness to the car seat, but we'd fixed that with the kind of steel safety pins a Highland wrestler wears on his kilt.

The Incredible Hulk couldn't have burst out of those restraints. David, however, was smarter than the average mutant superhero. At 70mph outside Pershore, I glanced in the mirror as I pulled past a lorry and saw my rear view was blocked by a boy on the parcel shelf.

He was lying on his side, crammed against the hatchback window, kicking the glass. I shouted at him, for all the good it would do: 'David, no!'

I couldn't remember latching the boot. Perhaps I'd slammed it, but I hadn't checked it. If the hatch flew open now, David would be flung out. One pothole, one lump in the tarmac would kill him: he would be sucked out of the car and under the wheels of twenty lorries.

My rear view was blocked, but in my side mirror I saw there was a left-hand-drive coach behind us, flashing its lights. The incomprehension, or disgust, of the coach driver helped me hold on to my nerves. This was David: he might look like a rioting brat, but he was just an ordinary lad who liked doing things differently.

I imagined the tour guide's commentary to the coachload of Scandanavian pensioners, or whoever they were: 'If you look ahead of us, ladies and gentlemen, you'll see a sad example of the decline in standards of British parenting. Many middle-class families now are unable to discipline their children ...'

The hatch didn't spring open. I started to believe that David wasn't on the brink of death – though if I stopped suddenly, he would decapitate me as he smacked into the windscreen. I'd just have to be careful not to stop suddenly.

David crawled head first down the back seat like a gecko. Hanging upside down, he fastened all the seatbelts. He tried dangling on the left. He tried dangling on the right. Then he slithered to the floor. I couldn't look away from the road, but I reached between the front seats and met David wriggling through to join me.

'Back in your seat!' I snapped, pushing on his head. He screamed. I stopped pushing.

'You're not getting in the front,' I said. 'No, David. No!'

He shoved at my arm and flung himself on the hand-brake. I groped for the scruff of his neck, but he clung on to the gear lever and shrieked.

'Let go of it! Stop it!' I yelled. I hadn't meant to look down, but in a heartbeat two wheels had drifted on to the hard shoulder. My right hand wouldn't hold the car straight. I tried to bolster the wheel with my left knee, and heaved at David's fingers on the plastic stump of the gear stick.

He was pulling so hard that the gears jerked out of fifth.

The engine whined like a siren. Stamping on the clutch, I tried to pull the stick down into fourth, but David was dragging it sideways and I hit second instead.

The car slowed with a lurch and a howl, and the Scandanavians behind hit the brake, the lights and the horn, but somehow didn't hit us.

'Let go of it! Let go!'

I wrenched the gear lever across to fourth and ground the accelerator into the rubber mat until we'd climbed above sixty again.

The coach rumbled past us in the middle lane. I couldn't look up, but I felt eighty elderly Norwegians glaring at me. With my left hand gripping David's wrists, I couldn't risk my right fingers to give them an English salute.

As David clambered on to the passenger seat, I indicated left, switched on the hazard lights and coasted on to the hard shoulder.

We slowed to a stop, and I reached across to take hold of his dungarees in case he opened the passenger door and tried to leap out. The rear doors were safety-locked and couldn't be opened from the inside, but he'd probably noticed that the front doors were different – noticed it, and filed the information away for future kamikaze fun.

With an arm around his chest, I wriggled on to the passenger seat and slid out. Every lorry that hurtled past pummelled us with backdraughts and noise. Their tyres made a ripping, crackling sound on the road surface, like packing tape being torn off bubble wrap. I clamped David to me, pulled open the back door, and thrust him into his seat.

He arched and bucked, but I pressed down on his hips till he sat, and the harness snapped tight. He was unclipping its buckle before I had straightened up.

'Very clever,' I said. 'If you can work that out, how come you can't drink from a cup? Eh?'

Holding David in place with a forearm across his stomach, I searched the car for something to secure him. Pulling my sweatshirt over my head, I slipped the sleeves under his shoulder straps and knotted them tightly. Then I wrapped the body of the shirt under and around the buckle.

For added security, I fed my belt behind the car seat, fastened it and rotated it till the buckle was behind him. Now I was shivering in a T-shirt that was too short to tuck in, and trousers that were too loose to stay up.

'Get out of that,' I told him.

He did.

The sweatshirt held him for half a minute, long enough to get us up to seventy. To wriggle out of the belt, he simply raised his arms, pulled back his shoulders and sank down the seat like a synchronized swimmer sliding into the deep end.

I didn't fight him as he scrambled into the front. A loud scolding would make him all the happier. This was a game, and a bellowing adult added flavour to any game.

Settling into the slow lane at fifty-five behind a caravan, I held my left hand tense, ready to grab him if he started fiddling with the door. When he buckled the seatbelt across himself, I relaxed, by a smidgeon of one degree: he had his feet stretched against the glove compartment and the chest strap against his throat, and if I braked, he would hang himself.

After ten miles, he slid into the footwell. Curled up like a cat, he wasn't safe, but he looked less likely to cause an accident. I moved to pass the caravan, and the increased noise and vibration must have made the footwell uncom-fortable because David clambered up again.

'Good chap! That's sensible, you sit yourself back in. Much more fun when you can see where we're going … No way! David! Not the dashboard. You can't.'

I seized his collar and thrust him on to the passenger seat as he tried to stretch his body along the windscreen. He shrieked, bashed his head against the seat, and then cracked it against the passenger window. When I hauled him towards me, he scrambled on to my lap, bounced on my knees, tried to wrench the wheel out of my hands and stood up. As we careered on to the hard shoulder again, he was full-length on the dashboard.

'What we need is a staple gun,' I told him, as I pulled the Houdini harness tight enough to turn his arms and legs numb.

In the end, I used my shoelaces. David screamed for twenty minutes as his fingers picked at the knots and then, accepting defeat, became serene. Staring out of the window at the Severn valley countryside, he suddenly looked like a vicar composing next Sunday's sermon.

I drove home in my socks.

Ten

And then, one day, David started talking.

It was as simple, and as unexpected, as that.

We'd always insisted that David didn't have learning difficulties, he had understanding difficulties. He could learn to do anything he wanted, such as unbuckle a Houdini harness or operate a video player; he wouldn't learn to do anything we wanted, because he didn't see why he should. David didn't understand … and without words, we couldn't make him.

When he started talking, we realized the problem was more complex. Words were just one twist of the puzzle. But it hardly mattered, because we were so overjoyed to hear his voice.

He paraded his vocabulary for the first time just after Christmas, aged five and a half, in the sitting room. It had become David's room: we'd stripped out all the breakables, installed a trampoline and a rocking horse, screwed the TV set to a table, replaced the carpet with a disposable wicker mat and the sofa with a cheap futon, and collected David's toys into colourful plastic buckets.

He had lovely toys because no one, least of all Nicky and

me, could accept he didn't know how to play with them – we gave him die-cast models of his favourite rides and of the planes, trains and bulldozers from his videos, hoping he would try to act out the stories with them. He'd started re-enacting Disney movies, rushing round the house and dancing down the stairs as he sang the soundtrack (perfect pitch, perfect tempo, incidental orchestration and all). But he didn't use props. David knew every note of the *Lion King* score, but he hadn't the first idea how to incorporate his plastic Simba or his cuddly Pumbaa into the retelling.

With a touch of New Year fervour, we'd tidied all the toys by theme – alphabet toys in one bucket, fire engines and police cars in another, and so on. David assumed we'd done this to streamline the mess-making experience: it's more satisfying to tip a toy bucket that contains, for example, only dinosaurs.

I treated this as a conflict – we wanted order, David wanted chaos, and David would always win. It's something to do with the Second Law of Thermodynamics, apparently. Nicky saw it as a chance to play with David – he tipped a bucket, she refilled it slowly and told him the name of each toy. She'd also spotted that he wouldn't upturn a half-filled bucket, so the more slowly she tidied away the toys, the less often David created a mess.

'David, what's this? What is it? It's a racing car. Can you say "racing car"? Let's put it in the bucket. And what's this? What is it? It's a helicopter ...'

I watched them through the crack of the door jamb, the way David peeped from one world to the next, because I didn't want him to notice me and be distracted. I marvelled at my wife's patience for a few minutes, and then I slipped away to the kitchen.

When I came back with mugs of tea, Nicky was wiping tears from her eyes. She shushed me before I could speak.

'Watch this,' she said. 'David, what is it?'

Nicky held up a tiny orange Kawasaki. David glanced at it and said, 'Motorbike.'

'He said "motorbike",' I gasped.

'And he isn't copying me,' Nicky said. 'That's what is really incredible. He knows the word. Look ... David, what is it?'

'Racing car.'

'Good boy! In the bucket ... and, what is it?'

'Ambulance.'

He was saying the words perfectly, without any prompting, and though his eyes only flickered at the toys, he was clearly loving the game and waiting for each challenge.

Nicky worked through every bucket of toys that morning, and David knew almost every name. He came out with words that would have taxed any five-year-old – 'narrowboat', 'rhinoceros', 'steamroller'. Then he repeated them, as his grandparents listened on the telephone.

'Some of these toys I showed him earlier,' Nicky said, 'but lots of words he must be remembering from goodness knows when. How long has he known "rhinoceros"? And how is he able to say it so beautifully, without any practice?'

He didn't want to be hugged. We were bursting to praise him and tell him how glad we were, but David wasn't interested in anything we thought. He couldn't imagine we even had opinions about him – he just assumed that our thoughts, and feelings, echoed his.

The truth was, we were feeling so much that we could hardly separate our emotions. Happiness, and frustration, and bewilderment, and excitement, and pride were all churning round together. The only feeling we could easily put into words was what a joy it was to hear David's voice. 'He says every word so sweetly,' Nicky kept telling me. And she was right – David sounded happy, and proud of himself, but most of all he sounded perfectly innocent.

For months, or years, he must have been listening to words and taking them in. Now he could say them, but he couldn't tell us why. All he could do was pronounce the name of each object. Although he seemed to be answering a question ('What is it?'), really he was responding to a cue: the game would have worked as well if Nicky had struck a gong or blown a whistle.

David had picked up these words – now he was putting them down again, in a place outside language. They had meaning, but not context. He dismissed even the most basic language rules: a car next to a lorry wasn't 'car and lorry', it was 'car ... lorry'. There was no 'and' anywhere to be seen. What was an 'and' – were we talking about this thing on the end of his arm? We discovered as the game developed that David knew lots of words for parts of the body ('eye', 'chin', 'knee', 'tummy', 'finger', 'hair'). If he didn't know a word, he could learn it and mimic it in a couple of repetitions. Suddenly, he understood about colours too – post vans were red, tennis balls were yellow, and David could tell us so.

He was enjoying the game so much that he kept playing as we set off on our walk. 'Pushchair ... blue car ... green car ... ambulance ... motorbike ...' he announced, not to draw my attention to them (David had seen them; therefore Dad-thing had seen them), but for the sheer fun of saying the words.

Excepting the colours, all the words were nouns, labels, names. David didn't attempt to use adjectives or verbs, to describe how things looked or what they were doing. When a police car blazed by with its sirens howling, I said, 'Noisy!' and David didn't answer. He looked unsettled. 'Police car,' I added, and his relief was plain: 'Police car!'

An airliner went over, heading for Bristol Airport. I said, 'Look, David, a plane!' and he stared round, even more puzzled. He had aeroplanes in his toy box. He knew what he should be seeing, but there were only cars and bicycles and people with dogs around us.

'Look up there,' I told him, leaning over the chair and pointing. 'Look!' I grabbed his finger and made it point to the sky. David pulled his hand away. 'Look' was a verb, an instruction. It wasn't a label, and David didn't understand it.

I thought again. 'Up!' I said. 'Aeroplane, up.'

David tipped back his head and saw the plane. A broad grin spread over his face. 'Aeroplane,' he said, and watched it for a few seconds before kicking the wheels of his buggy, like a cowboy spurring his horse on.

Even a two-letter word can be packed with overlapping meanings. 'Up' meant direction and movement, to me. To David, it was a place, a label on the sky. He was deploying words the way he'd learned to use songs at MusicSpace – each one had a definite, single application.

We couldn't have a conversation with labels. We couldn't even ask him a question, like 'Where does it hurt?' David knew the word 'tummy', but he couldn't tell us when he had a tummy ache.

But David didn't want conversation. Like Elvis, he just wanted a little more action. With words, he could make his demands more precise and achieve better results. Nicky felt strongly that when David managed to ask for something out loud, he should be rewarded whenever possible. It didn't matter how frivolous his requests – if he wanted it badly enough to force the words out, he deserved it. (The usual caveats applied: nothing laced with blue food colouring, for instance, because he'd still be crawling across the ceiling at 4 a.m.)

When he forgot his words and started flailing about in a tantrum, we tried to make him talk his way out of it. He'd get his milk when he said, 'Milk,' not when he head-butted the television.

A week later, he went back to school, and his teachers were as thrilled as we had been. It wasn't only that the classroom, like our home, became less fraught and more hopeful – it was the obvious pleasure David gained from being able to label his needs. He became more relaxed, less ready to fly into a rage when he didn't get exactly what he wanted first time: words, like old cars, didn't always work at the first attempt, but if he kept turning the key, they'd usually chug into life.

That school term, he learned to say, 'I want,' before he named an object. It was the first time he'd been able to describe his inner state in words. David had an eloquent musical vocabulary, with songs that meant, 'I'm tired,' or 'I'm getting angry,' or 'This blasted Dad-thing doesn't work properly, the useless heap of junk.' A few notes were enough to tip us off to his emotions, though he wasn't singing to tell us anything: he was simply supplying the soundtrack to his life.

The words 'I want' gave him a change of gears. He could look up, see a plane and say, 'Aeroplane,' for the fun of naming it. That didn't mean he wanted a private jet. He couldn't imagine flying, or any destination that couldn't be reached by car or buggy. But a few moments later, he could say, 'I want … cornflakes.' And that meant something very different – he was talking about how he felt, and what he expected to happen. When David said, 'I want,' he was using words in earnest.

This breakthrough grew from PECS, the picture-exchange system which he'd started to learn at Red House and which was used constantly at Briarwood. 'I want' was the first rule of grammar in PECS, the first step from labels to dialogue. And it's powerful – I've worked with news-paper editors who never really got beyond it.

David added his own word rules. He didn't understand adjectives, but he used colours: blue car, red fire engine, black cat. That told us something new about the way his brain was processing what he saw: colour was concrete to David. It mattered more than shape or size. A car was a car, whether it had a soft top, a bulbous bonnet or an aero-foil off the back of Michael Schumacher's Ferrari. 'Car' was a small word with a wide application. But 'red car' was much more specific. There was no leeway with 'red' – try telling David a pink car, or a maroon car, or an orange car, were red and he'd correct you smartly. Colour mattered to him, just as musical pitch did. To call a green car 'blue' was as contradictory as singing 'Heigh-Ho' in the wrong key.

He also tired of words easily. After that first day, we never heard him say 'rhinoceros' again. James always loved to try out new words in a variety of ways, repeating the sounds and sampling them in sentences; even now, at fourteen, he can't hear a new word without demanding to know its meaning, and testing it. David treated most new words as so much debris, and discarded them. He was like the men we saw on wet mornings at low tide in Weston-super-Mare, sweeping the beach with metal detectors – for every 20p coin they found, there were dozens of bottle tops and ring pulls. David had discovered hundreds of words, but he reckoned only half a dozen had real value. The rest, the 'penguins' and 'boomerangs' and 'handbags' and 'dinosaurs', were just bottle tops and ring pulls.

Some practical words were confusingly similar to completely useless ones: 'telephone' and 'elephant', for example. One was a source of entertainment, the other was a waste of good syllables. David had a plastic elephant: it was too big to chew, too small to sit on and it didn't break when thrown. Pointless. He tried to say its name: 'Elephone.' That set Mum-thing laughing, but it didn't make the toy any more useful.

A telephone, on the other hand, was lots of fun. Characters in videos were always grabbing hold of them and shouting, and then slamming them down. When our phone rang at home, David heard familiar voices: if he had the chance, he'd pick it up and listen, and sometimes squawk. David had no idea there were real people on the other end of the line – after all, he hadn't grasped the concept of 'real people', never mind telephones. But most of his victims couldn't understand that. 'I called your number,' a newspaper colleague complained, 'but a child answered and screamed at me. That was your son? You've got to teach him he can't do that!'

David could and did do it. We encouraged him instead to say 'hello', and suddenly he understood the five-point etiquette of phone calls: pick up receiver, say 'hello', listen to caller, say 'goodbye', replace receiver. David wasn't sure how long the listening part should go on, but surely a heartbeat was enough – any more was to court boredom.

Every time the phone rang, we raced for it. David often won. Grab, 'hello-goodbye', click, all over in a second and a half. The explanations took longer: 'Of course I didn't slam the phone down on you, Auntie ... We're always delighted to hear from you ... David was just playing a game ...'

He wasn't interested in play phones. Plastic mobiles that trilled cute messages in American accents were about as useful as toy elephants. He wanted the real thing, the ones that spoke with voices he knew, the ones that sounded like his Grampa and said, 'Hello, David.' But even those were a disappointment most of the time. Unlike the ones in videos, which rang whenever they appeared in shot, our phone was usually silent. So David started to experiment.

The first we knew of this was a buzz on the doorbell and three uniformed policemen outside the house. Two of them stood well back from the door as I opened it. The third was on the pavement with a radio, staring up at our windows.

I confirmed my name, and my first feeling was, illogically, relief – Nicky and our children were in the house. I knew they were safe. The police were here, probably to bring terrible news, but whatever had happened was not as awful as it might have been.

'Is your wife in the house?' one of the PCs asked. 'Is she all right? Can we see her?'

A hideous memory flashed back: I'd answered the door, aged about twelve, to a policeman who'd asked gently to see my mother, and I'd shouted up the stairs, 'Mum! Police are here! Hide the drugs!' In too many ways to list now, that had been wrong of me, and the lessons must have made a deep impression: this time, I bit back the reflex quips, asked the officers to wait a moment and fetched my wife.

They seemed surprised to find her not murdered and not dismembered. They were frankly sceptical when we insisted we hadn't been arguing and that Nicky hadn't dialled 999 in a desperate cry for help. They absolutely didn't believe the 'bonkers five-year-old *Fireman Sam* fan' defence.

Fireman Sam is the children's show that puts the 'arson' into plasticine. In every episode, a character runs to a call box and gasps, 'Nine, nine, nine.' We now knew that David could find the '9' on a keypad, which probably meant he knew all his numbers. The police officers at our door were less impressed by this than we were.

One of them came into the kitchen, to deliver the lecture on how hoax calls to the emergency services could cost lives, and Nicky made him a coffee. In a china mug.

Perhaps David could hear the difference as the hot water splashed in. Maybe he could smell hot pottery. He came motoring into the kitchen, eyes fixed on the mid distance, and as the PC said, 'So this is the culprit, is it?' David's hand flashed out and smashed the mug against the skirting board.

That was our last china mug. All the others were melamine or metal, and tea tastes vile from a tin cup. The sacrifice was worth it, though – our alibi was upheld. There really was a bonkers five-year-old loose in the house.

'Is that why all your cupboards are tied with socks?' the policeman asked.

Most people were too polite to mention the socks, the

way you'd ignore a pair of underpants drying over the radiator. Police don't have to be polite, though. And he was right – socks were the best deterrent we'd found. Plastic fasteners to clamp our cupboard handles together were useless: David could locate the levers and press the release tabs with one hand, and sweep a shelf of glass to the floor with the other. He could loosen string bows too, and knots would pull so tight that we needed scissors to get to the cereal bowls. Socks were ideal – David's fingers weren't strong enough to unpick the knots instantly, which gave us a few seconds to spot him and drag him away.

'What about banning him from the kitchen?' suggested the PC. 'Friends of mine have a toddler gate to keep their lad out, in case he gets burned.'

Questions like that can set me off on two-hour explanations. In the office, in the park or in parents' groups, my Ancient Mariner tendency kicks in. People think they've asked a simple question, but there are no simple answers with autism, because it isn't a simple condition. Autism is pervasive: it affects everything a child thinks and does, and so it soaks into every aspect of family life.

A gate across the kitchen seems sensible, at first glance. We keep David out of James's room with a hook, after all. David would like to slip in there and wreak havoc. He'd *like* to, but he doesn't *need* to.

The kitchen is different. His mother goes in the kitchen. Wherever Mum is, David needs to be. As long as he's in the house, he has to know she's in reach. There have been many days, and even entire weeks, when he hasn't let her out of his sight for a moment.

When he comes home from school, Nicky has to be there; when he's nodding off to sleep, she has to be there;

when he's on holiday or off school with a cold, she has to be there. For a few years, there was a ten-minute crisis once a week, when Nicky had to set off for work on a Tuesday morning before the school bus arrived. David took it badly. He didn't care that she worked just two days a week, during term time only, or count the constant sacrifices she made to be with him all the time – he just couldn't cope with seeing her leave the house. In a rage of jealousy and fear, David would smash his head from one wall to the other like a pinball.

In contrast, he'd get up early on a Saturday to watch me drive away. I was welcome to go whenever I fancied, and he wasn't especially anxious to see me return. He likes to have me around the place, but he *needs* his mother. The difference in intensity can't be measured; neither can the pressure it places on Nicky.

Even now, aged eleven, David refuses to be parted from his mum. Last night, there was a shriek and a splash from the bathroom, as he joined her in the tub. He didn't want a bath – he didn't even take off his shoes. He just wanted to be with her.

If David was separated from Nicky by a gate across the kitchen doorway, even if he could see her, he'd tear the walls down. He'd scream himself blind.

We didn't mind suggestions, of course. Most people meant well, and it gave us a chance to defuse their concerns. When professionals suggested similar solutions and dressed them up as 'recommendations', however, that made us seethe. It was bad enough that we had to submit to cross-examinations from strangers, simply because our child had been born with a disability – it was insulting when they had no understanding of autism.

One specialist was alarmed to read that David smashed glasses and crockery. That was dangerous, she said. People might tread on broken glass – as if she was the one who had sliced her feet open at three in the morning, while boiling another kettle for a bottle of hot milk.

'I advise you to set aside a special place in the garden,' she said, 'where David is allowed to break things. After a while, you can start to ration it, perhaps to a bottle a day, and eventually one a week.'

'And how do we make him understand that?' I snapped.

The specialist gave me a chilly smile. 'How do you usually explain things to David?' she asked.

'We don't. We can't. Sometimes he learns to associate certain songs with corresponding actions, but so far we haven't come up with a tune that means, "Go outside before you start smashing the crockery, my lad."'

Nicky caught my eye. I wouldn't help David by losing my rag. That would be worse than refusing to see the specialist in the first place. One day, we might need her report: it was another tick on our checklist. But my anger was over quickly – it flared up and I gave vent to it in sarcasm. Nicky felt these intrusions more deeply. They hurt her.

The worst was a series of discussions about David's behaviour with a clinical psychologist. For an hour on four Friday afternoons, he sat in our front room and asked questions about our family that were so intrusive that sometimes even I squirmed. Nicky was in tears after every session. But we couldn't refuse to see him: it would effectively mean we were rejecting all future NHS help ... and with David struggling to settle in to his weekly respite sessions, we couldn't put that in jeopardy.

For both of us to give up an hour when David wasn't at home was a significant sacrifice. To do it four times, when the sheer pointlessness was more blatant every week, made us feel like bashing our own heads against the wall. At one session, the psychologist likened David to a garden over-grown with weeds, or bad behaviour, and said we needed to root them out and fill him with flowers – as if we could solve his problems by putting our backs into it. We had to sit there, listening to these insulting banalities and pouring him fresh cups of tea, because by cancelling the sessions, we'd lose the game.

One of the psychologist's suggestions was almost worth the whole ordeal, though. We've never met anyone who can quite believe he said it.

Some impulses could never be eradicated, he told us – violent dogs would always have the instinct to bite. But those instincts could be controlled, with 'aversion therapy'. The dog was taught to associate bad behaviour with instant punishment. It couldn't enjoy its instincts, because pain kicked in simultaneously.

'One common method,' he explained, 'is an electric-shock collar. At the first sign of a violent move, the owner can press a button on a remote handset that sends an electrical pulse through the animal's throat. It's painful without causing permanent injury. Pretty soon, the dog realizes that if it even thinks about biting, it's going to be sorry.'

This nasty little lesson in animal obedience was obviously leading to some sort of analogy. We waited for the sentence that began, 'Now, I'm not suggesting, of course ...'

Instead, he said: 'How would you feel about ...'

We goggled at him.

Years of training and experience must have enabled him to interpret our expressions. We were leaning forward, not breathing, with our jaws dangling.

'You wouldn't feel comfortable with that kind of therapy?' he asked.

What we didn't feel comfortable with was sitting in our own front room, listening to a stranger outline a system for torturing our child.

More than ever before, we were aware of how vulnerable our family had become. We had a disabled child, and that justified any intrusion by figures of authority, who had licence to say anything they chose.

If one of James's teachers had suggested physical violence, even jokingly, the school could expect an official complaint. Threats of thick ears and the cane aren't tolerated any more.

It's hard to imagine the psychologist could have set up an 'aversion therapy programme' for David, even if we'd given permission – his teachers at Briarwood would have raised the alarm.

At moments like that, we felt like criminals. We'd broken the law (Unspoken Prejudices Act, 1996) by having a disabled child, and now we were outside normal, decent society. Even the forms we had to fill in for social services emphasized their system's contempt for our family – this was the same paperwork they used for abused children. One night, we might be trying to hold David as he punched his own face in an autistic frenzy, while in a different part of the city, another little boy's drunken parents could be beating him: to social services, there was no difference between us. Both sets of casework would be entered on the same forms.

We tried to protest – when care workers failed to turn up, week after week, or when the mandatory review of David's progress was typed up and distributed to all his carers, with dangerously inaccurate details. We couldn't get apologies or retractions from social services, we couldn't stop more mistakes from happening and, most of the time, we couldn't even get replies to our letters. When we filed an official complaint, the 'independent adjudicator' was a department head from social services; when we gave up in exhaustion, he declared our case was 'successfully resolved'.

No one who is looking after a severely disabled child can win a fight with social services. These public servants can't be held to account for their mistakes, and they know it. They're untouchable. It's a kind of bureaucratic gangsterdom.

David's straightforward innocence isn't affected by their attitude; that's one of his many appealing, rewarding traits. He's a joy to look after when he's happy, which is most of the time. 'I love David,' Nicky says, 'it's everything else that wears me down.' And it's 'everything else' which autism screens out. No wonder David often lies on the sofa and doubles up giggling.

Eleven

At six years old, David had discovered the secret of happiness. He couldn't tell anyone ... perhaps that's why it's a secret. The rest of us have to find it out for ourselves. And a lot of people have done that, just by watching David. Like all the best cosmic truths, it's short enough to put on a T-shirt: 'Do Whatever You Want. Repeat Until Bedtime.'

The lessons that self-help gurus spread across a shelf of books came naturally to David. He didn't care what people thought of him, he had no inhibitions and he bore no malice to anyone. That kind of confidence takes courage for most of us – to David, it came as easily as breathing. When people saw this, it could be a revelation, and an inspiration.

On a spring evening, after buckets of rain, David and I were strolling on Brandon Hill in the centre of Bristol. There are ornamental gardens at its top, and a pond: David had sent his shoes flying into the lily pads with a ballerina-style flick of his toes, and we'd spent fifteen minutes kneeling at the water's edge with a stick. Then we chased up and down the steps, David barefoot and me dragging the buggy.

A playpark, deserted after the rain, stood at the foot of a steep slope. We could have followed a winding path down, but David threw himself sideways into the thick, wet grass and started rolling, all the way to the bottom. I stood at the top, shaking my head – I knew he'd be back for more, and sure enough he scrambled upright and came staggering towards me. His hair was plastered to his head, his coat was sodden and I could hear his trousers sloshing all the way up the hill. And he was grinning. He wasn't just happy, he was radiant, beaming with joy.

A group of students had stopped to stare. The boys were guffawing – 'Look at that kid! Just a bit wet!' But as David lunged into the grass at the crest of the slope and started barrelling down again, one of the girls looked at me with brimming eyes. 'I wish my dad would have let me do things like that,' she said.

I wanted to say, 'Go on then! There's no one to stop you now.' But that wasn't what she meant. She wanted to have rolled down wet slopes when she was six years old.

We couldn't let him do quite everything he wanted. There are some obsessions that have to be thwarted. They're not hurting anyone, they cost nothing ... but we just don't do them. Opening other people's car doors, for instance. David could spot an unlocked car from twenty yards. His arm would dangle over the side of his buggy, he'd sing a happy tune at the sky, and as we rattled past, his fingers would flash out and flip the handle.

If a car's unlocked in Bristol, it's usually because the driver is inside, sipping a coffee and reading the newspaper. And when the passenger door explodes open, he's probably going to spill his drink all over his paper and his knees. When that happens, the best explanations are short ones, and the shortest ones of all are just a wave – a cheery waggle, as though jolting coffee across someone's trousers means 'good afternoon' in most European countries. No one wants to hear apologies and excuses about autism, or white lies about how David thought that it was his car. They just want to wipe cappuccino off their pinstripes and be grateful it wasn't a carjacking.

We also discouraged free chewing gum, the kind David found in blobs under tables or on lampposts. He didn't care where it had been – what mattered was whether he could get it gooey again. David's enthusiasm for found foods was a puzzle. I spotted him once in our garden, crunching on something with a ponderous face. Tucking two fingers into the side of his mouth, I scooped out a snail.

Another afternoon, he dragged his slide over to the garden shed and used its steps to climb on to the roof. For an hour, he sat there in silence, his back to the kitchen window, and we were naive enough to think he was simply enjoying his domain from a new perspective. It wasn't until he held out his arms and started singing an agitated tune that we wandered out to help him down ... and discovered he'd eaten half the roof felt. He'd been tearing it in tarry strips, rolling it into gobstoppers and chewing it.

He'll try anything, as long as no one's making him eat it. Soap, flowers, the dog's ear ... Yesterday, Nicky caught him sneaking out of the study with blue lips. He'd been drinking the ink.

But when his teacher persuaded him to lick a spoon during a cookery lesson, she was excited enough to email us: 'David actually trusted me enough to try a taste. He didn't expect to like it ... but as it was golden syrup, he did!'

If we could get him to taste a vegetable, or any hot food,

that really would be progress. Anything, of course, is progress after roof felt. Apart from cornflakes, he'll eat the crusts of bread rolls, the icing from doughnuts and the crosses from hot cross buns. He's gone off Weetabix completely. He won't eat sticky buns without currants, but he will eat currant buns once he's picked the currants out. He doesn't like chocolate, except for Rolos and Kinder eggs, which are a paper-thin chocolate shell around a plastic toy: David throws the toy away.

If you're reading this and thinking, 'What an over-indulged child,' remember that squadrons of nurses, teachers and special-school dinner ladies – as well as us – have tried and failed to make this boy eat anything he doesn't fancy. Even if you manage to slip a morsel into a mouth that's wide open – in mid scream, for instance – you can't make him swallow. Slap a hand over his face and he'll store the food in his cheeks, like a hamster, before spitting it out through your fingers.

David's diet is one thing we've discussed repeatedly with a succession of paediatric specialists. There's not much point in talking to doctors about his behaviour – they don't have a pill to make him normal. He wouldn't swallow it if they did. But we do want to know if his obsessive pickiness is putting his health at risk. It's hard to see where a boy who lives on dry cornflakes and the crosses from hot cross buns is getting his nourishment.

When he was born, David was in the 'hundredth percentile', the top 1 per cent of hefty babies, weighing 8 pounds 10 ounces. Ten years later, he was in the fiftieth, as average as could be. It's nice to know there's something ordinary about him, but he had to miss out on a lot of vitamins to become average.

To make David eat, we were ready to try any incentive. That meant treating him differently from James, and we needed plenty of long chats with our older boy to help him understand why his little brother was allowed so many liberties. James had to sit up to the kitchen table; David ate his cornflakes spreadeagled over the television with his nose pressed against the screen. James was expected to finish his plate before he had ice cream; David tipped his cornflakes over the floor when he'd had enough. James faced a scolding if he ate sweets before a meal; David had no mealtimes, and he ate what he wanted, when he wanted.

David's favourite treat was jam tarts from the bakery up the street. They had to be raspberry jam, and the filling had to be even, or he'd refuse them – though he never ate the jam itself. He nibbled the pastry all the way round, and discarded the centre.

In winter, jam tarts weren't a problem. I bought a bag of six each morning, and David munched his way through them (or rather, around them) after school. But in summer, the jam would be tacky, and that caused headaches. If a tart was smeary, he'd throw it in disgust across the room. And if two were stuck together, he'd declare a state of emergency.

The bakery staff humoured us, arranging David's tarts in cake boxes and accepting our power of veto over any imperfect pastries. Half-term came round, and David joined me on the morning visit – he stood obediently in the queue, clutching £1.25 in his hot fist, with my arm across his chest like a sash to stop him from leaning forward and licking the display case. We went every day, and when Sunday morning came, David pulled on his coat and shoes for his daily episode of tart trek.

Nothing could distract him. He didn't understand words like 'closed' and 'shut' and 'Sunday'. He did know what 'no' meant, and he wasn't having any of it. So we decided to let him find out for himself.

The bakery was dark. There was no one queueing. The door was shut, the pavement signs were stacked inside and through the window I could see the cabinets were empty.

None of this was significant to David. He ignored the signals that shouted, 'This shop is closed!' They were communicating a message, and David doesn't do communication. He wouldn't have cared either if the shop had been on fire, or filled with revellers in Hawaiian tops and straw skirts. Only one fact mattered: this was the place where he collected his jam tarts.

I let him rattle the door handle. 'It's shut,' I said.

The door opened. It wasn't locked. David marched in. I dragged him backwards. He shrieked, and I froze. The cake stands were empty, but the shelves were stacked with jars of pickled eggs, onions, gherkins and cabbage. The cabinets were glass-fronted and the fridge was full of Coke bottles. I didn't want to provoke a bout of the whirling dervishes in here.

'Who's there? We're closed,' a woman's voice shouted, and I remembered that the couple who ran the shop lived upstairs.

'It's OK, it's only us,' I called, as though David and I were in the habit of popping round every Sunday morning to help get the roast on. 'Sorry, door was open, David barged in, wasn't quick enough to stop him – he doesn't talk, you know – don't suppose, umm, you've got any, umm … jam tarts?'

There are people who'll fall over themselves to be kind

to David, and the baker's wife is one of them. She raided her stockroom for six of the finest raspberry-filled, folded a cake box for them, and wouldn't hear of taking any money. By the time we reached home, David had scoffed the lot and I was carrying a sticky stack of tart centres.

Those jammy centres forced us to ban David's treats in the end. They always landed gummy side down when he dropped them, and by the time we'd scraped one up, two more had hit the furniture. When he got one glued to his shoe, he'd grind it into the carpet all over the house; when he left one lurking on our red settee, it would splodge itself across Nicky's dress. The dog ate so many of them, he looked like a rugby ball.

I lost patience one Friday night when I lay down with the alarm set for 5.30 a.m. for a dawn train to Paddington – and pressed my face into a jammy pillow. Sticky, crumbly tart was smeared through my hair: I had to get up, change the pillowcase and take a shower.

Aside from pastry in bed, David liked eating on the move. He tucked into cornflakes in the car, guzzled milk on his swing, peeled his hot cross buns in his buggy and took bags of bread rolls out to the garage, where his own ride had been installed. It was a green racing car on a red plinth, which my parents had bought from an amusement arcade when its owner retired. They loaded it into a borrowed Transit van and drove it down from Wales, and David rode it hundreds of times that first day. It took 20p coins, so we collected a tenner's worth from the bank, but he fed them in so quickly that it was difficult to seize the moment between rides when we could reach round the back of the car, unlock the coin tray and retrieve the money.

The next day, David started experimenting. He tried pushing £1 coins and 50p pieces into the slot, and then pennies and tuppences, which jammed the mechanism; David was heartbroken. The coin slot was soldered into place, so I phoned the company which manufactured the ride to ask their advice. They supplied information which ought not to be in the public domain ... but if you ever need a safe-cracker, I'm your boy. Just call my publisher and ask for Fingers.

That was five years ago, and David still rides on his car every week. He has to sit on the boot these days – his legs won't fit under the steering wheel. When he plugs it in, the car chirrups, 'Have a ride with me!' in a Blackpool accent, and David imitates it perfectly. I can't hear him without remembering his first teacher's prediction that David would one day learn to talk, like the boy in his class who could say, 'Hold on tight! Super-fast ride!'

David has learned to say a lot that he doesn't understand. Words have meaning for him in the same ways as music: he invokes them for specific situations. To anyone who doesn't know him, it must sound as though he's chatting away normally. In fact, David has devised a way to use words which doesn't involve grammar or communication. 'Have a ride with me,' in that George Formby voice, has a meaning: it means his green car is working. The words are like five notes in a musical phrase, a fanfare that announces the fun is starting. David can echo it perfectly, but that doesn't mean he understands the sentence – he couldn't know it means the same thing as 'Jump in the seat' or 'Sit on, and off we go'. Those are different words, as dissimilar to David as the openings of Beethoven's Fifth and 'Bohemian Rhapsody'.

If David wants his mum to watch him having fun in the garage, he tells her, 'Have a ride with me.' If the car won't work, he grabs her hand and drags her, complaining, 'Have a ride with me.' He'd be horrified if she actually sat on the car: the words aren't an invitation to anyone but him.

Because David wants Nicky to be involved in everything he does, even in everything he thinks, he expects her to parrot all kinds of phrases. When he acts out his videos, David takes almost all the parts and recites nearly all the script, but a key role is reserved for Mum. He propels her up and down the kitchen, pushes her into the garden, shoves her back indoors, drags her up the stairs, and she can't step out of the play for a moment or David will scream and insist on starting again. He needs her; she has a starring role. It's probably just one line, maybe just one word, but in David's mind, the entire production hinges on it.

One favourite is the climactic fight from Disney's *The Jungle Book*, the battle between Shere Khan the tiger and Baloo the bear. David rushes around roaring, clawing, bellowing and grunting – at last the tiger is vanquished, the chairs are overturned, our cat Peggy is cowering on the highest cupboard, and Nicky has to step forward and say, 'Baloo! You're all right!'

Another touching scene is the end of *Beauty and the Beast*: David collapses (after another fight scene) and then jumps to his feet, becoming the heroine. Mum should be the beauty, of course, but life isn't fair. 'Beast!' David laments, and Nicky must croak, 'Belle!' When it's *101 Dalmatians*, she just has to stand and be hugged at the right moment ('Oh, Roger, darling, what are we going to do?' – big hug).

The first time I saw him act out a whole movie was in a

playpark, when he was six. We arrived at eight in the evening, with David singing the *Jungle Book* overture, and every frame of the film was recreated: 'The Bare Necessities' at eight-thirty, King Louie's scat jazz around quarter to, barbershop vultures on the hour. He wouldn't be distracted or dragged away until the credits rolled, when I got a walk-on part – David threw an arm around me and high-stepped through the gate. He was Baloo and I was Bagheera, walking into the sunset. I wasn't allowed to sing, though.

In the whole performance, he barely uttered a recognizable word: the script was reduced to shapeless phonetics. I could sometimes guess what he was trying to say – as he flung himself off monkey bars shrieking, 'Ah-ooo, a-a eee!' I knew he was imitating Mowgli's shout of 'Baloo, catch me!' But it was obvious David didn't understand what the words meant, and didn't care.

Within a few months, that had changed. He was starting to shape words with the same precision he'd applied to song lyrics for years. Now he could shout, 'Baloo, catch me!' and sound like his life depended on it. But he still had no idea what the words meant.

The medical term for this use of language is 'echolalia', which means 'speaking in echoes'. Until the early eighties, it was regarded as nonsense chatter, but echolalia is now recognized as a complex phenomenon which serves many purposes. The autism researcher Dr Barry Prizant published a paper in 1983, breaking echolalia down into fourteen categories: nine were 'interactive', directed at other people and objects, and five were 'non-interactive'. External functions of echo-talk included labelling objects, demanding attention, raising protests and asking for help;

internal functions were less clear-cut, but seemed to involve supplying a soundtrack, practising speech sounds and simply having fun.

Most children babble before they can talk. David's babble *is* his talk, and he isn't unusual in this: according to Prizant's research, about three-quarters of people with autism use some sort of echolalia if they can talk at all.

As David's speech developed, we realized we needed new ways to help other people understand what was going on when he caused a scene. Our standard explanation, 'David can't talk,' had been perfect for deflecting angry members of the public. It took a second to say, and most people understood in a blink: they switched instantly from 'What's the matter with that child?' to 'How do you cope?'

If he was stamping his feet and baying the script of *The Jungle Book* at the rooftops, it was pointless to claim, 'David can't talk.' The factual, 'David's autistic, he doesn't understand,' was sometimes effective, but, as autism became more common, the word seemed to lose its impact. 'My neighbour's son is autistic,' one woman retorted, 'and he doesn't do things like that.'

A woman walked up to me in a bookshop when David was jabbering and said, 'I know what his problem is – too many E numbers!' She had a prim, Edinburgh accent, and she shook a finger at me. 'I should know ... I'm a teacher.'

Another woman, as I carried David screaming out of a shop, yelled: 'I know what he needs – a bloody good hiding!'

Most people, even if they were thinking something like that, just stared and said nothing. When the disturbance was merely noise and shouting, I found the best explanation was a smile. People would be looking at David – when they realized I was smiling at them, they'd turn away.

If they didn't, I'd say, 'He's all right, don't be afraid.' And if they protested that they weren't afraid, I'd just raise my eyebrows. But I needed more than a reassuring smile when the broken glass was flying.

We were determined that David had to join in normal family activities, such as trips to the shops, no matter how much strange noise he was making. He was a real boy, and he deserved a real life. If other people couldn't deal with that, they should stay at home: we weren't going to keep David indoors.

The one exception was when he seemed hell-bent on smashing something – it's a bad start to the weekly shop if your seven-year-old tears off his shoes and lobs them at the special-offer display of Piat d'Or in the main entrance.

Sometimes, he hid his intentions. I wheeled his buggy into Sainsbury's one afternoon, when he was smiling dreamily after a ride on the Bananas in Pyjamas, and he dipped a hand into a passing trolley. Seizing a wine bottle by the neck, he threw it like a stick grenade – it cartwheeled over a checkout and detonated in a blossom of glass and red wine.

David whooped so hard with laughter, he could barely breathe.

No one was hurt. The staff treated it as just another breakage, and another bottle was brought for the shocked shopper. I wouldn't blame her if she drank it in the car park.

On another occasion, in the beer aisle at Tesco's, David got his fingers to a bottle of Guinness and shattered it at a middle-aged man's feet. The poor chap wasn't going for my shrug-and-a-reassuring-smile routine: 'He did that on purpose,' he roared.

'David does that,' I agreed.

'He threw it straight at me.'

'He was aiming to miss. Otherwise, he'd have hit you.'

'I could have been badly hurt!'

'But are you? No harm done, then.' And while he was trying to work that one out, we trundled away to find a cleaner.

Mostly, I could control David by keeping a physical grip on him. He accepted that, if he was aiming for breakages, I had every right to pin his wrists to the buggy handles. It made the game more of a challenge. And when David was winning, I treated it as a game too – it was the quickest way to assure other shoppers the situation was under control. A jar of beetroot would hit the floor, and I'd say, 'Well done, David. One-nil.'

As David got older, we left the buggy in the car, and he helped to push the trolley. I walked with my arms round him, clamping his hands to the push-bar. The position became second nature as we trooped up and down the aisles, whiling away a wet evening by labelling all our groceries out loud: 'Pasta, David.' *Pastadavid*. 'Look, Marmite.' *Lurmurmae*. 'Apples.' *Pulls*. 'What's that?' *Wotsat*.

I got so used to touring supermarkets this way that one Sunday in the biscuits aisle, I looked down at the red-faced, squirming boy in my arms and remembered I'd brought James instead. 'Dad!' he hissed. 'For God's sake, let go!'

High-security shopping worked well in supermarkets, but David had the edge in other shops. He caused so much damage one afternoon in a record store on Park Street that we were lucky to avoid arrest. The music usually lulled him: I'd thumb through the racks while he tranced out to Mogwai or Goldfrapp. This time, he woke up, grabbed a handful of CDs and flicked them like frisbees at the walls. As I started apologizing and wheeled him backwards, he hooked a foot under a CD rack and dragged it over.

The counter staff must have thought we were vandals, or maybe the heavy mob from a protection racket. I don't look much like hired muscle, but David was doing his best impersonation of Mad Frankie Fraser. We managed to carry him, upside down, in his buggy out of the shop, and he was laughing till the tears squirted out of his eyes like a circus clown.

'He enjoyed that,' I said.

'At our expense!' snapped the manager.

David saw breakables everywhere. A cider bottle in the gutter or a pint glass on a wall were easy targets – he'd shatter them across the pavement before I'd even seen them. People stared at us, and sometimes yelled comments from windows, but to my mind David was blameless. There were empty bottles within reach because university students were drinking in the streets, and well-paid office workers were staggering from club to club, and the city council was issuing alcohol licences to every third address for a mile and a half down Whiteladies Road. Anyone who blamed David was ignoring the real problems.

He wasn't the only person who could pick up the empties, either … he was just the only one who ever seemed to bother. One afternoon, he stretched a hand into a doorway and caught hold of a wine bottle, but he savoured the moment too long: I snatched it out of his fingers. The next day, his excitement gave him away. As we reached the doorway, the bottle was still there and David was fizzing with anticipation. I steered him round it. He dug in his toes and screamed, and smashed his head on my hands as I covered the struts of the buggy. 'Yell all you like,' I told him, 'we're not turning round.'

But the next day, the bottle was still there. I didn't have the strength for another tantrum. From my knuckles to my wrists, the backs of both my hands were bruised from David's headbanging.

So I looked away, and let him smash the bottle across the doorstep. The next time we passed, the shards had been swept away. He must have given someone's conscience a jab.

Other people's consciences were causing us trouble, though. Every Wednesday, the recycling boxes went out. David saw vodka bottles that would burst like balloons, brown beer bottles that could turn to crushed glass, dense green wine bottles that bounced, champagne bottles that exploded with a boom, Guinness bottles that became strips of fragments like a kite's tail, held together by a label; they were all jumbled in black crates, outside houses on every street.

David thought they were left out to tempt him. I thought they were there to make life just that little bit trickier. We steered round most of them, but if the pavement was narrow, or blocked by a badly parked car, we had to detour into the road. Sometimes David scored a point by smashing a bottle across a driveway; we never stopped to apologize, because David would assume he'd won a free go at the entire box. I'd just pick up pace, hoping we hadn't been seen and that the victim would blame rowdy students or drunken office workers.

The loudest, angriest, longest tantrum he ever staged

during a walk was triggered by one of those black boxes. David was out of his buggy, trotting along a cobbled road off Brandon Hill as I lumbered beside him. He'd been playing on the swings, and I wanted him to have as much exercise as possible before I strapped him back into the chair. When he saw the black box, he headed for it at a sprint – no craftiness, no disguise, just a full-pelt attack.

It was a steep hill, and I had no hope of stopping him unless I let go of the buggy. It bounced past parked cars as I skidded down the cobbles and dragged an arm around David's waist. He was dipping into the box as I caught him. My eyes were on the buggy, which was careering towards the junction with a busy road at the bottom of the hill. I couldn't stop David from smashing a beer bottle into the gutter, but I was able to pull him backwards. He screamed in rage.

The buggy somersaulted and landed on its side, about thirty feet from us. David was kicking and threshing so violently that I couldn't lift him, so I locked my arms around his chest and marched him backwards down the hill. It was the only way I could manoeuvre him and keep my balance.

He was livid. His fists battered his face. His screams filled the street. It must have sounded as if he was being murdered. A woman leaned out of her house, five doors up, and demanded: 'Can I help you?' She sounded angry and scared – she wasn't asking if we needed help, she was telling us to go away before she called the police. I wrestled David into his buggy, buckling him in and tipping it back to keep his feet off the ground.

The woman was still standing at the top of the street, glowering, and my body was awash with adrenalin and emotions. I wanted to yell back at her: 'How dare you! How dare you be angry at him – he's seven years old. Do you think he likes being like this? Do you think his mother and I wanted it this way? Do you think at all?'

I could have tipped over that bin and smashed every one of the bottles myself, hurling them as hard as I could. A hundred might have defused 1 per cent of the frustration I felt.

At that moment, I understood why our son needed so desperately to break bottles. I wheeled him home, his feet hammering on the footplate. With a mile to go, one of the buggy struts gave way, and the canvas seat folded around him like a collapsing deckchair. I towed him backwards the rest of the way.

Twelve

That wasn't the first buggy he'd broken. It wasn't even the third or fourth. The patient and forgiving people at Southmead Wheelchair Services suggested a tubular steel chair, a child-sized version of the adult wheelchair. Because I have long legs, they supplied the model with extended handles: the handles snapped on our first outing. I finished the walk bent double, pushing the chair by the armrests. We trundled past a guy we saw every afternoon: if it wasn't actually snowing, he'd always be leaning on his garden wall, wearing boxers and reading a book. 'Carry on like that,' he commented, 'and you'll need a wheelchair yourself.'

'It'll have a V8 engine and knives in the wheel hubs,' I promised. 'I'll be after revenge.'

I said it lightly, to disguise how earnestly I meant it. That's what inhibitions are for: they bury our darkest instincts and let them out only for glimpses, as jokes. But David didn't have any inhibitions. All he had was me, Nicky and his teachers, throwing ourselves on him before his destructive impulses built up too much momentum.

We often didn't succeed. If David could record his kills,

the way a wartime pilot tallies each victory on the nose of his plane, he'd be painted in skulls-and-crossbones from his toes to his chin. One of his finest, and earliest, was a brand new oven: it had a drop-down door and the engineer had fitted the unit that morning. We turned our backs to dump the packaging outside, and David pounced. Or bounced.

He flipped down the spring-loaded door, and leapt on it. Probably it looked like a foldaway trampoline. The oven toppled forward, the door dug into the wooden floor and David crashed through the Pyrex panel. We ran into the kitchen to find him standing in the splinters, the metal door frame round his waist like a hula hoop. There was nothing malicious about it: he was just an energetic boy, and the world was his climbing frame.

After a long argument, our insurers paid up, but our excess payment trebled. David, of course, wasn't hurt – he was born with the power to destroy £500 kitchen appliances in his socks.

Ovens, at least, could be replaced. One night, Nicky fell asleep as she was putting David to bed. He expects her to sit beside him till he's snoring, whether that takes thirty minutes or three hours. Now, David saw the chance to test a theory of his: Mum-things are bouncy.

Maybe it was the creaking bed, or simply a premonition, but Nicky woke to see David crouching over her like an imp, his toes gripping the headboard. Those feet could punch through Pyrex; a fleecy dressing gown wasn't going to save her ribs. She managed to turn as he landed on her chest, and though her arm was bruised, she wasn't badly hurt. It was a long time before she fell asleep again at David's bedtime, though.

He didn't mean to hurt her, of course. He loved her. Life without his mum was literally unthinkable. But the oven was replaced when he smashed it, and we had no way to make him understand that people were different ... including him.

One birthday, David was given a plastic glove filled with gel. It was soft and wobbly, with pointed knuckles, and he enjoyed wearing it. We thought he must be intrigued by the combination of sensations and textures. All these years we've known him, and we're still so naive ...

On a Saturday when I was at *The Observer*, Nicky was coping, as she always does, with both boys. James was upstairs and David was clinging to his mum, while she cut sandwiches in the kitchen. A scented candle was burning in the hall.

And then suddenly David wasn't clinging to Nicky. She didn't see him go – she just heard the fire alarm.

Slipping into the hall, David had peeled off his glove and dropped it on the candle. The gel exploded, spattering him from his nose to his knees, and the glove burned with a flame 18 inches high. Fortunately, it was almost directly under a smoke alarm, and Nicky was able to grab a schoolbag and smother the blaze.

If she hadn't been so close at hand, or if she'd had to run to find something to cover the flames, they might have caught on the woodwork – or on David.

He was delighted with the experiment. He certainly intends to try it again, if he ever gets the chance. Explosion, pillar of flame, destruction of a toy, mother shouting, fire alarm shrieking: an outstanding result. He had no idea, of course, that he could have been hurt, or that he might have burned down the house – he literally couldn't imagine the consequences. His brain is incapable of imagination.

We didn't usually have to imagine the consequences: we just had to find the money to pay for them. A computer drive full of coins; video players full of apple juice or jam tarts; plaster dripping off the ceiling under the bathroom; a pot of whitewash down the carpet on the stairs; splintered chairs; shredded books; CDs and DVDs between the floorboards; scratched, dented and smashed-in furniture; broken mirrors and picture frames; biro on every wall; car seats black with Ribena stains and ground-in cornflakes; hundreds of cups and plates and glasses destroyed, including a Wedgwood cheese dish that had belonged to Nicky's mother; mattresses and sofas sodden with milk; every scrap of wallpaper ripped down in one bedroom.

We joked that he was possessed by the ghost of Keith Moon, the demon rock drummer with The Who, who threw TVs from hotel bedrooms and drove a Rolls-Royce into a swimming pool. David was born to rock 'n' roll: his restraining device was even called a 'hard rock' chair. It was a snug wooden seat with a harness for his body and straps for his ankles, and a tray that clamped over his knees. The base was the size of a tabletop, and couldn't be overturned – this was a kind of high-security 'naughty step'.

The school introduced it, with our support, when David graduated to throwing objects at moving targets. He was about seven, and breaking mugs had become too easy – he needed the extra challenge of hitting something that was taking evasive action. It was a one-sided game. Other children didn't want to play, but David couldn't know that. You might as well tell Wayne Rooney that the football doesn't want to be kicked.

When David wanted target practice, anything would do for a missile. It could be as small as a toy car or as big as a chair: he never missed. His teacher reported he had hit another pupil with a paper cup full of red paint, by lobbing it up and over an onrushing adult. David saw the danger, timed his move and scored a direct hit. If paint throwing was a recognized sport, he'd be a gold medallist.

One Saturday, he took all the tin cans out of the cupboards and stacked them in towers, the way nice autistic children do in textbooks. Then he started throwing them at Nicky. She had to fend them off with a kitchen tray, and all her shouting wouldn't make him stop until he ran out of ammunition. After that, he climbed on to her lap and demanded a tickle because, of all the people he loves, David loves his mum far more than anyone.

As he grew faster and stronger, we started to be seriously concerned. The decision to use a 'hard rock' chair wasn't taken lightly – all our other efforts to teach David not to throw things were fruitless. We were lucky that the school was so supportive, and that David's classmates could ignore him so easily: at worst, the other children in the autistic unit saw him as a nuisance, like a yappy dog, something to be avoided if possible.

If we could make him see that throwing things earned him a spell in the 'hard rock' chair, he might learn to behave. It was a faint hope, but our choices were limited. We couldn't ever smack David: either we'd be using premeditated violence against a child who couldn't even talk, or we'd be lashing out in a blaze of temper. Both were unthinkable.

Briarwood had a 'hard rock' chair, and we installed one at home, to help him understand that the penalty for bombarding us was always going to be a session in the chair. We tried not to notice that he loved sitting in it: the chair was safe, comfy and familiar.

Not all the wreckage in our home was the result of David's target practice. He broke things for all kinds of reasons: because he was experimenting, because he didn't know what else to do with them, because he got bored and discarded them, because it was fun, because it had become a habit, because he enjoyed the fuss and attention, and because, sometimes, he simply wanted to be rid of things.

In one frantic summer term, he destroyed all the videos which he had guarded obsessively for years. He was glad to be rid of them. He loved them, but they were making his life a misery.

David had always enjoyed watching more TV than James. He liked the predictability of videos, and their completeness: each tape began in silence with a copyright notice; a fanfare and a logo arrived before the adverts for other videos, and then the opening credits rolled; at the end of the film, there were more credits, more ads and a final logo. David couldn't miss any of that. If the tape wasn't fully rewound when he pressed 'play', he reacted with the horror of a diner who's been served with a half-eaten plate of food.

At five years old, he'd watch a *Pingu* tape from end to end, with his eyes wide, hugging himself with anticipation as the episodes unrolled. Most people watching a TV story want to know what happens next – David wanted to know that what happened last time wouldn't change.

As long as the tape played, he was engrossed. Sometimes, on a good day, if she was discreet about it, Nicky could even leave the room. But when the tape ended, David switched straight into tantrum. He wanted the tape to reset to the start, instantly, and it wouldn't … so he screamed. One of us would hold him as the rewinder whirred, and he'd howl and kick and twist and bite his hand, and then we'd be back at the beginning of *Pingu*, with the copyright notice, and David was calm again.

We tried keeping two copies of his favourites, with one of them always rewound, but he wouldn't accept a switch. When he watched a tape, he needed to be convinced that all the same things were happening in the same order. It was no good if the same things happened in the same order on a different copy – that proved nothing.

Video cassettes deteriorate with repeated plays. They oxidize, depositing sooty residues on the machine's tape-heads, so that it too starts to fail. Some days, we'd insert a tape and get nothing but interference on the screen. Cleaning cassettes weren't much use. The second-best remedy was cheap: it involved a screwdriver, paper tissues and a boy who was so angry that he'd be trying to explode his own head by screaming while his father wiped down the VCR's innards.

The best remedy was to have a brand new video player stashed under the stairs. We bought so many over the years that my accountant wrote to query it – I think she suspected I was pirating Hollywood movies and selling them on a market stall.

We hoped DVDs would solve most of these problems. They wiped clean, they were always ready to restart, and they didn't disintegrate inside the player. They also weren't tape-shaped: we presented David with *Pingu* on disc and he watched two episodes in puritanical disgust. Then he put the DVD between the floorboards in our bedroom, where it joined £2 coins and credit cards and stray keys and a lot of other items David had no use for.

By the time he was nine, David had enough videos to tile his bedroom floor in a mosaic of black plastic. That was my own fault: I can't walk past a charity shop without checking the bookshelves and, as videos became obsolete and David's contemporaries grew out of *Teletubbies* and *Pingu*, the bargain bins at Oxfam and Clic were spilling over with 50p tapes. David bought them by the stack. He especially wanted anything stamped with the BBC brand – he'd sit through *Poldark* and *The Onedin Line*, *The Fast Show* and *Absolutely Fabulous*, David Attenborough documentaries and Reith lectures, sporting highlights and pop concerts, just to see the swirling Corporation logo and hear its chimes. He wouldn't watch these things twice, though – once was enough to be sure the logo appeared in the proper places.

Every night, before his bath, he'd put on a Singalong Songs video called *Let's Go To Disneyland Paris*, and spend the first couple of tunes arranging criss-cross rows of tapes on his bed. He'd peeled most of the labels off, yet he could still tell the cassettes apart at a touch – we had to pick them up and squint at the tiny letters on the side, but David could find the right one by shaking them. Perhaps they were fractionally different weights; maybe they just rattled distinctively.

Each tape had a particular place, and if he couldn't find the right copy of *Fireman Sam* to fill the gap between *Dad's Army* and *Top Gear*, he wouldn't be going to sleep that night. When the catalogue was complete, he'd nip downstairs and arrange another cascade of videos across the sofa. After that, he could afford to relax and slosh a few gallons of bathwater over the floor, before joining Jiminy Cricket for the finale of the tape, and a duet of 'When You Wish Upon A Star'.

It was a sweet, happy routine. And it was driving him up the wall.

David's dread of disrupting patterns had a superstitious intensity. Tug one stray thread in the fabric of reality and the universe could unravel. But there were lots of stray threads in his bedtime routine: so many videos to be mislaid, so many sequences to muddle up. He was living on his nerves, knitting the loose ends of the cosmos together every night.

When his *Disneyland* tape snapped in the machine, he was appalled, and thrilled. The world was going to end and, frankly, it would come as a bit of a relief. When we mended the video with Sellotape and the world didn't end, another layer of complexity was added to the routine: each night, he had to snap the tape with his finger and we had to mend it.

The curative powers of Sellotape were so marvellous that David started to apply them everywhere. If his hands were dirty, or his feet were sore, he bandaged them in yards of the stuff. When his pyjama trousers ripped, he used an entire roll to bind his legs together.

Each Monday, he went to the city's Central Library. He chose a video to borrow – but before he could watch it, he had to cover the label with strips of sticky tape. After exhausting the BBC tapes and the documentaries, he worked his way through a series of Disney movies dubbed into Spanish: one of the librarians would ask each week, 'You know this is in a foreign language, don't you?' and I'd say, 'It's all right, David doesn't speak English.'

When the librarian handed over the video, David would discard the case and hug the cassette. By the time we returned it, he would have double-glazed it in Sellotape. The staff never objected. They put up with my apologies for years, as I explained that David had thrown a video into the docks, or eaten the packaging, or snapped the tape, or shredded the label.

It helped to know that David was genuinely welcome in the library. The staff weren't paying lip service to some politically correct policy of inclusion: they were honestly determined to make the library available to everyone. One afternoon, when David was wrecking the hush by whooping like a cowboy at a rodeo, one of the librarians came across to say how nice it was to see such a cheerful child.

Nicky and I had resolved a long time ago that David was going to be included, and that anyone who didn't like that could stay at home with the curtains drawn. Nevertheless, the welcome we got at the library, and many other places, took a lot of pressure off us.

The librarians even listened patiently as I raved about David's latest linguistic advance. He'd discovered a rule of grammar and learned to apply it. All right, it was Spanish grammar and it was, in fact, completely wrong, but it made sense – he'd looked at their video of *Los Aristocatos* and realized he could create a Spanish version of any favourite film with a 'Los' and an 'os'. David had invented prefixes and suffixes. Now he was demanding his rewards – *Los Bambios*, *Los Robin Hoodos* and *Los Beauty and the Beastos*.

He adored his videos. He spent hours shuffling them, stacking them and studying them. Almost all his echolalia focused on them. That's why it was so unexpected when he destroyed them.

It started at Nanny's Chalet, the holiday home my parents had kept after they retired to the Welsh coast. Four or five times a year, I'd take David to stay there for a couple of nights. An assortment of his favourite viewing was always on hand, in a shiny cardboard carrier bag from Debenhams: the bag was regularly restocked by my Aunt Barbara, who collected armfuls of videos from the charity bring-and-buy sales that she helped to run.

David's task, when we arrived, was to empty the Debenhams bag across the carpet, liberate every cassette from its box, scatter the unwanted videos in an exact replica of the chaotic pattern he'd made with these same tapes the previous visit, and shove a copy of Disney's *Aladdin* into the player. That gave me about fifteen seconds to switch on the electricity and fit the batteries into the video remote, before I was required to read the words on the box and name every title on the advertising insert.

It was easy: by the time David was nine, he'd drilled all his family to become honed components in a precision machine. Nicky packed a suitcase of matching outfits and spare pairs of shoes for him, Nanny baked a tray of flap-jacks, Grampa stocked up on 20p and £1 coins for the arcade rides. All I had to do was switch on the electricity and make sure David didn't worry the sheep.

The video player wasn't such a honed piece of machinery. It was so old, there were still channels tuned to ATV and Southern Television. Most of the time, it wasn't used – when Nicky and I brought James to the chalet, during David's long weekends at Church House, we'd watch DVDs on a laptop if the weather was wet. But for bursts of forty-eight hours, when David and I went to Wales while Nicky spent time with James, that ancient VCR endured a bashing. And when it finally went under, it took *Aladdin* with it.

There was a groan, and a crack, and a puff of smoke. No genie.

David started to giggle. He liked things that exploded. I unplugged the player and unscrewed the casing. 'Broken,' I said, wincing at the thought of the fury he'd unleash when he realized this wasn't just a programme intermission.

I levered the blackened video out, trailing spools of tape. I rubbed David's fingers on the sooty rollers. 'Broken,' I repeated.

'Brw-oken. Brw-oken,' David said. He kept saying it, louder and louder, between bursts of manic laughter, until he collapsed, kicking helplessly, and giggled himself to exhaustion. When Nanny arrived, to hold his hand as he went to sleep – another of her component roles – it was all he could do to stagger into the bedroom. He lay gasping for breath as I brushed his teeth, and then he fell asleep, twitching with the giggles. All night he kept waking, shouting, 'Brw-oken!' and laughing himself to sleep again.

'He's a happy boy,' my mother told her neighbours – and it was true, in the same way that Billy the Kid was a naughty lad and Olga Korbut was an athletic girl.

By the next night, we had another VCR, and David was disappointed that this one didn't go bang. All through *Snow White*, he was twitchy and impatient. When the film ended – and he couldn't have conceived of doing this *before* it ended – he ran to the machine, pulled out the cassette, snapped the tape, shrieked, 'BRW-OKENNNN!' and hurled it out of the door and down the hillside.

He would have done the same to his entire bag of videos, but his Grampa hid them in the car boot.

When I told Nicky about his new game, she said, 'He'll expect to do that every time he visits the chalet.' What neither of us guessed were his plans for when he got home. At bedtime, according to sanctified ritual, he organized all his tapes as he watched the *Disneyland* Singalong, and at the end, he snapped it and chucked it down the stairs. The tape splintered and took a gouge out of the floorboards, but this time David didn't laugh. He just stood, staring down at the wreckage, his eyes narrowing and his head nodding, like Charles Bronson or Bruce Willis with the germ of a notion for citywide destruction.

That week, he smashed every video he could lay his hands on. He threw them at the walls, in the bath and down the garden. He flung each one again and again, until the tiny springs had popped and the cogwheels were hanging out and the plastic windows were caved in. Then he brought the corpse to Nicky, who had to touch it, read the name and pronounce it 'broken'. These were the last rites for a video; it could then be dumped in the bin.

Not one was spared. He was without mercy. Favourites he'd watched fifty times went into the heap with titles he had played once. Videos that were out of print and sold on eBay for extortionate sums were smashed and binned along with movies we'd recorded off the telly before he was born. He scoured the house to make sure not a scrap of magnetic tape survived – some sixth sense led him to the last remnants. I'd boxed up our home movies, the films of James and David as babies, and cached them on top of the tallest bookshelf in my study. The floor was concrete, so I don't think he heard the tapes vibrate as he stomped past: my best guess is that he smelled them. However his detectors worked, we caught him climbing the bookcase like a ladder to fling the box down.

When all his videos were dead, David relaxed. We were worried he'd been feeding an insatiable lust for destruction, and that books, clothes and furniture would be sucked into the purge. Instead, he started collecting Disney song CDs – not to destroy them, but to wear them.

David treated CDs as costume jewellery. If he'd wanted to use them as earrings, we'd have been concerned about the effects of prolonged exposure to social workers. In fact, he wore them on his fingers, in stacks ... bling you can sing.

The discs didn't stay playable for long, but he was happy to let us make copies of them. That way, when a CD snapped, or holes were scraped on the silvery side, we had a back-up ready with a home-made label. David had become so easy-going about his obsessions that he actually liked those DIY labels.

Every few days, David would choose a 50p video from a charity shop, watch it once and destroy it. He was determined never to be a slave to his collection again.

He introduced another change: all programmes were to be viewed upside down. That didn't mean David was going to stand on his head. His portable TV, with a built-in video player, was attached to the wall and to his wardrobe, but he wrestled it free and stood it on the carpet with its feet in the air.

The first video he watched this way was *Postman Pat*,

and Nicky called out to show me what was happening. I stared at the picture, and for a moment I didn't understand what I saw. A post van was marching across the ceiling of the screen, like a gecko, but much stranger than that were the colours. They'd all changed.

The sky was red. The fields were yellow. Pat's van was blue. By inverting his television, David had turned the colours inside out. Gravity had reversed the spectrum. David didn't seem to notice – the soundtrack was the same as before – but we could barely recognize the images.

'It's like the Beatles song, the one with marmalade in the sky,' I said, and hummed a line.

David scowled and clamped a hand over my mouth. My singing always has offended him.

I think of that inverted TV, whenever anyone comments that 'autism must have turned your lives upside down'.

It has. What's hard to express is how completely that changes everything. It's not just that the world is on its head – it's the way all the familiar elements of our marriage and our family life have changed beyond recognition. The skies are red, the fields are yellow, and our little boy is trying to make sense of it all as he stares down the wrong end of a kaleidoscope.

Thirteen

David's asleep as I write this. Nicky and I have been standing and watching him. She's coaxed me back to the keyboard, because she knows I don't want to write this chapter. I'll be ready when I've watched him long enough to know that he's in his bed, and he's safe. The windows are locked, the doors are deadlocked, the keys are hidden. He can't vanish.

He's eleven years old now, but when he's sleeping, he looks no more than three. There's not a mark of experience on his face: he's an angel of innocence. Golden curls fall around the smiling corners of his mouth, as if he'd been posed by a sugary Victorian painter. He doesn't look old enough for nursery, let alone secondary school.

It's a blissful sleep, because he has no fears. David never has nightmares. We're sure he dreams, because sometimes we see his eyelids flickering and he calls out words from his videos. But he's never woken up sweating and afraid. We think that's because he has no conception of death. Even in his unconscious mind, he can't imagine anything terrible happening to him or his family. He's not programmed for nightmares.

But Nicky and I have nightmares, and this is one of them.

On a Tuesday morning when David was eight, he almost died.

He was awake before six, watching his mum get ready for work, and lounging over the furniture eating fistfuls of dry cornflakes. At 7.45, he was dressed and ready for school, though his big brother wasn't even awake yet. We waved Nicky off. David wasn't happy to see her go, but he'd learned to accept that, once a week, she left the house. Lately, he'd dealt with it by shutting himself in the sitting room with breakfast TV blaring – he liked the *GMTV* logo and the title music.

David's school bus was due to collect him in fifteen minutes. I loitered in the kitchen, wearing jeans, a T-shirt and slippers, and read the paper. After a couple of minutes, it struck me that the television was too loud. I went to turn it down, and saw that the sitting-room door was open.

So was the front door.

To escape, David had undone a latch, a chain, a lock and a bolt. And he'd done it silently. That must have taken time, and Nicky had set off to work only a couple of minutes before. I was sure David couldn't be more than thirty seconds ahead of me, and I thought I'd find him on the garden wall, waiting for his bus. But he wasn't there. He had run out of the front door and disappeared, and that was something he hadn't done since he was two years old.

He wasn't acting on a whim. David thought about everything. This was planned. Wherever he was going, he had a destination, an objective.

My first guess was 'jam tarts', but I could see straight up the street and there was no sign of him. He must have headed down the hill, away from the bakery – unless he'd run along the lane beside our house.

I ran, flapping in my slippers, into the lane. Beyond the end of our garden, there were steps leading down to a cul-de-sac, and I paused at the top, listening for him. It was no use calling out, because David wouldn't answer, but if I kept my ears open, I might hear him singing.

All I could hear was the swish of the cars on the main road, further down, and the accelerating thud of my heart-beat.

I ran to the house, and double-checked that he hadn't slipped back inside. Then I set off down the street.

That was the way his bus went each morning. It took a sharp left, down the hill, to join the traffic that thundered into the city centre. The thought that David might have headed that way, that he could have set off to school without waiting for his bus, and gone running out between the cars, was too sickening to face. He'd been out of my sight for three minutes or so – that was long enough to reach the road. Even if I could be there instantly, it might be too late to stop an accident.

One of our neighbours, a man I'd seen but never spoken to, called out: 'Was that your son I saw running off just now? He didn't seem to pay attention when I spoke to him.'

'He didn't head for the main road, did he?' I pleaded.

The man looked uncertain. 'He wouldn't try to cross it, would he?'

I set off at the fastest run I could manage in my bedroom slippers. At the junction, I stood and stared down the hill at the traffic, a hundred yards away, racing past in both direc-tions. There was no sign of David. There was no suggestion of any accident either – the cars weren't slowing.

There was a fear in my mind, like a premonition, that if I ran down the hill, I would see David dash in front of a car and be killed – and whatever I did, I wouldn't be able to stop it. I couldn't bear that. There had to be something else, a different fork in the future.

He might not have been heading for school at all. He could have set off for the park, following our road past the junction and round to the right. That was the way we went on our walks. It seemed possible, it even seemed logical. And it meant I wouldn't have to go down to the main road. So I started to run again, craning my neck past every driveway in case David had slipped into someone's porch.

Halfway up the street, I started shouting his name. He'd take no notice, but if he was being held at bay by an alarmed householder, perhaps they'd call out. No one answered. Now I could see all the way to the park. David hadn't come this way.

I turned and started to run back. There was a lump like a cog in my throat. A car reversed out of a drive and I stumbled round it. As I ran past the junction again, I was staring at the traffic, trying to see if any of the cars had pulled up, looking back over my shoulder ... and I ran into a lamppost.

For a split second, I thought someone had punched me. Then I bounced sideways, and put a hand to my face, and felt blood oozing from my nose as my eyes welled up.

It hurt, but the pain was somewhere under the surface of my panic. I ignored it. The neighbour who'd seen David was still outside his house, and his wife had joined him – I seized on them as an excuse. They were the only reason I had left for staying away from the main road.

Tears were running down my face as I staggered towards

the couple. They weren't to know my eyes were watering because I'd just cracked my nose. The man asked if I'd been down to the main road, and I couldn't find the words to tell him why I'd gone the other way. 'What if David comes back to the house while I'm searching for him?' I said lamely. The couple promised to look out for him.

A car pulled up. I thought for a moment the driver was looking for directions – but then I glanced inside. On the back seat, smiling like a star at a movie premiere, was my runaway son. A woman I almost recognized was sitting beside him.

The driver stepped out. He kept his mouth closed, and he didn't seem to blink. He stared, the way people do when they're making up their minds to forget what they've just seen. In the passenger seat, a girl in her teens was gazing fixedly through the windscreen. Her face was white as paper.

'You've found David!' I said.

The driver nodded. I'd answered the only question he wanted to ask. He opened the back door, and the woman steered David out. He was beaming.

I knew we'd seen the woman before – she probably lived in one of the houses we passed on our walks. Perhaps we'd chatted to her when she was in her front garden. But I couldn't place her. She was pointing at the driver, trying to tell me something about him, but he was already getting back into the car.

The woman saw I was bleeding from the nose. 'Are you all right?' she asked.

'I am now,' I said, hugging David.

A horn beeped, up the street. David's bus had arrived. He wriggled away and trotted towards it as the car drove off. By the time I'd handed him over to the transport escort, the woman had gone.

I think now that David must have charged into the main road and that, somehow, the driver avoided an accident. By the look of him, he'd never know how he did it. Nor would the girl, probably his daughter on her way to school. I'd guess that the driver yelled at David, and then saw how bizarrely this child was acting. Perhaps David was dancing and singing, or perhaps he was lying on the tarmac, licking a manhole cover. He certainly wasn't behaving like an ordinary schoolboy who'd just had a miraculous escape.

The woman might have been waiting at the bus stop. I'm sure she screamed ... and when she realized the car hadn't knocked down the boy, she went to help. Perhaps she held up the traffic as the driver tried to coax David off the road. And then she must have recognized him, and they bundled him into the car to find his home – wherever that was, because he couldn't tell them.

I've imagined the scene, in nightmares and in moments of gnawing reflection, over and over. I never saw the woman again and I didn't think to note the car's number plate. If either of them should read this, both Nicky and I want to say we're more grateful to you than we can express. You saved our son's life.

After the school bus had gone, I made an instant coffee and took a glass of milk to James. He was still asleep – he'd be late for school, but I didn't want to wake him. I just sat on the end of his bed, watching him, until his eyes opened and he smiled at me.

The moments when Nicky and I thought we wouldn't be able to carry on coping with David were rare, but they left painful marks on us, like burns. That morning was one of them: how could we keep our boy safe when he couldn't tell the difference between fun and suicide?

Other incidents were over in seconds, but they burned us badly too. There was a trip in the car, no more than a run home from the supermarket, when David insisted on riding in the passenger seat. He stayed calmly belted up ... until we turned into our street and he opened the door to leap out at 20mph. I pulled him back in by his hair.

When I felt we were competing against impossible odds, my impatience bordered on aggression with people who didn't understand. The usual eagerness I felt to talk and to explain was replaced by a constant state of truculence, like a simmering road rage. Anyone who bridled at David's eccentricities was my enemy – if they couldn't see he was autistic, they must have spent their lives ignoring every kind of difference and disability, and they deserved no explanations. I was conveniently forgetting all the blundering comments I'd made to parents of other disabled children around the time of David's diagnosis.

On an evening at the mall, I scored a small victory by persuading David to try a packet of french fries. That was the closest he'd come to hot food in years – it wasn't exactly hot, and it wasn't exactly food, but it had to be progress. He plucked out each chip, inspected it, bit the head off and discarded the stump ... unless it had brown bits, which was sufficient cause to chuck away the whole thing. We left a scatter of mangled fries from one end of the mall to the other, little patches of grease for shoppers to slip on. Though I tried to catch the flying food, I didn't stop to pick it up: I couldn't risk letting David get two steps ahead of me. If people thought he was flinging litter

around, too bad – I really didn't care. He was eating something, and that was all that mattered.

Sometimes I did stop to explain, and the explanation
became a savaging. We were trundling home on a spring
evening after heavy rain, and I was steering the buggy
round big puddles and pedestrians – David was smiling at
the sky and I should have been contented, but the blood
pressure between my ears was high enough to power a
steam engine. A woman commented to her friend as we
sailed past, 'Oh, but he's big enough to walk, don't you
think?'

I carried on for ten paces, and then I stopped. I turned
and pushed David back – and that was a sign of how laid-
back he felt, because an about-face would often set him
howling. 'He is big enough to walk,' I snapped at the
woman. 'But he's also autistic.'

She started to stammer: 'I didn't … I …'

'If I let him out, the first thing he'll do is run into the
road. And be killed.'

She looked like a pleasant woman, and she was about
to cry. Her companion, an older lady, was scowling at me,
but she probably thought it was wiser to let me say my
piece and go away.

'However bad it gets,' I snarled, 'there are always people
like you to make it worse.'

'I didn't know he was autistic,' she said.

'You're so … bloody … stupid!' I told her, and marched
David away.

I was the stupid one, of course. I'd been angry at the
world – now I was angry and disgusted at myself, too.

My short temper didn't only make me rude. It made me
belligerent. Packing David's wheelchair into the car boot

in a disabled bay at Sainsbury's one evening, I glanced at the van parked beside me. The driver was in his twenties, with a neck that was broader than his skull and a T-shirt that was rolled back to reveal tattoos and steroid muscles. Rap music was blasting through the open window.

'Yeah,' I said, as I opened my door, 'I can see you're disabled.'

He was out of his van before I'd put the ignition key in the slot. I ignored the stream of abuse and the fist on my window, but then he wrenched open my door. Before he could reach in to drag me out, I managed to pull it shut – the handles in a Renault Scenic are bigger and heavier on the inside, and the weight of the door favours the driver, not the enraged bodybuilder.

A vein as thick as my finger was throbbing from his temple to his collarbone as he yanked again at the door and I simultaneously hit the lock. He scrambled into his van, aiming to box me in, but the car park was half empty. In the end, he settled for weaving in front of us for the next ten minutes, making hand signals which could have meant, 'I'm turning left,' but probably didn't.

'He'll think twice before he parks there again,' I said gamely to Nicky.

'Yes,' she said, 'next time, he'll bring a shotgun.'

I found it easier to brush off the insults from the drunks who were already staggering between the bars by 7 p.m. on Thursday and Friday evenings. Most of them were in their teens or early twenties – all of them must have had university places or their feet on the lowest rungs of long career ladders. David's prospects were very different, but he never wasted a moment of them.

Usually, I felt a little anger and a lot of contempt when

the knots of girls and boys copied David's noises or shouted, 'Timmmmm-yyy!' and 'Spazz!' Once, when a quartet of Hoorays in rugger shirts jeered, 'Look at that huge kid in a pushchair,' I turned round and told them, in two short sentences, what David was and what they were. One of them lurched at me, white-faced: I'd called him something he wouldn't take from anybody. His mates held him back. That was lucky for both of us.

David didn't mind. He never noticed any of it. People stared, pointed, made remarks, edged away and, on every possible level, it meant nothing to him. He didn't know what they were saying; he didn't care what they thought; he didn't acknowledge their existence. What mattered much more to him was his new word, 'tickle'. When he said it, people tickled him. To David, this word was like a free pass to Disneyland, and he used it all the time. He'd sit for hours, at a coffee-shop table or in a playground sandpit, saying 'tickle' and giggling till his face shone.

We tried to be happy that he was happy and, mostly, we managed. We knew there were many eight- and nine-year-olds in the city who had much tougher lives, and only a few whose days were filled with so much fun and love. If other people couldn't see how blessed we were, that was their worry, not ours.

But it was hard to hold on to that sense of perspective when we'd had a bad night or we were struggling to find enough hours for work as well as both our children. Those were the days when my fuse was a short trail of gunpowder. The only time I really blew up, though, was at a middle-aged couple who hammered on their car horn because David was lying down across the entrance to their tennis club. His wheelchair was overturned beside him, he was clearly distressed, and whatever I yelled at them they deserved. Yet it would have been more effective, and more satisfying, to keep my cool: 'My son's disabled. That's his chair. You can see he's upset. Why are you hooting?'

The flip side to that was the fun we had when people couldn't quite work out what David was doing. They could see, or hear, that he was disabled, and didn't like to ask more than that.

When the Imax by the docks screened *The Lion King*, a thousand times bigger than David usually saw it on television, we went every Sunday for a month. He sang along, to every note. Most of the words were beyond him, but there wasn't a bar of the soundtrack, from the opening choir to the climactic battle, that David didn't know and reproduce. He reminded me of the earnest, owlish boys at school who listened to gramophone records with their fingers following the score – except David's score was in his head.

We sat at the back, where there were gaps in the seats for wheelchairs, and people looked round sometimes. But since I didn't mind when their toddlers asked loudly if the hyenas were cross and why the warthog ate slugs, they could put up with my son being a tuba.

We really let rip at the free movies for families with autistic children, organized by the Bristol branch of the NAS. The first time David saw a cinema screen, he couldn't believe it was real until he'd climbed on to the stage and licked as much of it as he could reach. Then he went and found the best seat in the house, which happened to be occupied by someone else. So he sat on a stranger's lap and watched *Monsters, Inc.*

'No trouble,' the chap said afterwards. 'Better behaved than any of my lot.'

During the summer, we stopped most afternoons for tea, cornflakes and Ribena in the garden of the Boston Tea Party cafe. David serenaded the parasols, and laughed at his own thoughts, and kept an eye open for any defenceless teapots that strayed within his reach. There was usually a gaggle of schoolkids smoking around a table at the end of the garden, and they were always louder and coarser than David, so I didn't feel we were lowering the tone.

One of the staff joined us one afternoon and started to talk about her new partner's children. The youngest had special needs and, feeling a little out of her depth, the woman was trying to see how other people coped. I explained that David was autistic and how that affected every area of his life.

'Autism, right,' she said, nodding. 'I thought he was just, you know … a nutter.'

The Boston Tea Party was popular with business types, the sort of people who raised their voices when they answered their mobiles so that everyone would know how important the call was. Everyone except David, obviously: when people shouted into mobiles, he shouted too. The more they tried to drown him out, the louder he bellowed – from the corner of my eye, I watched one woman writhing in embarrassment as she tried to sound dynamic and go-getting to a client while David did elephant seal impressions. At last she shouted into the handset, 'I can't … I'll tell you later … There's *this child*!'

Tough, I thought. If she couldn't tell the difference between her office and a cafe garden, David was happy to provide helpful hints.

Sometimes I wanted to explain, and couldn't. On a car

journey to Wales, in heavy rain, David discovered he could contort his body in his harness until his head poked out of the offside window. He looked more like a dog than a boy, eyes shut against the blast of the wind and rain, his tongue lolling out and his hair plastered to his face. I couldn't keep dragging him inside because the road was narrow and I needed both hands on the wheel – wherever I found a lay-by, we stopped and I tried to tighten the harness, but David kept wriggling free.

The faces of the drivers in the oncoming lorries were aghast. They must have seen the head in the rain and thought it was a suicidal labrador, before they realized they were about to decapitate a child. David didn't try to headbutt the lorries, but I was terrified that a loose strap would whip across and blind him. The builders in the Transit behind us weren't impressed either: they flashed their lights and hooted constantly.

I needed big bumper stickers: 'Don't Blame Me, He's Bonkers!' 'I Don't Like This Any More Than You Do!' 'My Other Child's Quite Normal!'

Sometimes, when David was moving too fast, or I was losing control of a situation, explanations were impossible. A stately lady flagged me down as I pushed a wheelchair at racing speeds after a free-range boy who was heading for the pond on Brandon Hill. 'Excuse me, is this the way to the St George's concert hall?' she asked, and all I could do was gasp over my shoulder, 'Sorry … Can't … Stop!'

'Well!' she snapped. 'How rude!'

On another occasion, I led David, without his chair, into a shoe shop, with my forefinger looped through the tag on his coat collar. He wouldn't hold my hand, and this seemed a simple way to hang on to him.

To break my grip, he suddenly twirled round. That would have worked if my hand had been on his shoulder, but all it did was tighten the loop round my fingertip. 'No you don't,' I said, which was all the encouragement David needed to do it again. And again. And again and again and again.

I collapsed, whimpering, to my knees and tried to hold on to David's waist. My fingertip was like a scarlet football. The boy at the counter looked like he was hoping I was drunk and not having a heart attack.

'Scissors,' I yelped. 'Have you got any scissors?'

Now the boy was sure I was drunk. This was a shoe shop. Why would they sell scissors?

When I'd managed to pin David to the floor and pulled the coat off him, and my finger was deflating, I tried to explain. It was too late. The boy knew I was blind drunk. His hand was on the emergency button under the counter, but he hadn't pushed it – he was gambling that I wouldn't get abusive or start singing filthy songs while I had a child in tow.

We left. There are some things, however innocent, that can never be explained.

One of David's innocent pleasures was to ring doorbells and run away. It's an age-old favourite of mischievous schoolchildren. David's version was unusual: ring the bell, run away and your dad gets caught.

He invented it after Nicky and I taught him to ring our doorbell at the end of a walk. Of course, we had door keys in our pockets, but the front door wouldn't be opened until he pressed the button. 'Ring the bell,' we said, over and over, holding his hand and pushing it to the buzzer. The idea was to make him associate a spoken instruction with a simple action which would produce multiple effects – the bell rings, the door opens, David arrives home.

The lesson worked too well. On our rambles round town, when David was walking alongside his wheelchair, he'd suddenly turn and dart up a garden path. If we were on a hill – and all Bristol is built on hills – I faced a choice: let go of the chair and see it roll into the road, or let David ring the bell. If there were milk bottles to be smashed on the doorstep, I'd dump the chair on its side and lunge after him, but that was often the worst move possible. David would ring the bell and I'd be left stranded in a stranger's porch, praying there was nobody home. Other times, I'd tackle him before he reached the door, and he'd scream, and a face would appear at a window as I dragged my hysterical child to the garden gate.

As I chased him down the steps from a bungalow by a church, a frail and elderly lady opened her front door. 'Would you like to come in?' she called.

I turned to explain, and saw she was smiling hopefully. She wasn't afraid of the cavorting blond boy – she just wanted company.

'That's really nice of you,' I said, holding on to David, 'but he's a bit too wild, I'm afraid. He's not deliberately naughty, but he'd want to break things, you see.'

'That doesn't matter,' she said. 'Things don't matter so much when you get to my age.'

Most people were less forgiving, but David didn't care about upsetting anyone. I needed extendable arms, or a lasso – instead, I experimented with toddler reins, buckling the harness over his coat and letting the leash trail behind. It gave me something to grab.

That earned the righteous disapproval of a social

worker from the Disabled Children's Unit. 'It's inappropriate for a boy of his age,' she said.

'So is ringing doorbells and running off ... for me, at least.'

'You'll just have to teach him not to do it,' she said.

Obvious, really. Why hadn't Nicky and I thought of that?

David liked his harness. It turned him into Superboy. He could fly – or, at least, he could flop forward, arch his back and grip his ankles, and Dad-thing would have to lift him off the pavement. One afternoon, miles from home, he simply lay down in the Superboy position and refused to stand up. As often as I dragged him upright, he dropped down. That happened to be the first day we'd ever gone out with the harness, but without the wheelchair. I had hoped David would walk the whole circuit. Instead, I broke my back hauling him, flying him, dragging him and finally piggybacking him home.

We gave up on the harness.

He was too big for his chair, though. His legs had grown so long that when he was feeling obstinate, he could tuck his toes into the spokes, or jam a foot either side of a shop doorway. And those long legs were so quick when he was out of the chair that I could no longer push it and keep up. David's buggies and wheelchairs had changed our lives, but they were becoming a liability ... and we weren't quite quick enough to realize that.

One Sunday, I took him to Wildwalk and Explore, the twin science exhibitions on the dockside. He enjoyed the hands-on features, the beachball that floated on a jet of air and the lift that rose to the ceiling on a rope pulley. He loved to sit in the sensory room, and spin the bicycle wheel on the giant gyroscope. Best of all, he liked playing with the lock gates on the miniature canal. By keeping a grip on his collar and his belt, I could usually prevent him from climbing in with the narrowboats, though he always got his arms soaked to the elbow.

Then we'd follow the evolution trail, past tanks of crustaceans and along winding paths under prehistoric palm fronds. Now that David wouldn't go through doorways in his chair, I had to unbuckle him and let him walk. He charged ahead and I followed as briskly as I could, steering the empty chair round families. He was soon out of sight, but I wasn't worried: there was a sweet stall at the end of the walk, and the worst that could happen was that I'd find him helping himself to the pick 'n' mix.

Where I actually found him was in the newt tank.

The glass sides were higher than his head. He must have vaulted in. Hauling him out was a slippery, smelly, noisy business, and it wasn't any easier to do it under the gaze of visitors and two student Wildwalk staff. They tried to salvage newts and weed from David's sodden coat.

'Could have been worse,' I said. 'The next tank's got piranhas, hasn't it?'

One of the teenagers gave me a look that said, 'I can't think of anything better.'

That incident convinced Nicky and me to fold away the wheelchair. 'He doesn't need it anyway,' we told each other. 'He's perfectly capable of walking, and he knows all the routes so well. It'll be much better for him to tire himself out.'

Inevitably, there was something we hadn't thought of.

Fourteen

If I'd stopped to think about it before David was born (and I don't suppose I ever did), I would have guessed that dedicated professionals do the most to make the lives of disabled children easier. Without teachers, and carers, and nurses, many parents wouldn't be able to cope. David has certainly been lucky with his school and his respite care at Church House, but often it's been the unexpected people who have given us strength to keep going – people who have helped, even though they didn't have to.

Some of them knew David because he brought that little bit of extra chaos and clearing up into their day. We stopped most evenings at the Starbucks coffee shop in Borders bookstore, where he strewed cornflakes, squirted Ribena and competed energetically with the piped music. Despite my bloody-minded insistence on taking David everywhere that other children could go, we wouldn't have become regulars without the genuine friendliness of the staff. Some were students with part-time jobs, others had careers at the company, and not one of them ever told us that he or she had experience of children with special needs, but they welcomed David. He was treated like a favourite guest.

The shop's first manager, Richard, had a young daughter of his own. He was a tall man, and he seemed to float an extra couple of inches off the ground when he talked about her. As a besotted father, he treated our pride in David as completely natural. He would have been much more perplexed by parents who scowled and swore at their child than by our raucous recitations of Disney titles.

David enjoyed the boiled-sweet lollipops at Starbucks: he coined his own word for them, 'bumpipops'. When he threw a screaming, lie-on-the-floor-clutching-the-tables tantrum because, one day, they'd sold out of lollipops, another shop might have banned us – Richard responded by stashing a box of David's favourites under the counter so we'd never be disappointed again.

'Go bumpipop' was one of David's first two-word sentences. It combined an action word with a label, and it gave him a sense of mission. We could walk out of the house and turn left, right or get in the car – as long as he understood the destination, he could cope with variations. 'Go bumpipop' was a promise: he was heading for Starbucks, by one route or another.

We never lied to him. If he'd been told that 'go bumpipop' was the order of the day, that was what happened. We'd tried to bamboozle him once, years earlier, when he was first getting to grips with his Church House visits, and we'd paid a high price. Nicky had coaxed him into the car without letting him see his overnight bag, and when he'd realized where he was going, he'd tried to bite his way through the seats and out of the car. Ever since then, though he's now settled and happy at Church House, he will not get into a car on his own with his mum.

We learned our lesson. If we'd tried to fool David with

a false promise of 'go bumpipop', he would never have trusted us on a trip again.

We were sitting over cornflakes and coffee on one of their deep sofas, David with his shoes off, his head on the armrest and his feet in my lap, when he made another linguistic leap. It was a school holiday, and we'd made a trek of it that day: before settling in Starbucks, we'd hiked across the docks to the Industrial Museum and its transport display. David loved the Lodekka bus with its steep stairs and plastic seats – sitting on that was almost as good as sitting on his own school coach.

'That was a long walk,' I said. 'All the way to the green bus and back.'

David sat up sharply. 'No green bus!' he said. 'NO GREEN BUS!' And his face crumpled.

'No green bus,' I agreed hurriedly. 'Green bus all gone. Goodbye green bus.'

David held his breath. He didn't want to be dragged all the way back to the museum. We were in Starbucks: this was 'go bumpipop'. After that would come 'go Mummy'.

'Goodbye green bus,' I said with emphasis. And then, pushing my luck, I listed all the things we'd done on our walk, in order: 'Goodbye Bob the Builder, goodbye swings, goodbye boats, goodbye green bus, goodbye library, hello bumpipop.'

David opened his mouth to argue, shut it, opened it … and got the joke. He laughed. It wasn't a tickle-me giggle or a manic up-to-mischief chuckle – it was a full-throated, I-get-it laugh.

'Goodbye green bus,' he said, and snorted. 'Goodbye library. Hello bumpipop!'

That moment was the biggest development in David's

mind since the day he started naming objects. 'Goodbye' gave him a way to think about the past. Until then, it was an uneasy trail of debris behind him – now, he had a way to exist in the present moment and take a view of the past that didn't invite it to come rushing back and overwhelm him. Just as 'go' gave him a mission, 'goodbye' gave him a history.

It might seem as if I'm attaching too much importance to one word, but the change in David's thinking was breathtaking. By the time we'd walked home, he'd worked out that we could discuss all the day's events, in order, and safely dismiss them with a 'goodbye' – and that if this held for the past, it could work in the future, too. The future was just a past that hadn't happened yet. Events could be lined up, hours in advance: 'Go Mummy, go bath, go *Disneyland* video, go teeth clean, go bed.'

His itinerary grew. He counted through the days of his next visit to Nanny's Chalet, marking in all the essential activities (go fruit pastilles, go video, go walk, go Postman Pat ride ... his grandparents didn't exactly get a mention, but they were implied). Then he assembled a litany that charted every remaining day of the school holidays, listing all his excursions and routines until he arrived with a grateful rush at 'go bus, go Briarwood'. That recitation took him about five minutes, and Nicky had to repeat every phrase after him, as a reassurance and a promise. He'd go through it again with her, and again, until she was hoarse. But every day it became shorter, as future days became the past.

All of that happened by chance, because I happened to mention the museum's green bus after we'd put it behind us. I should have realized then how carefully David listened to our chatter, analyzing it for fragments he could understand – he was like a radio dish, pointing into the stars, scouring the heavens for bursts of intelligible language that could tell him if these alien life forms really did have brains.

At the chalet that summer, I finally understood how attentively David was tuning in. A neighbouring family were packing their car with suitcases, and I called out that they could take David home with them if they had room. 'Plenty of space, hop on in!' joked the father, and David did. He trotted across the path, popped open the back door and slipped inside.

It seemed rotten to drag him out of the car, when he'd done so well to understand. The family were going back to Birmingham, though, and I didn't think they'd enjoy the journey once David spotted they were taking the wrong route. On our journey up from Bristol, he'd demonstrated a sense of direction that was better than satnav – at every turn-off and every junction, he reminded me to turn left or right. He didn't say the words: he simply operated my indicators, with a sharp kick to the elbow. A hard jab with the tip of the shoe meant turn left; a harder jab meant turn right. Simple, effective and painful ... my left arm was blue with bruises.

So I held his hand and eased him away from his free ride to Birmingham, and his face was a picture of bemusement until I thought to point out that this car was the wrong colour: 'No red car! Red car? No! Go Mummy in David's *blue* car.' David smiled: how could he have made such an elementary error? To him, it was irrelevant that he didn't know this other family, and that none of his own bags was being loaded. The only clear clue that he'd picked the wrong ride was its colour.

If they were amused by David's literal-mindedness, the family must have been unnerved by what followed. For an hour and a quarter, he lounged by their chalet and watched them pack. When all the pets, cases and children were crammed inside, David stared and ignored their waves with a stony face. He waited for the engine to fire up – and then he ran off, shrieking with glee, without waiting to see them drive away.

That had become a habit, one we couldn't have predicted, since he'd dispensed with the wheelchair. At first, he simply stopped to see drivers start their engines – he'd be skipping alongside me, allowing me to hold his wrist as we headed for a park or a coffee shop, and he'd see someone unlocking their car. He'd stop: he had to stand and watch until they twisted the key and the engine revved. Then we'd walk on.

Soon, he was walking right up to the cars and peering through the windows, to see the moment when the key turned. Some drivers ignored him; others waved, and he'd ignore them. I studied the sky and clutched David's arm. It was useless to try to drag him away – he'd scream himself to jelly. Anyway, there was no law against staring at people who were starting their cars.

One or two wound down their windows and asked if they could help us. I'd smile and say that David was the nosiest boy in Bristol. Short, strange explanations usually worked better than long, earnest ones.

The obsession became broader. He'd stand and watch anyone in a parked car, even if they'd just pulled up, or they were eating, or reading a newspaper, or sitting in the passenger seat ... or sleeping. We stood and gazed at a middle-aged man in a Toyota, snoozing on a residential street, one evening – a cold wind was blowing, and my initial hope, that he was taking a quick nap while his wife popped in to see a friend, faded as the blood left my fingertips. David wouldn't be budged, and he showed no sign of feeling the cold, so I resigned myself to a long wait. Maybe the man's daughter was at the piano teacher's house, with its brass plaque by the gate. If so, she'd surely be out after half an hour. But 8 p.m. passed, and 8.20, and by now I was coughing loudly and whistling to wake the guy up. He didn't twitch. I started to think he was dead, and that David would stand and stare at him until we froze to death too.

When his eyelids finally flickered open, I made a big palaver of trying to drag David away. The man watched us wrestling, and must have wondered why the screaming boy was staring at him in that horror-movie way – I gestured to him to wind down his window and he did, cautiously, just an inch. When I explained the problem ('Autistic son, won't shift till you start the engine, would you mind?'), he was delighted to help. David charged away as soon as the ignition fired – he must have been as glad to go as I was.

After that, I had no qualms about asking people to switch on their engines. One or two drivers objected, but mildly: 'I'll be going in about five minutes,' they'd say, and I'd just smile and let David press his nose against their windscreens. When they turned the key, he'd go away.

Most people couldn't do enough to be helpful. One boy of sixteen or so, who was sitting in the passenger seat with a book, got out and walked 300 yards up the street to convince David that the car wasn't going anywhere till his mother came back. Other people insisted on driving off, though David just wanted to hear their engines start: they always waved as they went, and the only way I could make him wave back was to hold his wrist and shake it, in a rag-doll salute.

Waving seemed so simple to us, compared to the astonishing complexity of some of David's behaviours. He could not do it, though. He loved to watch me leave for the station on a Saturday, and he'd hang out of the upstairs window and repeat everything I said as he waited to hear the car start, but he wouldn't wave. He learned to say, 'Bye-bye Mummy,' when she helped him on to the school bus, but he wouldn't wave. He'd watch as his nanny and grampa windmilled their arms when we left their house, but he wouldn't wave.

He understood so many words now that I was certain he must know that 'wave' meant waggling the hand – he just couldn't see the point. People waved at him to bid him goodbye, but there was no point in doing it back because other people weren't really sentient. They didn't have minds … they weren't quite alive.

'David watches us,' I said to Nicky, 'the same way that we watch television. Think about *Crimewatch* – at the end of the show, Nick Ross winks at you. That's reassuring. You'd be upset if he forgot. But you don't wink back. That'd be bizarre. He can't see you. He doesn't really exist. He's just an image. And that's how David interprets us: he wants us to do the usual reassuring things, but he can't see the point of responding, because we aren't really there.'

It was a sad, lonely thought. Our little boy was surrounded by love, but he was as all alone as a recluse in his forgotten flat with just the people on the telly for company.

We redoubled our efforts to get David waving. It was a chance to show him that we really were there, that we could understand his signals just as he was learning to understand ours. When one day he turned round at the garden gate to give his mum a momentary, flickering wave, we both cheered – and we were also fascinated to get another glimpse into his mind.

When David waved, he kept his palm facing him.

It made sense. When we waved, he saw our palms ... so when he waved, he ought to see his own. If he could see the back of his hand, he wouldn't be doing it right.

The only viewpoint in the whole world was David's. He couldn't believe that anyone saw anything, or felt anything, except what he was seeing and feeling. No wonder he'd reached the conclusion that other people weren't sentient – since we couldn't see what he saw and feel what he felt, we were effectively brain-dead.

We've spent years trying to understand that. It's simple, and logical, and quite alien. Explaining it to other people is often impossible, though we find that different anecdotes or metaphors unlock the mystery for different people.

One Christmas Eve, for instance, David and I were climbing Cabot Tower, a Victorian lookout point on the highest hill in the city. It was dusk, and halfway up its 108 steps, we met a council worker coming down. He'd locked the door at the top, and he was on his way to lock the door at the bottom, and there was no way we were going anywhere but straight back down, he said.

I explained that David couldn't talk. I explained he was autistic. I explained he'd understand much more quickly if he could just march to the top and find the door locked. I explained he was the most stubborn child in England and if he couldn't complete his climb, there was a good chance that all three of us would be spending Christmas on the narrow spiral staircase.

The man from the council wasn't moving. He wasn't going to let us go up, and he wouldn't go down till we did.

David got fed up of hearing me say, 'No more stairs. Bye-bye stairs. Down we go,' and he screeched every time I tried to manoeuvre him downwards. So, to pass the time, I started to tell the man from the council about autism. In fact, I was hoping that between my monologuing and David's screaming, the poor man would crack and let us finish our run up the stairs – it wouldn't take us more than thirty seconds.

He hadn't heard of autism, but he recognized something in my description: 'I play cricket, I'm in the local club,' he said, 'and there's a home next to our ground, you know, for mental cases. One of them, he comes and watches us – and he can't half throw a ball. Every now and then, somebody hits a boundary, and if the ball rolls near this bloke, we yell at him to chuck it back. First time he did it, we all stood with our jaws down round our knees. I've never seen anyone throw a ball that hard, straight to where he wanted it. We tried to teach him the rules, but he didn't have a clue. We couldn't even get him to play catch. Pity, cos with a right arm like that, he'd have been straight in the England team.'

He looked at David with renewed interest. 'Reckon your boy could play cricket?'

'Might be the next W. G. Grace,' I said.

That was like a Masonic handshake. 'Come on then,' said the man from the council, 'can't hurt if you just climb to the top.'

And that was David's signal. Honour was satisfied. Without taking another step up, he turned and scooted straight to the bottom.

Other explanations were more succinct. Nicky heard James answer the phone one Saturday: the pharmacist was calling from Boots, to let us know a prescription was in. 'Can I speak to David Stevens?' he asked.

'No,' said James, 'he can't talk. He's autistic.'

The tragedy concealed in those half-dozen words seemed much more real, Nicky told me, when she heard them spoken by our other child.

Sometimes it wasn't David's oddness that affected people; it was how near he was to normality. His voice was clear and strong, and his musical ear had taught him to pronounce words without any hint of an impediment. Almost all his language was repetition and echoes, but it sounded like plain English.

We were standing at the Starbucks counter in Borders, waiting to collect David's bumpipop, when he announced, 'BBC videos, *The Onedin Line*.'

I grinned at Rob, the student who was serving up coffees.

'BBC videos, *The Smell of Reeves and Mortimer*.'

Rob narrowed his eyes, as if there was an obvious joke here that he was missing.

'BBC videos, *Absolutely Fabulous*.'

David gave up waiting for Rob to join in the game, and turned to me.

'BBC videos, *Absolutely Fabulous*,' I said obediently.

'*Absolutely*,' David repeated, wanting to hear that I'd got the word right. I said it again. '*Fabulous*,' he concluded.

I ordered a coffee and explained to Rob how the game worked, and how David especially loved BBC videos. A few days later, when we returned, I saw Rob slip away from the counter to the staffroom. He came back with a package in a plastic bag.

'I was in a charity shop,' he explained, 'and when I saw this, I thought of your son.'

He handed it over. 'BBC videos, *Fawlty Towers*,' announced David approvingly. He cuddled it all the way home, making me stop to read the label every few yards, and Nicky and I sat in his bedroom that night, watching the whole tape. He was so shattered he could hardly keep his eyes open, but he wouldn't turn the set off until Basil had thrashed his car and goose-stepped through the foyer for the last time, and the final logo had appeared. Then he took the tape out of the machine, and hugged it all night.

We wrote a card to thank Rob for his present, but he couldn't have guessed how much it meant to David, or to us.

Neither Nicky nor I are religious in a conventional sense. We don't often attend church services. Nonetheless, we both enjoyed taking James to the cathedral in Bristol, or visiting a country church on days when David was at respite, and lighting a candle as we said a prayer. There aren't many moments more touching than a child's impromptu prayer for a dead pet: 'Please God, look after my gerbils now they're in heaven, and I hope they're happy.'

As James gets older, his prayers won't be for gerbils any more – they'll be for himself, for his family and perhaps for his own children. But the ones that matter will be as simple as the words he said as a small boy.

Our prayers were raw enough. When David was at his worst, I found it helped to slip out of the newspaper office during my lunch break and go to St Bride's on Fleet Street, or to St Paul's, where a side chapel was open at no charge. Those Saturdays when I couldn't be at home were sometimes the most difficult – I'd ring Nicky and hear the tears in her voice as David howled, and I'd know that even if I took a taxi straight to the station, I couldn't be back in Bristol for hours. So I prayed for strength: strength for me, and strength for her. It helped, too, to sit in the pews and think about how desperate I'd felt at other times in David's childhood. We'd survived bad days. There would be others, and we'd find the strength to get through those, too.

On our jaunts round the West Country, David and I had started touring the cathedrals. They gave the days a focus: no matter how much David enjoyed his three-for-£1 rides on Thomas the Tank Engine, I couldn't shake the feeling that we'd wasted a day if we drove for four hours just to drop a coin in a slot. We were visiting cities with some of the most spectacular architecture in England – it seemed a pity to stick to the shopping precincts.

When David was a toddler, we wouldn't have had an option. He didn't do cathedrals, or anywhere with echoes. Churches and swimming pools were equally terrifying to him. In his first year at Briarwood, David's class visited a mosque, an experiment which his teacher noted they wouldn't be trying again in a hurry. 'David seems to have a strong aversion to religious places,' Nicky wrote in his daily book, the diary that shuttled between home and school. 'Maybe he is a vampire! Nope, it can't be that ... I can see his reflection in the mirror.'

His attitude changed when he discovered vaulted roofs

enhanced his singing. He could let out a high, pure note and hear it come back to him again and again. The delight on his face was wonderful to see – he was like a boy at the seaside, skimming stones across the water and counting the bounces. Instead of bouncing pebbles, he was bouncing sounds.

We visited the cathedrals at Wells and Exeter, as well as the abbeys at Bath and Tewkesbury. At Bristol Cathedral, David sang a perfect scale, starting and ending on the second note instead of the tonic. It was the sort of musical game I might have expected from a trained musician. He added one trick that a music student wouldn't dare try in a church: instead of singing 'lah, lah, lah' or 'tum, tum, tum', David sang 'help'. That was, 'Help, help, help, HELP, HELP, help, help, HELLLLPPP!'

People stared. I nodded and whispered, 'Super acoustics.'

These visits started when David was still using a wheelchair, and I hoped that other churchgoers would realize he was a disabled child who was enjoying the chance to explore one of the focal points of his community, and not just a noisy oik. Many did; one or two didn't.

David's songs had precise significance for him, though their meaning was entirely divorced from what anyone who heard the words might guess. 'Help' didn't mean 'help' to David, and when he burst out with 'Happy Birthday' in Bristol Cathedral one afternoon, it wasn't his birthday – he'd simply spotted the candles. He was hoping we'd light one, so he could blow it out. At Wells the week before, he'd blown out six, all of them lit by other people, before I could wheel him out of range.

The thought of this made him happy, and the acoustics

magnified his happiness by echoing his song. I stroked his head, to keep him calm, and looked around. Apart from two ladies with leaflets at the door, the cathedral seemed almost deserted.

I hadn't realized that a service was going on in one of the chapels, until a verger bore down on us, 'sshh'ing furiously. He made it plain that David and I were to leave immediately. When I explained that David was profoundly autistic, and that his noises were a celebration of God and a response to the surroundings, every bit as heartfelt as any other worshipper's, the verger suggested I could take him to the tearoom in the cloisters.

That really got my goat. We left, but I stopped at the door to tell the ladies how David had been welcomed at other churches. By the time we'd marched home, I had built up a head of steam. What made me most cross was the idea that David didn't deserve to be in the main cathedral building; he was fit only for the coffee shop.

Nicky was horrified by the story. That was my barometer – I was sometimes so touchy about other people's attitudes to our son that I needed to see her response before I knew whether I was overreacting. This time, it was obvious how upset she was.

We wrote to the Bishop of Bristol, Michael Hill, to complain: 'The appropriate response might have been to include prayers for David in the service,' we wrote. 'We certainly had not come to intrude, but to worship.'

The bishop's office emailed us immediately, promising to investigate, and two days later, we had a letter from the dean, Robert Grimley. It was a beautifully written and unreserved apology. The incident had saddened everybody at the cathedral; the verger 'acted in good faith, but he simply got it wrong'. The cathedral worked closely with special-needs schools in Bristol, and if we telephoned the dean before David's next visit, a staff member would join us, 'to enable him to enjoy the feel and sound of the building to the full'.

A week later, the bishop himself, Michael Hill, wrote to apologize and to assure us of a warm welcome on our next visit. We did appreciate the courtesy of those letters, but what really made us feel at ease with taking David into churches again was a spontaneous incident at Gloucester Cathedral later that year. On a busy afternoon, when school parties were bustling round and David was chatting animatedly to the ceiling, a lady came across, smiling, to ask whether David was autistic.

'I used to work with a child who made quite similar noises,' she explained. 'I always enjoyed them – he sounded so natural. I must say, it's a pleasure to see your son here. It makes me feel this is a place for everyone, whatever labels other people stick on us: in God's eyes, we're human and that's all.'

By the strangest coincidence, we saw a piece of stained glass a few minutes later which seemed to emphasize the truth of that kind woman's words. Gloucester's windows are spectacular, but the vignettes around the cloisters are just as lovely, on a tiny scale. They illustrate stories from the Bible, and under the verse from St Luke, 'Jesus … said, "Suffer little children to come unto me,"' we saw a picture of Christ with a small boy at his side. The child was blond, and his round face was the image of David's. If the glass hadn't been more than a century old, I could have believed it was modelled on a photo of our son.

Another favourite cathedral was Worcester. It was a

long run up the motorway, and a long climb up the 330 steps of the church tower, but the view across the river and the cricket ground repaid all of that. David was amazed to see so much of the world. He loved heights: if he could have climbed the flagpole to gain a few extra feet, he would have done.

He sang his heart out on the tower, and he was still singing when we rolled into the cafe across the road an hour later. It was called Capuchin's, it sold second-hand books as well as coffee, and it became one of our favourite stopping points. Sadly, it is closed now, but I'll always remember the concert David provided on our first visit. He didn't just sing like a lark – he warbled like a thrush and trilled like a linnet. The woman who ran the shop couldn't find enough words to praise him and, since boasting about my children is my favourite hobby, I added some extra. David sang until he fell asleep, clasping a toy in his hand. I showed it to the shop owner: 'Other boys like cars or Transformers,' I said. 'David's got a magnetic letter "Q" from the alphabet on our fridge.'

He twiddled his letter 'Q' all the way home, and he gnawed it till bathtime, and he grizzled at it long past bedtime, and we eventually realized that the only reason he'd chosen a 'Q' to be his inseparable plaything was because it was stuck on his finger. That finger was now the size of a wooden clothes peg, and about as flexible.

We tried soap, of course. We tried butter. We tried cutting the plastic with scissors and snipping it with pliers. David wasn't cooperating – his finger already hurt like blazes and now the Dad-thing was waving a pair of pliers around. He started screaming.

We ended up at Accident and Emergency – 'Go doctor,

go doctor!' we said. An ambulance crew were on standby in the car park, and as I helped David out of the car, they offered their services: 'Stuck on your finger, is it, mate? Get that off in a jiffy.'

Four of them gathered round. David screamed. Someone touched his hand. He really screamed. The ambulance crew backed off: 'Needs a doctor, that does, mate. Can't help you. Through that door, they'll help you. Nothing wrong with your lungs, though, mate.'

It was twenty past eleven by now, just after chucking-out time in the pubs, and A&E was full of men doubled over on plastic chairs, and the reek of blood and vomit. David kept screaming. Most of the men barely glanced at him. He was just the soundtrack to a bad night. We were seen first, though – nothing jumps the queue like a banshee with a throbbing finger.

In the end, it took a doctor, two staff nurses, a student nurse, a porter and me to remove that letter 'Q'. Four people pinned David's limbs as he struggled in his wheel-chair, I held his head and chest as I chanted words to calm him, and the doctor cut the plastic away. As soon as it was off, he calmed down. Right until the moment we let him go, he was terrified, unable to understand what was happening. When he looked at his hand and saw the 'Q' was gone, he relaxed – suddenly, it all made sense.

As he waited for his bedtime bottle of milk, some time after midnight, he plucked a magnetic letter 'P' off the fridge and tried to push his finger through it. We threw the whole alphabet away, even the harmless-looking letters like 'J' and 'T'. He'd probably get them stuck up his nose.

Three years later, we took him to the hospital again. This time, he knew what was happening – he'd even asked to go. 'Tooth, doctor, ouch,' he'd told his teacher, Freja. We had to book him in for a general anaesthetic: he's come a long way, he'll even let people take a look in his mouth, but there was no way he'd sit still to have a cavity drilled. The whole episode passed without a single scream, even when the anaesthetist inserted a needle into the back of his hand: David sang a song to keep himself calm, recited a few lines of Disney script and flopped back unconscious.

'What a great soliloquy,' remarked the dentist.

That night, I dreamed I was walking with David to school. He was holding my hand, in the unaffected way of a ten-year-old who doesn't know it's uncool to show such childish affection. And I was happy, because I could sense he was relaxed and that he wasn't planning any outrages … and because he couldn't run into the road when I had him by the fingers.

Even when I'm asleep, I'm worried he'll get himself run over.

'I love you, David,' I said.

'I love you,' he echoed.

That made me smile. Half of all human communication amounts to repetition, chiming in with what's just been said.

'I'm feeling happy,' I said.

'Yes, I'm happy too.'

I squeezed his hand. He really sounded as if he understood what he was saying, as if he knew that I could comprehend his feelings and compare them to my own.

'You like your school,' I told him.

'Yes, I like school.'

'Who's your favourite teacher?'

'Claire. No, Freja. Err, no … Nikki. I like all of them.'

That's an answer, I thought. It's not an echo. I've just heard a breakthrough. David and I are having a conversation.

I thought of the promise my dad made to David, not long after the autism diagnosis: 'We'll have a proper conversation one day, mate – a conversation, you and me.'

Dad was right after all, I thought.

And then I woke up.

Fifteen

We've saved our favourite story for the end of David's book. Our first idea was to begin with it, because it seems so remarkable, so extraordinary – in David's entire childhood, this has happened only once. But to anyone who didn't understand our family, the story would seem mundane.

This is what happened: one Sunday afternoon, we went for a walk in the country and the boys played together.

All four of us got in the car. We'd been encouraging David for weeks to allow Nicky out of the house with him: usually, he'd go spare if she tried even to wave him off from the front gate. We joked that he was the original male chauvinist, hard-wired with caveman instincts about a woman's place. The truth wasn't so funny – David was terrified that one day he'd come home and his mum wouldn't be there.

It's hard to imagine a fear that intense. Think of yourself as a child ... and now suppose that, whenever you left the house, you knew your mother could be gone for ever. You didn't know why she would go, or where, or who would take her: nobody could explain these things to you. And you were forbidden to speak of your fears.

Try to hold that thought in your head. I can only begin to imagine it, for a fraction of a second – as soon as my imagination tastes it, my mind pushes the fear away. It is, quite literally, too horrible to think of.

For David, it was an ever-present terror.

Nicky was often confined to the house for days at a time, especially during the school holidays. She couldn't walk up the street to the shops, or go across the road to see friends – to David, she might have been walking out of his life for ever. He would not let her take him out of the house, even for a drive to his favourite places. At Briarwood during the summer, a playscheme ran for three weeks: Nicky helped to set it up, but David wouldn't let her drive him there when James and I were away. Freja, David's tireless and devoted teacher, came to the rescue in the school minibus.

He guarded his mother so jealously that other people, even children, were often barred from the house. If neighbours, or even his grandparents, tried to come in, David would lie screaming on the floor, smashing his head against the floorboards. These episodes of intense jealousy could last for weeks, and between outbreaks we trod cautiously, afraid of setting off another.

When we tried to explain David's exhausting demands to professionals, such as doctors or social workers, we felt they regarded us as part of the problem. 'We'll have to make David understand this isn't acceptable behaviour,' they'd say – as if autism was a bad habit, something David had picked up from poor parenting. The staff at Briarwood and Church House understood the reality; but then, they worked with David.

So when, one Easter, his authoritarian regime began to

tolerate hints of freedom, we were eager to encourage them. Nicky was able to sit with me and James at the table on the patio, while David splashed in a pool; she stood in the front garden and chatted to Vanda; she and James joined us for a car ride to the shopping mall. We took precautions – David didn't see Nicky get out of the car, or leave the garden. Those liberties would follow, if perestroika continued.

David seemed to want it as much as us. He was now almost nine, and he was tired of trying to control every element of the chaotic machine around him. He wanted to take more of it on trust … and he wanted to be more a part of his family.

We planned the trip to Bournstream Farm several days ahead. It was one of David's favourite places, a playground in rolling fields beside a Gloucestershire farmhouse, set aside for children with disabilities and their families. We'd been members for years, and it was a great place to take James as well as David – but we'd never been as a family before.

David accepted our laboured announcements of the day's agenda: 'Go Bournstream in the blue car. David go Bournstream. James go Bournstream. Mummy go Bournstream. Daddy go Bournstream. Mummy and David and Daddy and James … in the blue car.'

We expected anxious noises and a last-minute attack of the wobbles, but David wriggled into his harness on the back seat as comfortably as if he always sat next to big brother for a run into the country on Sundays. The rest of us were swallowing twice before we spoke, but David was relaxed.

At the playground, David permitted all of us to join him

in the open air. That hadn't happened since he was four. He lined up all the pedal-cars and trundlers on the path, in exactly the order that he always arranged them. Then he let James push him up and down the field in one.

The boys clambered up the rope climbing frame together. They clung on to the roundabout as Nicky and I spun it. They sat side by side on the swings.

We set off through the fields behind the playground, past huddles of sheep, and into the woods on the escarpment. There were rabbits, and above the trees a pair of goshawks patrolled, their wings raking forward, like Spitfires.

Beyond a stile, James scrambled up a muddy bank and slid down on his backside. David copied him.

The boys sat astride a log, as if they were paddling a canoe. Then David climbed on to my shoulders, and James hugged me. Nicky took photographs.

We followed the path for half a mile before we turned back, David striding silently beside his mother and James asking me questions about the burrows and the trees.

As we neared the stile again, we spotted a fallow deer and her fawn in a thicket. James was rapt.

We haven't been back since, to Bournstream, together. After that Sunday, the trust which made it possible ended, like a narrow gap crashing shut. If David sees Nicky put her coat on now, he starts to scream. If James tries to leave with us, David holds up his hand like a traffic policeman and shouts, 'Goodbye!'

We don't know what particle of normalness struck David's brain and allowed us to be an ordinary family for a few hours. No one who saw us crossing the stile would have given it a second thought – but to us, that afternoon was so rare and bizarre that we remember every minute of it vividly.

As David has grown, we have hung on to one constant hope. His autism ebbs and flows, and whatever improvements he makes soon fade away – but the improvements always come back, more strongly. 'If he did it once,' we say, 'eventually, he'll do it some more.' One day, the four of us will go for a walk in the woods again.

There's one sign of this which renews our hope every year: each Christmas, David remembers how to join in the fun. He unpacks the boxes of decorations, and races round the coffee table on a scooter while Nicky and James hang baubles on the tree. He and James bounce on tiptoes, huffing and puffing, trying to blow out the candles on our highest shelf. He sings along to carols, and curls up in a ball with his fingers in his ears when we pull crackers, and wears bangles and braces made of tinsel.

On Christmas Day, he finds all the presents that could be videos and shreds the wrapping from them. Everything else is untouched in this purge, though we have to be careful to hide books and computer games intended for James – all the presents under the tree belong, in David's eyes, to him, until he has generously rejected the ones that aren't video-shaped.

He didn't always cope well with Christmas. When he was two years old, I sat for hours with him in the car – he knew strange rituals were happening inside the house, with noisy toys and coloured paper everywhere, and he couldn't understand it. So we sat, him in his harness and me in the driver's seat, not driving anywhere but safe, at least, in a familiar place that hadn't been garnished with paper chains.

Nicky brought my dinner out, and I ate it with gravy and Brussel sprouts slopping in my lap. (A day or two later, she took the photo of David that's on the front cover of this book.)

The Christmas when David was four, he had to be taken to the deserted car park of the supermarket and the locked doors of the zoo, so he could see that his favourite places were off-limits – closed for one day of the year, though for all David knew, they might be shut for ever.

By the time he was six, he'd begun to see possibilities in Christmas. Those candles, for instance ... He left us to eat our lunch, and slipped away for an experiment. His sound-track gave him away: every song he sings has a meaning, and we realized he was singing 'Happy Birthday'. 'Matches,' said Nicky suddenly, and we raced up the stairs to find David in the study, feet up on the desk, blackened spots on the carpet showing where he'd dropped lit matches. He was watching a spill of paper burn in front of the computer.

The following year, he knew what the rituals were about. The zoo would be shut and the rides put away, but they would come back; the gaudy tree wouldn't be there for ever; a stream of people would ring the doorbell, but none of them took his mother away. There would be presents, and David liked presents. The awestruck look on his face when he spotted his rocking horse on Christmas morning is something we'll never forget.

There'd be hugs as well, and David had become very fond of hugs. He didn't often put his own arms round anyone, but he loved to be grabbed and squeezed. He liked to make other people hug, too – he'd grab my wrist and drag me to Nicky, and clamp his hands against the smalls of our backs, and compress us.

We were cautious. We didn't expect too much. He'd had a good Christmas; he could have a bad one next year. But good Christmases have become part of David's pattern – and he won't break his patterns lightly.

For one day of the year, he'll sit on Nicky's lap and watch James and me playing with presents, and listen to all of us talking and laughing at once. He falls about laughing himself, sometimes because we are tickling him and sometimes because life is worth a good giggle.

For one day of the year, all his routines are suspended. David lets us control the show. He is happy to join in, one of the family.

Hopefully, a time will come when David understands that he can live like that all the year round. Until then, corny as it sounds, we really do wish it could be Christmas every day.

One other aspect of Christmas has been significant to both Nicky and me. When we first talked about writing this book, neither of us was sure we could find the words. I didn't want to start making promises to publishers about chapter lengths and deadlines, and end up making excuses about 'too many things to say' and 'emotional strain'. We decided that, to test the water, we would both write a short piece, about an episode from David's life – any incident, the first thing that came into our heads, just something that summed up a little of the intensity, the pain and joy, the contradictions of loving our little boy.

We disappeared to different rooms. Two hours later, we printed out rough drafts and compared them … and laughed. We'd chosen the same incident: the school Christmas play.

That wasn't such a coincidence. David loves his school – it's one of the most important things in his life, but we don't often have a chance to see him in that setting. We wave him off every morning as he boards his bus, and the devoted escort, Cheryl, takes the satchel that he thrusts into her arms; eight hours later, he dances down the bus steps, singing the theme from *Emmerdale*, which, we think, means, 'I'm home and I'm bursting for the loo.' What happens in those eight hours, we can only learn obliquely. David can't tell us what he gets up to, and though the staff write diligently in his diary, they can only hint at what he's been doing. When he comes home wearing another child's trousers, or with green glitter gel in his hair, or with gold wellies on his feet and his own shoes, sopping wet, in a plastic bag ... we have to assume he's been having fun again.

Once a term, we sit down with David's teacher and the learning support assistants, and leaf through his workbooks or examine the snaps on the walls. Once a year, we visit the school for their Christmas play. Every year, we're staggered by the amount of work the whole staff have poured into making the occasion marvellous: lots of scenery, lots of music, and a chance for every child to be involved. A teacher narrates, and the children walk, or are wheeled, or cavort, through the story.

One year, David was the Artful Dodger in *Oliver Twist* – he's a naturally accomplished pickpocket, and he looked thoroughly rascally in cap and waistcoat.

His great dramatic triumph, though, was as the Snowman. He knows it, too: when he's feeling pleased with himself, you'll hear him trilling the soundtrack. I jotted some notes about that day, and I thought I'd captured some of the pride and the heartache, until I read what Nicky had written:

Living with David can be quite an isolating experience. Apart from Chris, myself, David's teachers and the other staff who work with him, nobody understands our son. It is impossible for anyone else to look after David: his behaviour is too difficult for that.

Someone who knows David once described him as 'a man of extremes'. This sums him up completely. He is such a rewarding and such a demanding child. He can display the most challenging and unimaginable behaviour, yet he can also sing like an angel, and he has a wonderful sense of humour, with the most amazing and captivating smile. It is so appealing, you can't help but think how lucky you are to have him for a son.

We love David so much that it is quite overwhelming. Having a severely disabled child makes you count your blessings – almost too much at times, but it is a good thing. James, David and Chris are the whole world to me. I am so lucky to have them to love and to be loved in return.

David attends a school for the most disabled children in Bristol. Occasionally, one of the pupils dies. It really shocks me when that happens – our son goes to a school where sometimes children die. This is part of our world, and it is always so sad.

I was thrilled at Christmas because David got the starring role in the Briarwood play. As with many school productions, every child at David's school gets a part in the play. However, I had noticed during past performances that the autistic children were often brought on and off stage as quickly as possible, presumably because they have exceptional chaos-creating abilities. This is why I was so amazed and proud when David landed the leading role.

I was really excited, and wanted to tell everybody. I tried telling some friends that David had been given the starring part, but I could sense in their reactions that, in their opinion, as he was disabled, it didn't really count. Sometimes, those who do not know what it is like to have a child with a disability find it hard to see why you would be proud. I think they imagine that you are constantly disappointed. Some friends often feel sorry for me. To be truthful, I probably would have been the same if I had not become part of the world of disabled children.

So, I stopped telling people that he was the star, but I was still as excited and thrilled as any parent would be. More so, in fact, as David does not understand the rules of society and consequently he has to try even harder than most people, as the 'normal' world does not make any sense to him.

He was to be the Snowman character from The Snowman *by Raymond Briggs. I got a hint from David that this might be the Christmas play when, one night in early December, he woke up in the middle of the night singing the song 'Walking in the Air' in his pitch-perfect voice. He sings so beautifully that you don't mind if he wakes you up … you just feel sorry when the singing stops.*

The news about the play got even better when I found out I didn't have to make a costume for him, as the school already owned a snowman costume. I am fairly hopeless at making costumes – the previous year, I had had to make him a sheep outfit, but in all honesty, he ended up looking more like a cloud.

I once commented to someone that the school play was the social highlight of my year. They thought I was joking, but it is true. I love the productions at Briarwood – they are amazing. The children are so severely disabled that it would be easy to assume they have little comprehension of what is going on (though, of course, it's impossible always to know what a child who can't talk is thinking). Yet the teachers are so creative and so intelligent that they get every child involved in the most suitable and appropriate way for that student. The staff could so easily not bother – but they do bother, and it is the respect that is shown for each pupil that is so utterly moving. It seems to sum up the true spirit of Christmas. It is an extremely emotionally draining experience, but it is one of the very best things about having David. I would have missed out on seeing the very best side of humanity if I had not witnessed the school plays. It really is a privilege.

The children in wheelchairs opened the play that year. They were dressed as snowflakes and their chairs were festively decorated with stars, tinsel and bells. The staff involved them in a wheelchair snowflake dance to the overture from The Snowman. *It could have made you cry – with a combination of sadness and joy, amazement at the work the teachers had put in, and an overwhelming sense of love and compassion for the performers.*

I wonder sometimes if there is a limit to the amount of tears I can cry. I imagine it to be a bit like the menopause: when you have used up all your tears, there are no more ... but no, that doesn't seem to be the case – there are always plenty left!

These children have some of the most difficult lives imaginable, and yet they create so much love. They are complete innocents: they do not have the capacity to be malicious or mean. They allow the best qualities that people have to be highlighted. They really make you think about what is important and how to behave towards other people.

David looked fantastic in his snowman costume and pink floppy hat, and the teachers had used make-up to give him big, rosy red cheeks. The lady behind me commented on what a good-looking boy he was. I felt like turning around and boasting, 'That's my son, you know ... Yes, the starring role.'

David did everything he was supposed to do. He maybe got a little over-enthusiastic in the part when he had to switch on the fairy lights decorating the Christmas tree. On ... Off ... On ... Off ... On ... Off ... And he was a little reluctant to get out of the freezer in which he had been cooling down. And, yes, perhaps there was a little too much exuberance in the dance with Santa ...

Nevertheless, providing that he got rewarded with fruit pastilles regularly, he was very cooperative. At the end of the play, the Snowman melts. David demanded a fruit pastille loudly, and then obligingly melted beautifully.

I looked at Chris. There were tears in his eyes, too. But they weren't tears of sadness. We were both crying, because we were so proud of our son.

The kindness and the patient understanding of the staff that morning was beyond anything Nicky and I could ask for. They treated our son, and all the children, with real love. Every one of the pupils was brought into the production, and given a moment in the spotlight. And after our own leading snowman had melted, and the crumple of clothes on the floor had lifted its head to demand one more fruit pastille, the children were brought back for a disco under coloured lights. Some of them ran around, and some swayed, and some just smiled. They were all loving it.

There are only a few dozen children at the school, and the parents can cram on to four rows of chairs in the school hall. We took our places at the back, hoping David wouldn't spot us: a couple of years earlier, he'd caught sight of Nicky and, when the initial disbelief was over, he'd staged a protest that threatened to turn a tranquil nativity scene into an outtake from a disaster movie.

That reaction meant we could never peep into a classroom to watch him at work or playtime. Our appearance would confuse him, and create the kind of sensory overload most people experience if they try to watch TV and listen to the radio at the same time. That's enough to give anyone a headache. David knows one cure for headaches – bashing his head against the table, the floor, the walls and anything else he can reach. It doesn't work, but it's the only thing he can do.

It's easy to tell he loves his school, not just because his teachers report how happy he is, but also because he can't wait in the mornings to pull on his coat and run to the bus. David's emotions are transparent, and if he didn't want to go, we'd hear about it. So would the whole street. But every morning he's eager, and we appreciate that it's because everyone at Briarwood shows him the same patience, kindness and love that we see on show once a year, at the Christmas play.

It's not all games, of course. David has to work in lessons. He enjoys sums and counting, and his maths ability is about the same as that of an average child two years younger than him. Since the average child can listen to the explanations, and read the workbooks, and ask the teacher questions, that's a phenomenal achievement: David has learned to add and subtract without using language. The acclaim for that belongs both to him and to his teachers.

He knows his alphabet too, and loves to write his letters. It fascinates him that a written word will always be spoken the same way, though he doesn't understand the meaning of anything but label words. Any adult with a finger can be used as a reading machine: he grabs their hand, jabs it on to the page and waits to hear the words. His favourite sounds are the titles on his video covers. If his teacher shows him a word that he knows with a letter missing, he can write it into the gap – and he can sign his own name, too. It's 'David Stevens', and if an address is required, that's 'Church House'.

He is, at a basic level, numerate and literate. He just can't communicate properly.

During the holidays, he's counting down the days to the new term. He has fun, because we insist on it, but he's like a workaholic businessman with his family on a Spanish beach, desperate for an excuse to escape and check his email.

His love for school is not unusual, and the Briarwood staff know this. Lots of their pupils would prefer to be in school during the holidays. And plenty of the staff would be glad of the chance to earn some extra cash; and there's that big building, standing empty for twelve weeks or more in the year.

It took the exceptional drive and commitment of David's teacher, Freja Gregory, to turn all that from a parent's grumble into a playscheme which now runs not only for three weeks in the summer, but for a week at Easter too. There were thousands of pounds to be raised, a tangle of legal requirements to be straightened out, transport to find, staff to recruit, and Freja's enthusiasm inspired a committee of parents to conquer it all.

When people wonder, 'How do you cope?' the answer is that David loves life, and this is possible because of the staff at Briarwood, and Church House, and all the others who do far more for him than we would dare ask. He's eleven years old now, and he can stay at Briarwood and its sister unit till he's nineteen. As far as he's concerned, he'll be a schoolboy for ever – there's no way to make him understand that he'll grow up, and we wouldn't want to upset him by spoiling the illusion.

We don't know if he'll learn to hold a conversation, and understand us. Some autistic children make a breakthrough in their teens; others reach a plateau, never learning new skills.

We don't know if he'll ever understand that other people have thoughts and feelings, that they know things that can help him and that they can't always guess what's in his mind.

We don't know where he'll live after his teens, whether he'll be able to settle into some kind of sheltered accommodation or if he'll stay with us. The best solution would be a Devon farmhouse, with a barn conversion for David and his round-the-clock carers, but the Idyllic Future Fund is currently several million quid short of its target.

Nicky's great fear is that we'll die, and David will be left with only his brother to love him. I'm more hopeful: he'll probably find a Californian heiress in need of great-looking arm candy who won't criticize her conversation. Nicky says I'm wildly unrealistic, and I tell her she worries too much, and that side of our marriage hasn't changed much in ten years.

Nor has David, come to that. He loves all the things he's always loved, like Rolos, and chewing the tyres off toy cars, and the adverts at the start of videos, and being with his mum. The day we moved into our house, I had to take him to the zoo, for a 20p go on the plastic elephant ride; this weekend, nine years later, we'll probably do the same. He won't care if it's raining. He won't notice if people stare at the big boy on the baby's ride. He'll just be having fun. Lots of fun.

Acknowledgements

So many people have worked tirelessly and selflessly to help David, it's impossible to name every one of them ... but we'd like to try. One of the best things about bringing up a child with a severe disability is the support and friendship offered by inspirational people. Our lives have been made much richer for knowing all of you.

We can't praise the staff of Briarwood school highly enough. There simply aren't the words. The head teacher, David Hussey; David's classroom teachers, especially Freja Gregory and Claire Bullick; the learning support assistants, the administrators, the kitchen staff – it's an astonishing team, and anyone who is lucky enough to visit the school will know how happy the children are to be there.

Our heartfelt thanks and gratitude also to:

Tracy O'Neil and all the staff at Church House, who have worked with endless patience and determination to give David a home away from home. Tracy has supported David and fought his cause ardently for years, often giving up her spare time, and she's been a real force in his life.

The transport staff, who chauffeur His Lordship from door to door and often risk damage to their hearing –

David is a noisy back-seat driver. Special thanks to Cheryl Young, who has been so kind for years, and to David Griffiths, for the extra support.

Everyone who has made Briarwood's New Friends Playscheme possible, especially Freja Gregory, Deborah Smith, Sheila Clark, Carol Bold and the inexhaustible playscheme leader, Lisa Foster. Thanks too to the school staff who give up their holidays to work with the children, and to the many donors who support the playscheme.

The Community Care workers, in particular Kate, Stephanie and Anna.

Rosemary Baker, Maggie Kirby and all the staff at the Red House Nursery, Redland.

All the nursery staff who worked with David over several years at the Time Zone creche in the mall, Cribbs Causeway.

So many patient, friendly and forgiving workers at Starbucks in Borders, Bristol, especially its former manager Richard, and also to Rosario and all the members of the team at the Boston Tea Party on Park Street – we owe both these coffee shops a shelfload of new crockery.

Jane Ling and her colleagues at MusicSpace in Southville – you set David on the right path.

Everyone at the Avon Riding Centre for the Disabled in Henbury, Bristol ... most of all the bombproof horses.

The friendly staff of Bristol Central Library, whose quiet is often disrupted by loud singing.

The staff at Bristol Zoo, especially everyone in the canteen who has bustled round after David with a dustpan.

The remarkably tolerant staff of @Bristol, not only at Explore, but also at the sadly defunct Wildwalk, and the much missed Industrial Museum.

Barbara Saxton, whose Bournstream Farm playpark for disabled children and their siblings in Wotton-under-Edge, Gloucestershire, is an invaluable resource as well as a beautiful haven.

Our friends and colleagues at Connexions and *The Observer*, for their help and support with this book and in general over the years.

Heather Holden-Brown, whose insight and support have made this book possible.

Barbara Reeves, who helped us keep the chaos at bay for many years.

Vanda Cream, for all her friendship and support.

And last but most of all, our family and friends – thank you for the emotional and practical support.

Thank you to everyone who has remembered David at Christmas and birthdays, and treated him like a real boy.

The National Autistic Society

The National Autistic Society is the UK's leading charity for people affected by autism. It was founded in 1962 by a group of parents who were passionate about ensuring a better future for their children. Today it has over 7,000 members and 80 branches, and provides a wide range of advice, information, support and specialist services to over 100,000 people each year. It campaigns and lobbies for lasting positive change for people affected by autism.

The National Autistic Society
Head Office
393 City Road
London EC1V 1NG

Switchboard: 020 7833 2299
Autism Helpline: 0845 070 4004
Minicom: 020 7903 3597
Fax: 020 7833 9666
Email: nas@nas.org.uk
Website: www.autism.org.uk